The Coming

Our Only Hope

for a Better World

Allan Stewart Maitha

The Coming

Trilogy Christian Publishers A Wholly Owned Subsidary of Trinity Broadcasting Network

2442 Michelle Drive Tustin, CA 92780

Cover design by: Grant Swank

Editing of this book by Margaret Lehman, who made a host of suggestions not only about corrections in spelling and grammar but also about how to make many aspects of this book more reader-friendly.

For information about special discounts for bulk purchases, please contact Trilogy Christian Publishing.

Manufactured in the United States of America

10 9 8 7 6 5 4 3 2 1

Library of Congress Cataloging-in-Publication Data is available.

ISBN: 978-1-68556-895-5

E-ISBN: 978-1-68556-896-2

Dedication

Dedicated to my son, Richard, a godly young man who loved the Lord with all his heart and who lived in anticipation of "the blessed hope—the glorious appearing of our great God and Savior, Jesus Christ" (Titus 2:13, NIV). Now he is with his Lord in heaven, awaiting the resurrection that will occur at that future day of Christ's coming.

Endorsements

How often does your conviction that Jesus is returning someday influence your decision-making today? Do you reflect upon God's future judgment of evil, reward for faithfulness, and creation of a new heaven and new earth as you battle traffic, choose what movie to watch, or feed your family dinner? Allan Maitha not only lays out the evidence from the whole Bible for a comprehensive and clear view of the future but also challenges the reader to make this "blessed hope" a conscious factor in daily life now. Biblical, accessible, irenic, and practical, Allan has written a page-turner that will become a valued and challenging resource for theological scholar and ordinary Christ-follower alike.

—Michael Maggard
Missionary, Strategic Impact International

Thorough—well-researched—thought-provoking. This book highlights and explains the linkages between Old Testament prophecies, the New Testament teachings of Jesus and others, and poses some challenging thoughts about our world today and what remains to be fulfilled as we draw closer to the return of Jesus Christ. Regardless of your views on the timing of the Rapture, the author leads the reader to explore things that they may not have previously considered, and he causes the reader to more thoroughly examine the facts, as stated in the Bible, and how those facts shape one's understanding in terms of what we might face when God's perfect timing is satisfied.

—Richard Cook
Retired Corporate Executive

I have known Allan Maitha for almost twenty years and have always admired his theological scholarship, reverence for the Word of God, and his commitment to steadfast discipleship of younger believers. In the manner of a true pastor of God's people, he presents a clearly articulated case for end-time events that cause the reader to really consider—and maybe challenge—the order of events as we've been taught. I am thankful for his research and his heart to equip us to know the truth. Readers will be as well!

—Jill Romine
Principal, Ambleside School of Ocala

Allan Maitha has put together a very well-researched and clearly stated treatise on biblical prophecy. His historical and theological scholarship comes through in each chapter, and yet his down-to-earth manner and approachability keep each page relatable for all readers. Allan has a real clarity about which things we can know and which things we cannot. Regardless of whether you have never thought about it or you have a firm stance on what the "end times" look like, this book will present you with a very scripture-based view of the second coming of Jesus and the events that surround it.

—Dax Romine
Pastor, Live Oak Christian Fellowship

Table of Contents

Preface

This book is a book about the future—the future of our planet and the future of your life. It is based upon the writings of the ancient Hebrew prophets and upon the teachings of Jesus and the apostles of the early church.

From the dawn of human history, God has promised the coming of a Messiah who would rescue us and our world from the damaging and deadly consequences of our own rebellion against God as our Creator. That Messiah is Jesus of Nazareth.

He came once to bring forgiveness and the gift of eternal life for those who, by faith, will receive His grace. He's coming again to establish an everlasting kingdom of righteousness and peace on earth where those who receive His grace will live with Him forever.

No man knows the day or the hour of His coming, but Jesus, Himself, has given us clues to be looking for as an indication that His coming is near. The important thing is to be ready when He comes. This book will help equip you to do that.

Introduction

The Journey

One of the great promises that we find running like a mighty river through the Bible from Genesis to Revelation is the coming of Christ. He came once as our suffering Savior. Through His death and resurrection, He has provided salvation from sin and death and the gift of eternal life for all who will put their trust in Him as Savior and Lord. He is coming a second time as our triumphant King to abolish sin and death for all time, to deliver the earth from the curse of the fall, to establish the kingdom of God on earth, and to allow His redeemed people to share His glory forever on a new earth "where righteousness dwells" (2 Peter 3:13).

Jesus said, "If I go and prepare a place for you, I will come again and receive you to Myself, that where I am, there you may be also" (John 14:3). The apostle Paul refers to this promise as our "blessed hope" (Titus 2:13). Again, Paul tells us, "When Christ, who is our life, is revealed, then you also will be revealed with Him in glory" (Colossians 3:4). And the apostle John adds, "We know that when He appears, we will be like Him, because we will see Him just as He is" (1 John 3:2).

I invite you to join me on a journey to explore what the Scriptures teach about the coming of Christ. Our primary focus will center around simply allowing the Scriptures to speak for themselves. Some people prefer to start a study like this from a particular theological position and then go to the Scriptures for evidence that they think will prove their position correct. I prefer to take a different approach. My approach will be a biblical and expository approach to the Scriptures rather than a theological one. I could begin with a particular theological perspective that I am committed to and hope to prove. I prefer to start with the Scriptures themselves and simply see where they lead. And I can think of no better focal point than to structure our examination around what Jesus Himself has to say about the subject in His Olivet Discourse.

The Olivet Discourse is recorded in all three of the synoptic Gospels (Matthew 24–25; Mark chapter 13; Luke chapter 21) but not in the Gospel of John. Bear in mind that each of the Gospel writers provides his own unique perspective on what Jesus is saying. For this reason, one Gospel writer may furnish details that may or may not be included by the others. It's interesting to note that Matthew is the only one of the three synoptic Gospel writers who was actually present on the Mount of Olives to hear this teaching of Jesus with his own ears. Mark was not one of the original twelve disciples but was a close associate of Peter, who refers to Mark as "my son" (1 Peter 5:13). Mark most likely wrote his Gospel based on Peter's account of what he saw and heard. Luke was not one of the original twelve disciples either. He was a close associate of Paul (Colossians 4:14; 2 Timothy 4:11; Philemon chapter 24). As a historian, Luke based his Gospel account on the testimony of those who were eyewitnesses—primarily, though not exclusively—the original twelve disciples (Luke 1:1–4). John does not include the Olivet Discourse in his Gospel at all. Keep in mind that none of these Gospel accounts of the Olivet Discourse is a word-for-word rendition of Jesus' speech. It is rather a summation of Jesus' teaching in the words of the writer himself (as directed by the Holy Spirit, which is the essence of what the inspiration of Scripture means). Also, keep in mind that Jesus most likely taught in Aramaic, while the four Gospels represent a Greek translation from the original Aramaic by the writer under the direct inspiration of the Holy Spirit.

As we examine what Jesus tells about His coming in the Olivet Discourse, we need to understand that even the Olivet Discourse does not include every detail of His coming or mention every event that will occur during the last days leading up to His coming. Developing a comprehensive understanding of what the Bible teaches about the coming of Christ is much like putting together a gigantic jigsaw puzzle. No single passage of Scripture—not even the Olivet Discourse—gives us the full picture of everything the Bible teaches about His coming. There are many passages in both the Old and New Testaments that give us additional bits of information about the coming of Christ. These are details that either Jesus doesn't mention in the Olivet Discourse or the Gospel writers, for whatever reason, did not record. Each passage gives us a little piece of the puzzle, which, when put together, give us a much more complete understanding of His coming. We're going to spread the puzzle pieces on the table and then put them together.

My job as we approach this subject will be to carefully explore with you what each of these passages is telling us about the coming of Christ. We will look at how they help to explain or expand upon things that Jesus says in the Olivet Discourse. Then we will look to see how everything fits together to give the full picture. We will be looking at each passage in its immediate and overall literary and historical context, allowing Scripture to interpret itself in the light of other Scripture. We will be looking closely at what keywords mean in the original languages of the Bible to discover any additional clues that may not be evident simply from using an English translation. We will be looking at parables and metaphors that are frequently used to teach spiritual truths through analogies from the world in which we live. These are analogies that ordinary people living ordinary lives can relate to and understand. We will also be looking at prophetic and apocalyptic visions and their highly symbolic language. In doing so, we will make every effort to interpret these challenging passages in light of the immediate and broader context of Scripture. While it can be helpful at times to use our God-given imagination in our attempt to understand Scripture, we must be careful not to imagine things that are not really in the text and that are not consistent with the broader context of what Scripture clearly teaches.

In the book of James, we discover that just hearing (or reading) the Scripture, or even studying the Scripture, is insufficient if we do not take the next step of putting what we now know into practice.

James says,

> But prove yourselves doers of the word, and not merely hearers who delude themselves. For if anyone is a hearer of the word and not a doer, he is like a man who looks at his natural face in a mirror; for once he looked at himself and gone away, he has immediately forgotten what kind of person he was. But one who looks intently at the perfect law, the law of liberty, and abides by it, not having become a forgetful hearer but an effectual doer, this man will be blessed in what he does.
>
> James 1:22–25

Jesus, Himself, makes the same point when He says, "If you know these things, you are blessed if you do them" (John 13:17).

Whenever we read, hear, or study the Scriptures, we should first ask ourselves the question, "What?" But that needs to be followed by the question, "So what?" The question "What?" has to do with the content and meaning of the text. The question "So what?" has to do with how I think God wants me to live out the "what" in daily life on a practical level. Asking "What?" merely increases knowledge, but asking "So what?" can and will change your life. I would encourage you to look deeply as you read to discover how God wants you to put the truth of the text into practice on a personal level in your own life. Hopefully, in the end, we will not primarily see and understand the coming of Christ from a theologian's perspective but from the perspective of a biblical expositor who simply wants to examine the Scriptures and allow the Scriptures to speak for themselves on the subject.

During the course of our journey, I will not challenge the theological arguments that others may use to support their particular point of view on the coming of Christ. Let me say again that we will be taking an expository approach to the Scriptures, not an apologetic one. As we reach the end of this exploration, my hope is that we will have put all the pieces together in a way that is cohesive, consistent, and complete. Even so, we would do well to remember the words of Paul when he says, "For now we see in a mirror dimly, but then face to face; now I know in part, but then I will know fully just as I also have been fully known" (1 Corinthians 13:12). In that day, mirrors were made out of polished bronze that could partially reflect a person's image. However, it could not do so with the clarity of detail that would come from looking at a person face to face. When it comes to our understanding of Scripture on this or any subject, it's like looking into such a mirror. We may be able to see God's revealed truth, but not with the same clarity as when we see Jesus face-to-face at His coming. This is why biblical expositors and theologians can often look at the same passage of Scripture and arrive at very different conclusions.

The challenges we will face on this journey of exploration together will be great, but so will be the reward of greater understanding and excitement about the promise that Jesus is truly coming again. His second coming will not be to die on a cross but to rule in power and glory forever. May taking this journey together fill us with a sense of awe and anticipation as we eagerly wait for the coming of our Savior. And may the cry of our hearts be summed up in one simple phrase—"Come, Lord Jesus" (Revelation 22:20b). Now let's get started!

Chapter 1

The Promise

I will put enmity between you and the woman, and between your seed and her seed; he shall bruise you on the head, and you shall bruise him on the heel.

Genesis 3:15

It seemed like an ordinary day, just like any other, as the man and his wife ambled through the beautiful garden. Trees as tall as a twelve-story building brandished beautiful flowers that radiated a sweet aroma, and gorgeous butterflies flitted from one flower to the next, extracting their sweet nectar. Little did they know that something would happen that day to bring a curse upon their world. This curse would not only inflict great suffering upon them. It would have a disastrous impact on all their descendants for generations to come. As they moved through the garden, occasionally grabbing a luscious piece of fruit from one of the dozens of varieties of fruit trees in the garden, they could not foresee the unimaginable, tragic change ahead.

Coiled beside the path sat a beautiful, though somewhat strange-looking serpent. It's not that they had never seen a serpent before in the forest, but they had never seen one like this. It seemed to radiate light in all the colors of the rainbow. While the man stood back at a slight distance, contemplating this strange creature, his wife moved closer for a better look. It never occurred to either of them that this serpent was something to be feared, but the woman's curiosity got the best of her, while her husband was just a little more cautious. Then the strangest thing of all happened: the serpent began to speak with eloquence, the likes of which neither had ever heard before.

Speaking directly to the woman, though aware that the man was not far away, the serpent asked her a question:

> "Indeed [said the serpent to the woman], has God said, 'You shall not eat from any tree of the garden'?" [...] "From the fruit of the trees of the garden we may eat" [replied the woman]; but from the fruit of the tree which is in the middle of the garden, God has said, 'You shall not eat from it or touch it, or you will die.'"
>
> Genesis 3:1–3

The woman had not heard these words directly from God, for she had not yet been created when God spoke these words to her husband. She had heard these words from the mouth of her husband, who had heard them directly from God. The serpent immediately challenged the woman's words, impugning the character of God and essentially calling God a liar with impure motives.

> "You surely will not die!" [the serpent replied to the woman with a very cynical look upon its reptilian face] For God knows that in the day you eat from it your eyes will be opened, and you will be like God, knowing good and evil."
>
> Genesis 3:4–5

Someone has said that the most convincing lie is the one that is sprinkled with truth. The part about their eyes being opened to know good and evil was entirely true, but the part about their not dying was entirely false. The serpent knew that!

Apparently, the woman chose to believe that God was the liar without ever considering that the real liar might be coiled right in front of her. When the woman saw how beautiful and delicious the fruit looked and considered the possibility of obtaining wisdom that would make her like God, she grabbed a piece of the fruit and took a bite, savoring the exquisite flavor as the juice ran down her chin.

You might think the man would have known better and tried to stop her. After all, he had heard the command not to eat and the warning of lethal consequences directly from the mouth of God. Instead of stopping her, he also took a bite. The decision was disastrous.

What's wrong with our world? I sometimes think to myself. Maybe you ask yourself the same question. It seems that I can't open the morning newspaper or turn on the evening news without reading or hearing about war and the threat of war, civil unrest, ethnic violence, crime, acts of terrorism, and a hundred other terrible things. We live in a world of sickness, sorrow, suffering, pain, and death. When my son was diagnosed with terminal cancer at the age of thirty-nine, a friend of mine, sympathizing with my pain, simply said to me, "It just isn't right!" And it's not! I still remember the day when a friend of mine living in South Carolina went to her job just like she would any other day. What happened that day came completely without warning. She was brutally murdered in a robbery at the bank where she worked. My heart still grieves over what happened and over the great suffering and loss that it has brought to her family.

Don't get me wrong. I'm not saying that there's nothing good about our world or that no good people exist anymore. It just seems to me that what's good about our world always struggles to keep its head above water in a swirling cesspool of evil, suffering, violence, and death. Sadly, this is the kind of world we live in. I ask myself, *Why is our world the way it is, filled with suffering and pain? Has it always been this way? And even more importantly, is it always going to be this way?* The answer to all these questions is found in an ancient book written by forty different authors over a span of fifteen centuries and preserved for thirty-five centuries of human history. I'm talking, of course, about the Bible, which I consider to be the true and living Word of God. Yes, there were forty different human authors who penned the words, but there was only one true and living God directing their thoughts as they wrote (2 Timothy 3:16–17; 2 Peter 1:20–21). This book literally begins at the beginning when God created our universe and the planet we call earth (Genesis 1:1).

What did God think about all that he had made once the work of creation was done? We don't have to speculate because the Bible tells us that when God looked upon the world He had made, He thought it was exquisitely beautiful.[1] As God looked at the finished product, it was everything that He wanted it to be—exceedingly beautiful—perfect in every way, and He was totally pleased with how it turned out. There was no sickness or suffering, sorrow, pain, or death. As you look at our world today, is that how you would describe it—perfect in every way? I doubt it! I certainly wouldn't!

So what happened to our world? What morphed it from the perfect world God created at the beginning to what it is today? It must have been catastrophic. And indeed, it was. In a beautiful garden, a man and his wife, believing a lie, committed an act of willful disobedience against the explicit command of God. And the rest is history—a very painful, destructive, and deadly history—for the human race and for this world in which we live.

The trouble started when the man in the garden (Adam) took the piece of fruit from his wife (Eve), who had been deceived by the serpent.[2] And then

---

[1] The Hebrew word for "good" (*tob*) is translated by the English word "beautiful" eleven times in the Old Testament (*New American Standard Updated Edition Exhaustive Concordance of the Bible, Robert L. Thomas, ed., Logos Research Systems, 1994*).

[2] This "serpent of old" is identified in the New Testament as "the devil and Satan, who deceives the whole world" (Revelation 12:9).

he did exactly what God had directly commanded him not to do. It was the man through whom sin entered the world and death as the result of sin, along with all the pain and suffering that has characterized our world ever since. The reason the man is held responsible for what happened, and not his wife, is that she was deceived, but the man deliberately disobeyed God with full knowledge of what he was doing (Romans 5:12). Don't misunderstand! The issue at stake here is not simply a matter of eating a piece of fruit (how silly would that be). The fruit was a test of whether Adam and Eve would trust God and, by their obedience, demonstrate their willingness to live by God's design and under God's authority over them as their Creator. The alternative would be to believe a lie and, through their disobedience, reject God's design and rebel against God's authority, declaring their own autonomy from God. Sadly, they failed the test, bringing devastating consequences upon the earth and all future generations of the human race.

Sin, by its very nature, corrupts everything it touches. God's intention from the beginning had been for mankind to "be fruitful and multiply, and fill the earth, and subdue it; and rule over [...] every living thing that moves upon the earth" (Genesis 1:28). To put it in simpler terms, they were to bear children and so populate the earth with people and to care for the earth and use earth's natural resources to develop civilization and culture that would be in harmony with God's design. This mandate didn't change after the entrance of sin into the world, but now sorrow, suffering, pain, and death would accompany the human race as their constant companions. With sin has come corruption in every conceivable area of life. The human body now experiences physical sickness and disease, aging, and ultimately death, resulting in its returning to the dust from which it was made. Sin brought corruption to the environment. Weeds and unproductive soil now make it a challenge to cultivate enough food to eat (Genesis 3:17–19).

Once sin entered into our once perfect world, our world wasn't perfect anymore. Hugh Whelchel, in his book *All Things New*, provides an excellent analysis of how Adam and Eve's rebellion has brought corruption and ruin upon our entire world. He says,

> This rebellion of Adam and Eve against God in the Garden of Eden broke the command he had given to them and introduced sin into the world (Genesis 2:16–17). Sin contaminated every aspect of human life and the created order (Genesis 3:7–24). The unity and peace God had woven into his world, shalom, began to unravel. Every part of the created order was damaged; even the environment was altered. Everything was broken, including our relationship with God. Today, we see the effects of the Fall in every facet of our lives. We seek independence from God and look to idols to fulfill our longings. We experience despair, hurt, pain, sadness, anger, and envy in broken relationships. We toil internally, wrestling with self-doubt, insecurity, pride, and depression. The earth itself aches from the physical effects of the Fall, groaning from famine, drought, floods, and other natural disasters. Sin has touched all aspects of Creation.[3]

This fully coincides with the apostle Paul's words,

> For the anxious longing of the creation waits eagerly for the revealing of the sons of God. For the creation was subjected to futility, not willingly, but because of Him who subjected it, in hope that the creation itself also will be set free from its slavery to

---

[3] Hugh Whelchel, *All Things New* (Institute for Faith, Work & Economics, McLean, Virginia, 2016) 8–9

corruption into the freedom of the glory of the children of God. For we know that the whole creation groans and suffers the pains of childbirth together until now.

Romans 8:19–22

The book *When Helping Hurts* provides further insight when it says,

> Their relationship with God was damaged, as their intimacy with Him was replaced with fear; their relationship with self was marred, as Adam and Eve developed a sense of shame; their relationship with others was broken, as Adam quickly blamed Eve for their sin; and their relationship with the rest of creation became distorted, as God cursed the ground and the childbearing process...Because these four relationships are the building blocks for all human activity, the effects of the Fall are manifested in the economic, social, religious, and political systems that humans have created throughout history.[4]

So what is sin anyway? That's an interesting question—especially in a world that thinks there is no such thing as sin because they think there is no such thing as moral absolutes. A biblical definition would be that sin is lawlessness (1 John 3:4). Sin is really the rejection of and total disregard not for just a particular law but for the very idea that there is such a thing as right or wrong in the first place. Sin rejects the idea that God, or anyone else, has the right to tell me how to live my life. Sin is choosing personal autonomy over submission to authority—any authority outside myself. This is the very thing that Adam did when he willfully chose to eat the fruit that God had commanded him not to eat. Needless to say, he failed the test!

---

[4] Steve Corbett and Brian Fikkert, *When Helping Hurts: How to Alleviate Poverty without Hurting the Poor...and Yourself* (Chicago, IL: Moody Publishers, 2012)

Mankind has been failing the test ever since Adam. In just a few generations after Adam, because sin had taken root in the human heart, what had once been a perfect world was now filled with wickedness. It had become corrupt. It was filled with violence. And every man's thoughts were continually intent upon evil (Genesis 6:5–11). Sound familiar? It sounds just like something I might read in today's newspaper. Sin is essentially a rejection of God as having any authority over us, even though we owe our very existence to Him as our Creator (Acts 17:28). In a sense, sin is essentially making ourselves our own god. It isn't difficult to see where this kind of thinking leads, is it? If I make my own rules, and everyone else makes their own rules, if I think that "It's all about me and I can do whatever I want," and everyone else thinks the same way, how well is that going to work in a world of nearly eight billion people? Not very well, I'm afraid.

Everything that's wrong in our world essentially flows out of the kind of thinking that embraces a spirit of lawlessness. Nations go to war, marriages fall apart, children rebel against their parents, and people commit acts of violence, murders, and all sorts of horrid crimes against their fellow man. Why do people do such things? Because, after all, "It's all about me, and I can do whatever I want—nobody is going to tell me what to do!" The very nature of sin motivates people to do whatever it takes to get whatever they want, regardless of how their actions may impact other people. This doesn't mean that every human being is as bad or as evil as he potentially could be. Because man has been created in the image of God (Genesis 1:27), all goodness in man has not been totally destroyed. Nevertheless, all the problems of our world can still be traced back to one man and his rejection of God's will and authority over him. By his rebellion against God, Adam brought sin into what had been a perfect world and passed on his rebellious heart to the next generation and the next and the next in our long, sad history. It all sounds pretty bleak, doesn't it? What is the future of our world? Just more of the same until one day we completely destroy what's left of our once perfect planet? Or is there hope for a better future?

When I read the newspaper or check the latest news on my phone, I certainly find no evidence that things are getting any better. On the contrary, this world gives every indication that things are getting worse. Our world is struggling today with problems that didn't even exist fifty years ago—international terrorism, mass murders, antibiotic-resistant germs, identity theft, and global warming. There are wars and conflicts around the world that seem to keep popping up like "whack-a-mole," each one a potential threat to world peace and a possible trigger for global thermonuclear war that could completely destroy the human race and even the entire planet. We have to wonder what kind of a world we're leaving to our children and grandchildren.

It certainly would be easy to throw up our hands in despair, saying, "What can we do?" And the reality is that there is very little that we can do. The reason that we can't fix the problems in our world is that we are the problem. But there's hope for the future of our world in the promise of God that at the proper time, He is going to resolve the problem and fix our world. Though it might not seem evident by what we see happening in our world today, God is even now working a plan to restore our world to what He originally intended it to be and even better. Just as the problem with our world is defined in the book of Genesis, so is the solution.

Only God can fix the problem of sin by stepping into human history and changing the heart of man because our own sinful hearts are the source of the problem. And that's where "the promise" comes in. After Adam's rebellion, God pronounced a curse on our world that, because of sin, would make everything in this world change, and definitely not for the better. But along with the curse, He offered a glimmer of hope with a promise that things would not always remain as they are. Turning to Satan, who had taken upon himself the form of a serpent, God said, "Because you have done this [...] I will put enmity between you and the woman, and between your seed and her seed; he shall bruise you on the head, and you shall bruise him on the heel" (Genesis 3:14–15).

Sounds a little mysterious, doesn't it? What He's saying is that a descendant ("seed") of the woman will be wounded by the serpent (Satan) but not destroyed, yet he will ultimately crush the head of the serpent (Satan) by completely destroying him and all the evil that he has done. In reversing all that Satan has tried to do, ironically, God will use the very woman who was deceived in the garden to bring forth the Savior who will one day rescue the human race and restore our world by undoing all that Satan has done. This prophetic promise in the book of Genesis does not specifically identify this Savior by name. Nor is any indication given of a timeline for when He will appear on the scene of human history.

Fortunately, many more prophecies would come, providing more detailed information about this Deliverer who would come to crush the head of the serpent. This Deliverer would eventually come to be known by God's people in the Old Testament as the Messiah, which means "anointed one" (Daniel 9:25–26). His name is Jesus of Nazareth. Born of a virgin, Jesus came into the world at just the right time to rescue mankind from the curse of the law (Galatians 4:4). He came to destroy the works of the devil (1 John 3:8) and to render powerless the one who had the power of death (Satan), in order to set free those who, through fear of death, were subject to slavery all their lives (Hebrews 2:14–15).

Jesus has already come and intervened in history to rescue mankind from the penalty and power of sin in their lives. And He's coming to intervene in history again to finish the job and rescue mankind and our world from the corruption of sin itself. Ultimately, we will live forever with Him in a new world on a new earth in which everything wrong with this present world will be made right (2 Peter 3:10–13), where there is no longer any death, mourning, crying, or pain (Revelation 21:1–4), when God says at last, "[...] Behold, I am making all things new" (Revelation 21:5a).

I am greatly encouraged when I hear the apostle Paul speak of this hope for the future of our world and how this hope should make a difference in our lives. He calls it "the blessed hope" (Titus 2:10–13), and with good reason. Paul is not talking about an "I hope so" kind of hope, which is just wishful thinking or an optimistic view of the future that everything will eventually turn out okay. He's talking about an "I know so" kind of hope that does not rest upon wishful thinking or an optimistic outlook on life but upon the certainty of God's promises and the faithfulness of God to keep those promises.[5] This kind of hope rests in the confidence that the writer to the Hebrews is talking about when he says, "Let us hold fast the confession of our hope without wavering, for He who promised is faithful" (Hebrews 10:23).

What is this "blessed hope" that we have to look forward to? Paul says our "blessed hope" is "the glorious appearing of our great God and Savior, Jesus Christ" (Titus 2:13). Jesus is coming, you know. And how do we know that? Because we have the promise of God and are trusting in the faithfulness of God to keep His promise. The "seed of the woman" has already come once in the person of Jesus the Messiah nearly two thousand years ago. He came to pay the price of our sin through His death on the cross and His resurrection from the grave. He came to bring us forgiveness of sin, to bring us into a right relationship with God, and to give us the gift of eternal life. All it takes for any of us to experience this is repentance and faith. What is repentance? It

---

5 The Greek word translated "hope" (*elpis*) in the original text means "a favorable and confident expectation." (*Vine's Expository Dictionary of Biblical Words*, Copyright © 1985, Thomas Nelson Publishers).

is choosing to forsake a life that is "all about me" and to embrace a new life that we receive through the grace of Jesus, the promised Messiah. This means choosing to live under the rightful authority of God, our Savior and Lord. It means believing the "good news" that Jesus alone is the One who has made all of this possible through His death and resurrection and putting our trust in Him for eternal salvation.

But this is only part of the package. This is only the beginning of what He came to do. He came once to rescue us from our sin, but He's coming again to rescue our whole world from the corruption of sin and death. Our present world will disappear in a puff of smoke. But we have God's promise that this is not the end of our world but its restoration into a new world in which everything that is wrong with our present world will be made right (2 Peter 3:23). Our blessed hope is more than just the coming of Jesus the Messiah in the fulness of His glory. It is also all that He will accomplish when He comes. It will be the birth of His kingdom on earth when, as the ancient prophet Zechariah tells us, "[...] He [the Messiah] will speak peace to the nations; and His dominion will be from sea to sea, and from the River to the ends of the earth" (Zechariah 9:10b). Furthermore, Zechariah says of that future day, "And the LORD will be king over all the earth; in that day the LORD will be the only one, and His name the only one" (Zechariah 14:9). And ultimately, He will "make all things new" (Revelation 21:5).

How should having this "blessed hope" make a difference in the way we live right now in the present? Again, the apostle Paul says,

> For the grace of God that brings salvation has appeared to all men. It teaches us to say "No" to ungodliness and worldly passions, and to live self-controlled, upright and godly lives in this present age,

while we wait for the blessed hope—the glorious appearing of our great God and Savior, Jesus Christ, who gave himself for us to redeem us from all wickedness and to purify for himself a people that are his very own, eager to do what is good.

Titus 2:11–14 (NIV)

Likewise, the apostle Peter says, "Therefore, beloved, since you look for these things, be diligent to be found by Him in peace, spotless and blameless" (2 Peter 3:14). May we live each day in a manner that honors and pleases our Savior, confident that He is coming, just as He promised, and eagerly looking forward with assured confidence to that day when we shall see Him face to face and live forever with Him in a glorious new world.

Chapter 2

The Prophecy

Seventy weeks have been decreed for your people and your holy city, to finish the transgression, to make an end of sin, to make atonement for iniquity, to bring in everlasting righteousness, to seal up vision and prophecy and to anoint the most holy place.

Daniel 9:24

The winds of war were blowing at gale force throughout the ancient Middle East as the army of the greatest superpower of its day was on the move, leaving a path of death and destruction in its wake. A new world empire was rising as the mighty kingdom of Babylon swallowed up smaller kingdoms like a ferocious predatory animal on the rampage. The ancient prophecy of the Jewish prophet Habakkuk provides a vivid description of what the Babylonians were like, and it's not pretty. He says,

[They are] a cruel and violent people [who] will march across the world and conquer other lands. They are notorious for their cruelty and do whatever they like. Their horses are swifter than cheetahs and fiercer than wolves at dusk. Their charioteers charge from far away. Like eagles, they swoop down to devour their prey. "On they come, all bent on violence. Their hordes advance like a desert wind, sweeping captives ahead of them like sand. They scoff at kings and princes and scorn all their fortresses. They simply pile ramps of earth against their walls and capture them! They sweep past like the wind and are gone. But they are deeply guilty, for their own strength is their god."

Habakkuk 1:6b–11 (NLT)

It was only a matter of time before the Babylonian army showed up at the gates of Jerusalem, intent on their mission to rule the world. Under the leadership of General Nebuchadnezzar, who would soon become king of the mighty Babylonian Empire, they breached the defenses of Jerusalem in a blood bath and captured the city.[6] Jerusalem became just one more trophy to the prowess of Babylon's seemingly invincible war machine.

Then, on Nebuchadnezzar's command, many of the brightest and best young men were taken from Jerusalem back to the city of Babylon. They were to be educated in the Babylonian culture and language and prepared to serve in the king's court. A young Jewish man named Daniel was among them (Daniel 1:1–7). Daniel excelled in his new environment, so much so that he eventually became ruler over the whole province of Babylon (the main province within the greater empire) and chief prefect over all the wise men of Babylon (Daniel 2:1–49). Daniel continued to rule under the reign of Nebuchadnezzar until the king died forty-three years later.[7]

The Jewish people chafed under the oppressive rule of the Babylonians, reaching a breaking point that led to a Jewish rebellion. King Nebuchadnezzar was swift to put down this rebellion in a tsunami of blood and tears. He made an example of the Jews to other nations that might be tempted to do the same by completely destroying the city of Jerusalem, including the Jewish temple, turning it all into a pile of rubble. Then he marched them off to Babylon in chains to live in exile (2 Chronicles 36:17–21).[8]

Over time the political landscape began to change as another mighty army arose to challenge the oppressive rule of Babylon. The city of Babylon was captured by a stroke of military genius when the Persian army diverted the Euphrates River that flowed under the virtually impregnable walls of the

---

[6] This occurred in 605 bc.
[7] This occurred in 562 bc.
[8] This occurred in 586 bc.

city, allowing them to conquer Babylon simply by marching under the wall on the dry river bed.[9] Now, in an ironic turn of events, the mighty Babylonian Empire had itself been conquered and swallowed up in the jaws of the Persian Empire under the rule of King Cyrus the Great.

The former Babylonian ruler Belshazzar, decadent grandson of King Nebuchadnezzar, was dead, and a man by the name of Darius the Mede was appointed by the Persian king to serve as the new ruler of Babylon (Daniel 5:30).[10] Apparently, Daniel had been living in relative obscurity after the death of Nebuchadnezzar. But now, as Darius the Mede began to set up a new administration in Babylon, he brought Daniel out of obscurity and appointed him to serve as one of the leading officials in his new administration (Daniel 6:1–3). Darius was astute enough to know that, as a former ruler of Babylon during the reign of King Nebuchadnezzar, Daniel would be well suited to help him establish his new administration during this time of regime change. I can only imagine how the Jewish people who were living in exile wondered what would be coming in this time of political and social upheaval.

As this regime change played out in Babylon, Daniel was well aware of Jeremiah's prophecy that the Jewish people would remain in exile in Babylon for a period of seventy years, and then God would restore them to their homeland (Jeremiah 29:8–14). Daniel also knew that the time for the fulfillment of this prophecy was rapidly approaching. A man who believed in the power of prayer, Daniel began to intercede, reminding God, in a sense, of His promise given through Jeremiah's prophecy to restore His people to their homeland (Daniel 9:12–19).

---

[9] This occurred in 539 bc.

[10] The Darius mentioned here as being appointed ruler of Babylon in 539 bc by King Cyrus the Great is not to be confused with King Darius I, who became ruler over the entire Persian Empire in 522 bc, and who ruled in the days of the Jewish prophets, Hosea and Zechariah.

As Daniel was praying, he was interrupted by an unexpected visitor. The angel Gabriel suddenly appeared in his presence (Daniel 11:20–23). It isn't every day that a person receives a visit from an angel of heaven. I have to say that in all the years I've lived on this earth, an angel from God has never paid me a visit. Yet, in Daniel's case, he had already been visited by the angel Gabriel twelve years earlier.[11]

Now Gabriel was back again, this time with a prophecy of God's future plans for the Jewish people and a revelation of how those future events would impact them as a nation. What an encouraging message to assure them, in a time of great uncertainty and anxiety about their future, that God was not finished with them. What a soothing balm to their troubled and anxious souls. Through this revelation to Daniel, God reaffirmed and spelled out some of the details of His promise spoken through the prophet Jeremiah at the beginning of their captivity in Babylon when he said, "'[...] I know the plans that I have for you,' declares the LORD, 'plans for welfare and not for calamity to give you a future and a hope'" (Jeremiah 29:11).

In revealing this prophecy to Daniel, the angel Gabriel explains,

> Seventy weeks have been decreed for your people and your holy city, to finish the transgression, to make an end of sin, to make atonement for iniquity, to bring in everlasting righteousness, to seal up vision and prophecy and to anoint the most holy place. So you are to know and discern that from the issuing of a decree to restore and rebuild Jerusalem until Messiah the Prince there will be seven weeks and sixty-two weeks [...]. Then after the sixty-two weeks the Messiah will be cut off and have nothing, and the people of the prince who is to come will destroy the city and the sanctuary.

---

[11] This was 551 bc.

And its end will come with a flood; even to the end there will be war; desolations are determined.

Daniel 9:24–26

One of the amazing things about this particular prophetic revelation given to Daniel is its specificity in terms of some of the details given for future events affecting the Jewish nation and, in reality, the whole world. This specificity of detail in so many of the prophecies found in the Bible is truly one of the strongest evidences that the Bible is not only true and therefore trustworthy but that it is the Word of the living God, not just the word of men (2 Peter 1:20). No human being has within himself the ability to predict the future. Only God does! Men may guess at the future and may use various techniques, such as computer algorithms, in an attempt to predict the future, but they are only dealing in probabilities. God alone knows the future, and in the prophecies of the Bible, He reveals the future to us.

Prior to the time when Daniel received this revelation, many other prophecies had been given over the course of centuries, providing more details about the "seed of the woman," who later came to be identified by the Jewish people as the Messiah, which means "anointed one"[12] in the Hebrew language. For example, Isaiah, whose prophetic ministry was 200 years before Daniel, prophesied that the Messiah would be miraculously born of a virgin and would be called "Emmanuel," which in the Hebrew language means "God with us" (Isaiah 7:14; cp. Matthew 1:18–25; Luke 1:26–38). The prophet Micah, a contemporary of Isaiah, said that the Messiah would be born in the city of Bethlehem and that he would be "a ruler in Israel [whose] goings forth are from long ago, from the days of eternity" (Micah 5:2; Luke 2:1–20).

---

[12] The Hebrew word translated "Messiah" (*maschiach*) means "anointed one," which is equivalent to the Greek word for Christ (*christos*) (*New American Standard Updated Edition Exhaustive Concordance of the Bible*).

These prophecies provide incredible detail about the Messiah's birth, which should make any reasonable person stop and question how a mere mortal could predict such things apart from divine revelation. Both were fulfilled by only one man—Jesus of Nazareth. I find the detail and accuracy of these prophecies, and so many others like them, truly amazing and reaffirming to my faith. However, this prophecy given to Daniel provides even one more incredible detail about the coming of the Messiah that none of the other Hebrew prophets specify. He prophesies the exact year when the Messiah would show up in history.

Daniel's prophetic revelation begins with the statement that God will complete His work of rescuing mankind from the curse of sin and of creating a new world order characterized by everlasting righteousness over the course of a period of 490 years (Daniel 9:24).[13] The prophecy goes on to break these 490 years down further into three distinct periods of 49 years + 434 years + 7 years (Daniel 9:25–27). As we've already seen, the city of Jerusalem had been destroyed by the Babylonians with nothing left but a pile of rubble. At the time that this prophetic revelation was given to Daniel, the city had been in ruins for nearly half a century.

Now according to this prophetic revelation, at some point in the future, a decree would be issued for the rebuilding and restoration of Jerusalem. Such a decree, from a human perspective, would have seemed highly improbable, if not impossible, at the time. Yet history tells us that this prophecy was fulfilled by the Persian king Artaxerxes nearly a century later, long after Daniel's bones

---

[13] When Daniel speaks of a "period of seventy 'weeks,'" in the Hebrew language, the word translated "week" (*sheba*) simply means a "period of seven" (*New American Standard Updated Edition Exhaustive Concordance of the Bible*). While the English text reads seventy "weeks," it really says seventy periods of seven. The Jews measured time in heptads (periods of seven years), just as we measure time in decades (periods of ten years) or centuries (periods of one hundred years).

had turned to dust.[14] You can read about the fulfillment of this prophecy in the Old Testament book of Nehemiah. Nehemiah, himself a Jew and a close advisor to the king, was the one commissioned by Artaxerxes to restore and rebuild the city when the decree was issued.

The prophecy goes on to say that the restoring and rebuilding of Jerusalem would extend over the first forty-nine of the 490 years. The book of Nehemiah tells us that the rebuilding of the city walls was completed in record time—less than two months—which was an extraordinary, even miraculous, accomplishment (Neh. 6:15–16). However, it says nothing about how long the complete restoration and rebuilding of the city took. Considering the immensity of the project, it would not be at all unreasonable to think that it took forty-nine years to finish.

The prophecy continues to be one of the most incredible predictions in the entire Bible about the coming of the Messiah. It says that from the issuing of the decree to restore and rebuild Jerusalem to the time when Messiah the Prince would appear on the world scene would be a period of 483 years.[15] Taking into account the differences in calculating months and years between the Jewish calendar and our modern Gregorian calendar, this brings us to the year AD 33, the very year when Jesus presented Himself to the Jewish people as their Messiah at the beginning of Passover week.[16] How amazing is that!

But wait! There's still more! This prophetic revelation also says that once the Messiah appeared on the scene, He would be killed and seem to

---

[14] Secular history tells us that this decree was issued in 444 bc, whereas the prophetic vision was given to Daniel in 539 bc.

[15] Seven periods of seven years (the time it would take to restore and rebuild Jerusalem) + sixty-two periods of seven years = four hundred eighty-three years.

[16] For more information on the chronology of the life of Christ, see Harold W. Hoehner, *Chronological Aspects of the Life of Christ* (Grand Rapids: Zondervan Publishing House, 1978).

have accomplished nothing (Daniel 9:26).[17] In other words, it would appear that after Messiah's death, His life had ended in complete failure. And this is exactly how it would have seemed to Jesus' followers when they saw Jesus dead and buried, at least until His resurrection. According to the Gospel of Luke, two of His disciples even expressed this conclusion before they realized that Jesus had risen from the dead.[18] Of course, appearances can be deceiving to those without all the facts, as in the case with Jesus' disciples until after the resurrection.

The prophecy goes on to say that, after the Messiah is killed, war would bring about the complete destruction of the city of Jerusalem and the Jewish temple for a second time. We know from history that this part of the prophecy about the destruction of Jerusalem was fulfilled in AD 70, just thirty-seven years after the crucifixion of Jesus, when the Roman army came to put down a Jewish rebellion against Roman rule. According to Josephus, the ancient historian who was an eyewitness to what happened, the Romans captured Jerusalem and left the city in total ruin, with 1,100,000 people killed during the siege and 97,000 people captured and enslaved.[19]

This event marked the end of Israel as a nation, with the surviving Jews eventually being scattered across three continents. The story temporarily ends right here, leaving one more period of seven years before God's plan and program

---

[17] The Hebrew word here translated "cut off" (*karath*) literally means "to cut, to cut off [or] to kill" (*The Online Bible Thayer's Greek Lexicon and Brown, Driver & Briggs Hebrew Lexicon*, Woodside Bible Fellowship, Ontario, Canada, 1993, Licensed from the Institute for Creation Research).

[18] "But we were hoping that it was He who was going to redeem Israel" (Luke 24:21). Notice the tense of the verb, "[...] we were hoping..." Clearly they had been hoping that Jesus was the Messiah, the One who would redeem Israel, but not any more after the crucifixion (and before the resurrection) because they could not reconcile the death of Jesus with a Messiah who would show up, judge the nations, and rule the world.

[19] "Siege of Jerusalem (ad 70)," htpps://en.wikipedia.org/wiki/Siege of Jerusalem (ad 70) (accessed 25 April 2022)

for Israel and the world would be complete. The prophecy itself gives no clear indication that there would be a break in the timeline after the appearance of the Messiah in AD 33, followed by His death, and then thirty-seven years later, the destruction of Jerusalem by the Romans in AD 70. However, from our present historical perspective, we can look back and see that this is so. This final seven-year period that will bring about the completion of God's prophetic program for His people, as revealed in Daniel's prophecy, has not yet arrived, even though the break in the timeline has lasted nearly 2,000 years.[20]

In the New Testament, the apostle Paul makes an interesting statement, not just about the coming of the Messiah in fulfillment of the ancient prophecies but about the timing. He tells us, "But when the fullness of the time came, God sent forth His Son, born of a woman, born under the Law, so that He might redeem those who were under the Law, that we might receive the adoption as sons" (Galatians 4:4–5).

Notice three important things that Paul tells us in this passage. First, God sent His Son into the world, whom we know to be Jesus the Messiah. Secondly, He would be born of a woman, which is an interesting description of the Messiah since the Messiah is depicted in the original prophecy as the seed of the woman (Genesis 3:15) who would come into the world through a virgin birth (Isaiah 7:14). And thirdly, it says that the Messiah came right on time in the outworking of God's plan. In the Greek language, it says that God's Son came in the fullness of time (Galatians 4:4).[21] This means that He came when the precise number of years appointed by the Father was completed according to His plan for the Messiah to come on the scene.

It's wonderful to see that God is so precise in His timing. He's never early, and He's never late. He always takes action at just the right time. And because

---

[20] We'll talk more about this final period of seven years in chapter 7.

[21] The Greek word translated "fullness" (pleroma) is derived from another word (pleroo), which means "to fulfill, complete" (Vine's Expository Dictionary of Biblical Words).

this is true, we can be confident that Jesus will come again to complete what He started the first time, just as He promised, and at just the right time in the Father's plan.

Whether you are contemplating the outworking of God's plan of redemption, or His personal plan for your life, God's timing is always impeccable. It was "when the right time came" (Galatians 4:4, NLT) that God sent His Son into the world. Whatever you may be waiting on God to do in your life, you can rest assured that God will take the necessary action when the "right time" comes, even in the smallest detail of your life.

The reason we can confidently wait for the Lord to act is what the Lord Himself tells us through the prophet Isaiah, "Those who hopefully wait for Me will not be put to shame" (Isaiah 49:23c). Just keep on waiting without getting discouraged or losing hope. Isaiah assures us that when it comes to waiting on the Lord, it will always pay off; he says,

> He gives strength to the weary, and to him who lacks might He increases power. Though youths grow weary and tired, and vigorous young men stumble badly, yet those who wait for the LORD will gain new strength; they will mount up with wings like eagles, they will run and not get tired, they will walk and not become weary.
>
> Isaiah 40:29–31

God is never early, never late, but always right on time. And because that's true, you can also rest assured that when Jesus the Messiah comes again as He promised, He will be right on time in the outworking of God's plan. Count on it!

Chapter 3

The Question

As He [Jesus] was sitting on the Mount of Olives, the disciples
came to Him privately, saying, "Tell us, when will these things
happen, and what will be the sign of Your coming, and of the end
of the age?"

Matthew 24:3

It was a year of great expectation among the Jewish people. The year AD 33
marked the time of fulfillment for the ancient prophecy of Daniel regarding
the coming of Messiah the Prince (Daniel 9:25). The prophetic clock had
been ticking for 483 years from the issuing of a decree by the Persian king
Artaxerxes to restore and rebuild the city of Jerusalem, destroyed by the
Babylonians nearly 150 years earlier. At last, the time had come. There's a
good possibility that many of the Jews living at that time were aware of this
ancient prophecy.[22] Certainly, this was true among those who were godly and
familiar with the ancient Scriptures. These would have been the ones filled
with a sense of expectancy and excitement for the Messiah to reveal Himself
to the nation. This was especially true as the Passover season was now rapidly
approaching.

It was the Tuesday before Passover—two days after what we have come
to know as the triumphal entry of Jesus into Jerusalem. Jesus and His
disciples were making their way out of the temple complex in Jerusalem.
Their destination was a secluded garden located on the Mount of Olives
on the other side of the Kidron Valley opposite the city. This is where they
would spend the night. As they crossed the valley and began the ascent up

---

[22] See Appendix 1

the mountain, they were undoubtedly exhausted. They were eager to relax beneath one of the gnarly and venerable olive trees populating the garden.

Ever since their arrival in Jerusalem, Jesus had been teaching the people in the temple every day with His disciples and then spending the night on the Mount of Olives (Luke 21:37–38). Today had been an especially grueling day for Jesus as He faced a hostile confrontation with the Jewish leaders. Their opposition to Jesus had come to a head, ultimately leading to His arrest and crucifixion (Mark 14:1). As they were leaving the city, Jesus had turned to the crowd and expressed His bitter grief over what He knew was coming. The Jewish people had not only rejected Him but the prophets who had been sent to them throughout the nation's history. Soon they would reap the consequences of that rejection.

I can picture Jesus with tears streaming down his face as He cried out, "Jerusalem, Jerusalem, who kills the prophets and stones those who are sent to her! How often I wanted to gather your children together, the way a hen gathers her chicks under her wings, and you were unwilling. Behold, your house is being left to you desolate!" (Matthew 23:37–38)[23]

Jesus is talking about the fulfillment of that portion of Daniel's prophecy that we examined in chapter two when He speaks of the desolation of Jerusalem (Daniel 9:26). As we saw in chapter two, we know from history that this part of the prophecy about the destruction of Jerusalem was fulfilled just thirty-seven years after the crucifixion of Jesus. The Roman army came to put down a Jewish rebellion against Roman rule in AD 70. They destroyed the city and the temple, brutally killing or enslaving the people. This event marked the beginning of the end for Israel as a nation as those Jews who had survived eventually were scattered across three continents. Truly the words

---

[23] The Greek word here for "desolate" (*eremos*) means "solitary, deserted," and the corresponding verb carries the force "to lay waste, make desolate" (Leon Morris, *The Gospel of Matthew,* Grand Rapids, MI: Wm B. Eerdmans Publishing Co., 1992, 591), (footnote 50.)

of Jesus were fulfilled as He had said, "Behold, your house is being left to you desolate!"

As Jesus and the disciples were leaving the temple after this prophetic utterance, the disciples began to point to the temple buildings in wonder and amazement. Then, according to Mark's account, one of the disciples said to him, "Teacher, behold what wonderful stones and what wonderful buildings!" (Mark 13:1b) It's not difficult to understand why the disciples would be awestruck by the beautiful temple buildings and the beautiful stones used to construct them. Remember that these were just simple men from rural Galilee. But their fixation on the stones used to build the temple would seem to indicate that they didn't hear a word Jesus had just said about the destruction of the temple and the entire city. Here they were, staring wide-eyed at these beautiful stones after Jesus had just said that all of this would be obliterated.

In response to their fascination with these stones, Jesus reiterated His earlier point, "Do you not see all these things? Truly I say to you, not one stone here will be left upon another, which will not be torn down" (Matthew 24:2). In essence, Jesus was asking them, "Don't you get it? Have you not heard a word I've been saying?" Jesus was predicting that not only would the stones of the temple be torn down, but the destruction would be so complete that literally not one stone would be left upon another. He was amplifying what He had just spoken to the Jews gathered in the temple. He wanted them to grasp just how extensive and complete the destruction would be.

Imagine how confusing and troubling it would have been for the disciples to hear these words from Jesus. Even though they may have been familiar with Daniel's prophecy, what they heard Jesus say was certainly foreign to the prevailing Jewish theology of the day concerning the Messiah, especially the part about Jerusalem being destroyed.

We know that the disciples were convinced Jesus was truly the Messiah of Israel. This is evident from Peter's response to the question that Jesus had presented to the disciples several weeks earlier, just before they started on their journey to Jerusalem to celebrate the Passover. Jesus and the disciples had taken a rest stop in a city called Caesarea Philippi. This city was located some thirty miles north of the Sea of Galilee near the base of Mount Hermon and approximately 120 miles north of the city of Jerusalem. Once in Jerusalem, they would celebrate the Passover along with other Jewish pilgrims coming not just from Judea and Galilee but from all over the Roman Empire and beyond.

The disciples had been journeying now with Jesus on the dusty roads of Judea, Samaria, Galilee, and beyond for nearly three years at this point. Before they set out on their physical journey to Jerusalem, however, Jesus challenged them in regard to their understanding and belief of who He really is. Before they set out on their physical journey to Jerusalem, it was time for Him to bring up the issue of where they were on their spiritual journey of faith. He challenged them regarding their understanding of His identity. "Who do people say that the Son of Man is?" (Matthew 16:13b)

It's significant that in asking the disciples this question, Jesus refers to Himself as the Son of Man. The term "Son of Man" hearkens back to another ancient prophecy of Daniel (Daniel 7:1–14). In what He calls "the night visions," Daniel sees someone who appears to be human doing something that no mere human can do—coming "with the clouds of heaven." He describes this human-like being as "One like a Son of Man." This "Son of Man" comes to be presented before the "Ancient of Days," and He is given "dominion, glory and a kingdom, that all the peoples, nations and men of every language might serve Him."

Daniel goes to say of this "One like a Son of Man" that "[...] His dominion is an everlasting dominion which will not pass away; and His kingdom is one which will not be destroyed" (Daniel 7:14b). This is not the only time that Jesus would identify himself as the "Son of Man." In fact, He refers to Himself as the "Son of Man" thirty-one times in the Gospel of Matthew alone. The disciples would have clearly understood that Jesus was claiming to be the Messiah because they knew that "Son of Man" was a messianic title. This is the kind of Messiah that the disciples, and indeed all Israel, were anticipating. They were expecting a mighty, conquering king who would establish an everlasting kingdom on the earth and rule over the nations forever.

In answering His question, the disciples reply that some are saying He is John the Baptist risen from the dead. Others are saying that He is Elijah or Jeremiah or one of the other prophets (Matthew 16:14). Without comment, Jesus immediately raises a second question, which is where the first question was intended to lead: "But who do you say that I am?" (Matthew 16:15) What matters most at this point is not who other people think Jesus is but who the disciples think Jesus is. Do His disciples truly believe that He is the promised Messiah?

Simon Peter, in his usual role as spokesman for the group, replies, "You are the Christ [Messiah], the Son of the living God" (Matthew 16:16). Right answer! Jesus immediately indicates that Peter has answered correctly. He says to him, "Blessed are you, Simon Barjona, because flesh and blood did not reveal this to you, but My Father who is in heaven" (Matthew 16:17). The disciples were clearly convinced that Jesus was indeed the Messiah of Israel.

The disciples would have known that this was the year when, according to the ancient prophecy of Daniel, the Messiah, this "Son of Man," would present Himself to the nation of Israel. And with the Passover rapidly approaching, I can imagine that they were probably thinking to themselves that this would likely be the time when Jesus would reveal Himself as the Messiah/King that everyone was waiting for. Unfortunately, they were in for a disappointment. Their understanding of all the prophecies regarding the Messiah and how they all fit together was incomplete and incorrect.

Yes, they were likely familiar with Daniel's prophecy foretelling the Messiah's appearance on the scene that very year. But they simply had no category for a plotline that included the Messiah being killed and the city of Jerusalem and the temple being destroyed—again. Either that or else they conveniently overlooked it. Why would they do that? Because it simply didn't fit in with the Jewish theology of the day. The Jews were expecting not a crucified savior but a conquering king. In all fairness to the disciples and to the Jewish people at large, the messianic prophecies of the Old Testament were not presented in a linear fashion. They were presented more like a random collection of individual photographs of the future.

Let me suggest another metaphor. You might say that for the Jews, the messianic prophecies of the Old Testament were like individual pieces of a jigsaw puzzle not put together. The problem is that they were trying to put it together without the benefit of a box cover showing the finished picture. If you've ever tried to put together a very large jigsaw puzzle, you can understand exactly what I'm talking about. Even though the Jews knew the prophecies, there were no instructions to explain how to put the pieces of the puzzle together. The Jewish theology of that day was a human attempt based on human reasoning to make sense out of all these hundreds of puzzle pieces. They got parts of it right, but there were others that they got totally wrong. This explains why the disciples just didn't "get it." Jesus was putting the pieces together correctly for them, but differently from the theology they knew.

After Peter's statement of faith, Jesus began to confirm Daniel's prophecy about the Messiah being killed. He explained that He must suffer and die at the hands of the Jewish leaders during Passover week (Matthew 16:21). Here Jesus is again making reference to the prophecy of Daniel that we looked at in the last chapter. This prophecy states, "Then after the sixty-two weeks the Messiah will be cut off and have nothing" (Daniel 9:26a). Imagine how hearing this would have confused and upset the disciples. When the disciples heard that Jesus would be killed by the Jewish religious leaders and then be raised up three days later, it didn't really go well. Can you believe that Peter actually took Jesus aside and began to rebuke Him? Peter actually said to Him, "God forbid it, Lord! This shall never happen to You" (Matthew 16:22b). Can you imagine Peter actually rebuking the very person whom he had just acknowledged as the Messiah, the Son of the living God?

Again, as they continued their journey to Jerusalem, Jesus further reaffirmed that He, the "Son of Man" of Daniel's prophecy, would be put to death at the hands of the Jewish leaders. But then He would be raised from the dead on the third day (Matthew 16:22–23). They were grieved by what they heard, but they still just didn't seem to get it. To them, it made no sense at all that the Messiah would come only to be killed. And if He were killed, how would He possibly rule the nations, as the prophets said He would? The part about Jesus being raised from the dead apparently went right past them. They had no category for such a thing happening. This despite the fact that they had already witnessed Jesus raising Lazarus from the dead (John 11:1–44).

It seems clear that the idea of the Messiah being killed instead of welcomed by the Jewish religious leaders simply did not have a place on their radar. This despite the fact that, as we've already seen, it is clearly stated in Daniel's prophecy and now elaborated upon by Jesus Himself. They were expecting a Messiah who would come riding on the clouds as the Son of Man to establish a kingdom that would never end. They were not expecting a Messiah who would come to an end by hanging on a Roman cross to die. None of this made any sense to them. A crucified and risen Messiah simply did fit with the prevailing theology of the day. And that's probably why the vast majority of the Jewish people in that day utterly rejected Jesus as their Messiah. They, like the disciples, held fast to a theology based on an incorrect understanding of how all the individual prophecies fit together.

Now, let's come back to where we started. The disciples were resting on the Mount of Olives. They probably had not been there for very long before the conversation reverted to what Jesus had said earlier about the destruction of the temple. They were trying to make sense of it all with no success. Finally, they decided it was time to ask Jesus the big question that had been on their minds for quite some time. They simply wanted to know when these things that Jesus was telling them would happen. What "sign" would indicate that the time of His coming[24] to establish His kingdom at the end of the age was drawing near? (Matthew 24:3) The disciples weren't expecting it to be in the far distant future, but probably before the end of Passover week.

The disciples were expecting that His coming to establish His messianic kingdom on earth would occur immediately (Luke 19:11). They had no concept of Jesus going away for an extended period of time (so far, more than two thousand years and counting). In asking about the sign of His coming, they were expecting some kind of signal—possibly an unusual occurrence of a supernatural or miraculous nature.[25] This sign would indicate that He was about to come in power and glory to present Himself officially as the Messiah/King of Israel. They were certainly not expecting Jesus to die and rise from the dead and then go away. And they certainly didn't expect Him to come again to fulfill the rest of the prophecies at some point in the far distant future.

---

[24] According to Gustav Adolf Deissman, (*Light from the Ancient East: The New Testament Illustrated by Recently Discovered Texts of the Graeco-Roman World*, 1908) "[...] the Greek word parousia occurred as early as the 3rd century bc to describe the visit of a king or dignitary to a city—a visit arranged in order to show the visitor's magnificence to the people" ("Second Coming," *https://en.wikipedia.org/wiki/Second_Coming*), (accessed 22 April 2022).

[25] The Greek word for "sign" (*semeion*) is frequently used in the Gospels in this way (Vine's *Expository Dictionary of Biblical Words*).

I'm sure that in asking this question, the memory of Jesus' "triumphal entry" into Jerusalem two days earlier would have still been fresh in their minds. As Jesus entered the city of Jerusalem, riding on a donkey, the crowds went wild. They were shouting, "Hosanna to the Son of David; BLESSED IS HE WHO COMES IN THE NAME OF THE LORD; Hosanna in the highest!" (Matthew 21:9b) It would seem likely that the disciples understood this as Jesus' fulfillment of Zechariah's prophecy spoken hundreds of years earlier— "Rejoice greatly, O daughter of Zion! Shout in triumph, O daughter of Jerusalem! Behold, your king is coming to you. He is just and endowed with salvation, humble, and mounted on a donkey, even on a colt, the foal of a donkey"[26] (Zechariah 9:9). Matthew certainly made the connection since he references Zechariah's prophecy in regard to this incident in his Gospel (Matthew 21:4–5). They saw Jesus presenting Himself and affirming His identity as Israel's promised Messiah.

You can imagine how the expectations of the disciples after the triumphal entry would now have risen higher than ever. The welcome that Jesus received from the crowds, who were likewise entering the city to celebrate the Passover, would only serve to confirm what the disciples were already thinking. They were obviously not the only ones who believed that Jesus was the Messiah and that He would soon declare Himself as Israel's Messiah/King. This is evident from the fact that in calling Jesus the "Son of David," the crowds were actually declaring Him the Messiah of Israel. In saying, "Blessed is He who comes in the name of the Lord," they were quoting from a messianic psalm (Psalm 110:26). This explains why Luke's Gospel says that the Pharisees wanted Jesus to rebuke His disciples and tell them to stop making these affirmations (Luke 19:39).

---

[26] Zechariah 9:9. I think it is significant that when Solomon was crowned king over Israel and Judah that he rode a mule (closely related to a donkey)—specifically the mule belonging to David, his father, King David, to the place of his coronation (1 Kings 1:38–40). Don't make the mistake of thinking that Jesus riding on a donkey into Jerusalem was "unkingly."

I'm sure the disciples were convinced at this point that Jesus' triumphal entry was merely the prelude to His coming in the power and glory of His kingdom. After all, the rest of Zechariah's prophecy continues, "I will cut off the chariot from Ephraim and the horse from Jerusalem; and the bow of war will be cut off. And He [i.e., 'your king'] will speak peace to the nations; and His dominion will be from sea to sea, and from the River to the ends of the earth" (Zechariah 9:10). During the "triumphal entry" the disciples must have been thinking, "This is it! It's all finally beginning to happen!" But after all that, nothing seemed to be happening. No miraculous sign! No Jesus coming in the power and glory of His kingdom. Nothing at all!

For the next few days, all Jesus did was go into the temple and teach the people. So when was He going to come as the mighty conquering Messiah/King in all the power and glory of His kingdom? The disciples clearly expected more than what they had already witnessed in the triumphal entry. And they certainly expected it would all happen very soon. Now, as they gathered around Jesus on the Mount of Olives, they wanted to know how soon the "rest of the story" would play out. They wanted to know when Jesus would come as the mighty King "in power and great glory" to rule over the nations. They simply had no clue at the time that His coming in that capacity would occur in the far distant future, centuries beyond their lifespan. They had no idea that His words were not just for them but for future followers right up to the generation that would actually be living on the earth when he came.

Before we go any further on this subject, it's important that we identify the audience Jesus is addressing as He answers the question raised by His disciples. Of course, it's obvious that Jesus is speaking face to face with His disciples. But clearly, He is also speaking to future generations yet to come. And in particular, He is speaking to those who will actually be living in the last days before His coming and the birth of His kingdom. So here's the real question!

Is He speaking to the disciples as representing Israel (since the disciples were all Jewish)? Or is He speaking to the disciples as representing the Church (since, as Christ's apostles, their teaching and ministry would become the foundation of the Church)? (Ephesians 2:19–20) Are the disciples to be seen here as the Church or Israel? I'm personally inclined to think that the question forces an unnecessary dichotomy because the disciples represent the people of God, including both Israel and the Church.

The people of Israel, the Jews, have always been God's special people, His covenant people—they still are and always will be. This has been true ever since God made His covenant[27] promise to Abraham, saying,

> I will establish my covenant as an everlasting covenant between me and you and your descendants after you for the generations to come, to be your God and the God of your descendants after you. The whole land of Canaan, where you are now an alien, I will give as an everlasting possession to you and your descendants after you; and I will be their God.
>
> Genesis 17:7–8 (NIV)

That covenant has never been rescinded, nor can it ever be rescinded because it represents an everlasting covenant. For this reason, the promise of God to Abraham is irrevocable, just as Paul says of the Jewish people, "[...] from the standpoint of God's choice they are beloved for the sake of the fathers; for the gifts and the calling of God are irrevocable" (Romans 11:28b–29). Paul is saying that because of God's promise to Abraham, Isaac,

---

[27] In the Old Testament, a covenant is "an agreement between two people or two groups that involves promised on the part of each to the other" (Ronald A. Youngblood, F. F. Bruce, R. K. Harrison, "Covenant," *Nelson's New Illustrated Bible Dictionary*, Thomas Nelson, Print Publication Date: 1995, Logos release date, 2001).

and Jacob (the fathers), He will not and cannot change His mind about Israel being His special people.

This is true even though, as a nation, they are now living in disobedience and are under judgment because of their rejection of Jesus as the true Messiah. Though Israel as a nation has rejected Jesus, God has not permanently rejected them. Nor will He ever. God's covenant with them still stands and can never be revoked. Even today, there is a remnant of the Jewish people who have put their trust in Jesus as the true Messiah. Many of these call themselves messianic Jews. This actually includes the apostle Paul himself when he says,

> I say then, God has not rejected His people, has He? May it never be! For I too am an Israelite, a descendant of Abraham, of the tribe of Benjamin. God has not rejected His people whom He foreknew. [...] there has also come to be at the present time a remnant according to God's gracious choice.
>
> Romans 11:1–2a, 5b

Paul continues,

> For I do not want you, brethren, to be uninformed of this mystery [...] that a partial hardening has happened to Israel until the fullness of the Gentiles has come in; and so all Israel will be saved; just as it is written,
>
> "THE DELIVERER WILL COME FROM ZION,
> HE WILL REMOVE UNGODLINESS FROM JACOB."
> "THIS IS MY COVENANT WITH THEM,
> WHEN I TAKE AWAY THEIR SINS."
>
> Romans 11:25–27

Israel has been God's covenant people ever since the time of Abraham, and the entire remnant of Israel who will live to see the coming of their Messiah will all come to genuine saving faith in Jesus when "the deliverer will come from Zion." But what about the Church? Ever since the day of Pentecost, those who are non-Jewish members of the Church, which now has become the Body of Christ, have become just as much a part of God's special people as the people of Israel (Ephesians 2:15–16). I'm not suggesting for a moment that the Church and Israel are the same entity or that the Church has replaced Israel as God's special people. What I'm saying is that Jew and non-Jew alike, through the work of Christ, have now become equally the people of God. Neither one is better than the other, but both are the same in their standing before God. Israel is still Israel, and the Church is still the Church.

But here's the deal! Both have now been joined together in a unique way. Yes, there is, only has been, and only will be one people of God. But that one people of God will now and forever include both Israel and the Church. It has also always included those ancient saints who preceded Abraham and the nation of Israel, going back to Adam (Hebrews 11:1–7). The people of God, then, whether of Jewish or Gentile descent, are the ones in the spotlight as Jesus responds to the questions raised by the disciples there on the Mount of Olives. Jesus especially has in mind the future generation of the people of God, both Jew and Gentile, who will live through the "great tribulation"[28] (Matthew 24:21–22). These are the ones who will see His coming and who need to be prepared for the things that will precede it.

In answering these two questions, "When will these things happen?" and "What will be the sign of Your coming and of the end of the age?" Jesus actually reverses the order in which they were asked, answering the second question first and the first question second. In answering the second question,

---

[28] More will be said about the "great tribulation" in chapter 8.

Jesus does not actually tell them what the "sign of His coming" will be. He simply tells them that those who are looking for His coming will recognize it when they see it (Matthew 24:29–30). However, He does reveal some of the things that will indicate when His coming is near.

In the Gospels of Matthew and Mark, He specifically mentions deception, war, earthquakes, famines, persecution, apostasy, lawlessness, and the proclamation of the gospel to all the nations, as well as the abomination of desolation and the great tribulation. The Gospel of Luke adds to the list plagues (pandemic diseases), terrors, and great signs in the heavens. Jesus specifically says to them that the generation of God's people who sees these things happening will know His coming is near, and they will actually live to see His coming as Israel's promised Messiah/King. But as to the exact time when He will actually come as their King, He essentially says that nobody knows except God the Father alone, but that it will be when people least expect it to to happen (Matthew 24:36, 42, 44).

Obviously, this was not what the disciples wanted or expected to hear. And apparently, they still didn't get it, at least not until after Jesus' death, resurrection, and ascension. They still didn't understand that Jesus had come this time as a Savior to suffer and die for the redemption of mankind from sin and death through His own death on the cross. Nor did they understand that the rest of the story would be coming at a later time in the future. In that future day, Jesus would come again to finish what He started, and this would be the time He came in the power and glory of His kingdom. However, as I've already said, we shouldn't be too hard on the disciples for not getting it right since even the ancient prophets themselves who wrote of the Messiah's coming weren't able to "connect the dots" in trying to understand the connection between the suffering of the Messiah and His glory to be revealed (1 Peter 1:10–11). Nevertheless, even though Jesus doesn't say when He is coming to establish His kingdom, we still know that He is coming because that's His promise to us, just as the prophets foretold. Jesus' response to the disciples' question on the Mount of Olives that day must have "rocked their theological boat." He didn't tell them what they were expecting to hear and instead told them things that they weren't expecting to hear—and, frankly, didn't want to hear.

I think the words of the two disciples on the road to Emmaus pretty well express what all the disciples were thinking after the crucifixion. They said, "[...] we were hoping that it was He who was going to redeem Israel. Indeed, besides all this, it is the third day since these things happened" (Luke 24:21). Notice the past tense of the verb here. They "were hoping," with the implication, "But now we don't know what to think." Probably the best words to describe their state of mind would be confused and disappointed. What they were expecting to happen never happened, and what they never expected to happen did.

So what about you? What are your expectations about the coming of Jesus the Messiah? Maybe you've thought about it a lot, or maybe you've barely thought about it at all. Maybe you have studied the subject or heard sermons about it, or maybe this is your first time to even hear about Jesus' coming. Whatever your understanding about the coming of Jesus, I encourage you to check it out for yourself in the Scriptures. Don't just rely on what you heard in a sermon or read in a book, even this one. Just remember that the disciples thought their theology of the Messiah's coming was right. But they were obviously mistaken, and they ended up confused and disappointed until the risen Jesus showed up and straightened them out. How did He do that? He took them to the Old Testament Scriptures and explained them. Beginning with the writings of Moses and ending with the writings of the prophets, He showed them how the Scriptures spoke of Him and all that God would accomplish through Him (Luke 24:27).

When Paul came to the Jewish synagogue in the city of Thessalonica and preached the message of Jesus the Messiah as Savior, Lord, and coming King, only a few of the Jews believed, along with a large number of Gentiles. As a result, the unbelieving Jews became jealous and ran Paul out of the city (Acts 17:1–9). Yet when Paul visited the city of Berea, just down the road, and preached the same message in the Jewish synagogue there, the people "[...] received the word with great eagerness, examining the Scriptures daily to see whether these things were so. Therefore many of them believed..." (Acts 17:11b–12a) Did you pick up on the difference between the response of Paul's audience in the city of Thessalonica and the response of his audience in the city of Berea?

The Bereans eagerly welcomed the message they were hearing, but they didn't believe it just because it sounded good or even because it made sense to them. Before they believed the message to be true, the Bereans made the effort to "check out" what Paul was saying. And they did so by going back to the authority of the Scriptures (in their case, what we refer to as the Old Testament). They carefully scrutinized what[29] they heard in the light of the clear teaching of Scripture, and they weren't afraid to ask the hard questions about what they were hearing (Acts 17:11b). The only reason they believed was that they could see how his message was in sync with the Scriptures.

Don't take my word for it or anyone else's. Human arguments or interpretations can sound very plausible, but sometimes they don't stand up to a thorough examination in the light of Scripture. Go to the Scriptures. Ask the hard questions. Check it out. Before you make up your mind what you believe about the coming of Jesus, make sure it passes the Scripture test, just as the Bereans did.

---

[29] In the Greek language of that day, the word translated "examine" (*anakrino*) means "to investigate, examine, inquire into, scrutinize, sift, question" (*The Online Bible Thayer's Greek Lexicon and Brown, Driver & Briggs Hebrew Lexicon*).

Chapter 4

The Deception

[...] See to it that no one misleads you.

Matthew 24:4b

"You can do this," he said. "You can make more money over summer break than you ever imagined." The young college student seemed bewildered at hearing these words since he had never thought of himself as a salesman. At the young man's hesitation, the older student continued, "Just think about the pile of cash you can have in your pocket if you decide to join my sales team for the summer. Selling Bibles door-to-door isn't really as difficult as you think. And I know you can do this," he repeated.

Even though it seemed too good to be true, the younger student began to think of all the things he could buy with that "pile of cash" he would have in his pocket. The older student was very persuasive, his sales pitch very convincing, and most of all, the younger student really wanted to believe it was true. To his chagrin, he found that it wasn't true at all. Selling Bibles door-to-door was a lot harder than he had been led to believe, and his sales ability was far less than what the older student had convinced him he had. By mid-summer, he had quit the sales team and was scrambling to find another summer job to pay for the next semester's tuition.

This story is real. And I know it's true because I was the younger college student. I found out the hard way that if a person really wants to believe something, he can easily allow himself to be persuaded. But a lie is still a lie, no matter how beautifully it's packaged. Believing a lie can have devastating consequences. As the ancient sage writes in the Old Testament book of Proverbs, "There is a way which seems right to a man, but its end is the way of death" (Proverbs 14:12).

As Jesus begins to warn His disciples about the things that will occur on the earth prior to His coming and the birth of His kingdom, the first issue He addresses is the very real danger of people being deceived by religious charlatans and spiritual shysters who try to convince them to believe a lie. In giving this warning, Jesus says, "See to it that no one misleads you. For many will come in My name, saying, 'I am the Christ [Messiah],' and will mislead many" (Matthew 24:4–5). Certainly, false messiahs are nothing new on the world scene. Over the course of history, there have been at least sixteen so-called messiahs in Judaism and at least thirty-three false messiahs in Christendom, either self-proclaimed or acclaimed as such by their followers.[30] Clearly, the world has had its share of false "messiahs" over the centuries, just as Jesus said they would.

The apostle Paul expands upon this warning that Jesus gives and describes a deception that the followers of Jesus will encounter in the last days before His coming and the commencement of His kingdom. This deception will ensnare people throughout the entire world. Paul writes to the Thessalonian Christians some twenty years after Jesus warned in the Olivet Discourse about religious deceivers. He warns the Thessalonians not to be deceived by a false teaching being circulated among the churches. This false teaching claimed that the coming of Christ (here referred to as the day of the Lord) had already occurred and that his readers somehow had missed it (2 Thessalonians 2:1–2).

Paul moves from the deception in his day regarding the day of the Lord to this future deception. He says that the day of the Lord will not come "[...] unless the apostasy[31] comes first, and the man of lawlessness is revealed, the son of destruction" (2 Thessalonians 2:3b). Paul tells them that this "man

---

[30] "List of Messiah Claimants," https://en.wikipedia.org/wiki/List_of_messiah_claimants (accessed 22 April 2022)

[31] We'll talk more about this "apostasy" in chapter 6.

of lawlessness" "[...] opposes and exalts himself above every so-called god or object of worship, so that he takes his seat in the temple of God, displaying himself as being God" (2 Thessalonians 2:4). This man of lawlessness will be empowered by Satan himself to perform miraculous signs and wonders (2 Thessalonians 2:9). He will deceive those who neither love nor believe the truth but prefer to believe what is false because they find pleasure in wickedness (2 Thessalonians 2:10–12). As a result, the whole world will be beguiled by the most outrageous deception ever perpetrated in the history of mankind. And, as Paul makes clear, all this will happen first—before the day of the Lord (Christ's coming) will occur.

Before we can understand this deception, we must first understand who this man of lawlessness is. And this requires us to understand how the word "lawlessness" is used in Scripture. Lawlessness is not just a disregard for the law or a violation of the law but an utter contempt for the law.[32] And while this will likely include a disregard or contempt for civil law, it is most often used in the New Testament for a total disregard and contempt for the moral law of God. The apostle John puts it this way: "Everyone who practices sin also practices lawlessness; and sin is lawlessness" (1 John 4:4). As one writer explains it, lawlessness is "the rejection of the law, or will, of God and the substitution of will of self."[33] This man of lawlessness will practice, encourage, and promote a total disregard and contempt for God's moral law. In other words, the world in that day will be entirely given over to a hedonistic philosophy that says— "It's all about me." Such thinking produces a mindset that shouts—"The only thing that matters in life is me—my pleasure and my happiness" and "Nobody is going to tell me what to do or how to live, not even God!"

---

[32] In the Greek language, the word translated "lawlessness" (*anomia*) means "contempt and violation of law, iniquity, wickedness" (*The Online Bible Thayer's Greek Lexicon and Brown, Driver & Briggs Hebrew Lexicon*).
[33] *Vine's Expository Dictionary of Biblical Words.*

The prophet Daniel appears to be describing this same individual in one of his ancient prophecies (Daniel 7:25; 11:36–37). The picture he portrays is of a man who will stand against God as an adversary and persecute God's people. He will do so because of their firm commitment to follow God and to respect for His moral law. This man will reject God's moral law and replace it with his own laws. He will declare every other law except his own null and void, creating a state of spiritual and moral anarchy in the world.[34] In doing so, he will totally reject the authority, established order, and moral law of the only true and living God of heaven.

It's evident that the lawlessness of this man is clearly directed not only at God's moral law but at God Himself. This man of lawlessness will not only oppose and exalt himself as greater than any so-called deity, but he will actually claim to be God. He will set up the seat of his government in the very temple of God in Jerusalem[35] (2 Thessalonians 2:4). In claiming to be no mere mortal but God himself, he will allow no rivals and will demand that he and he alone be worshipped. As such, he will be the ultimate false messiah when he claims to be God in a human body.[36]

Actually, claiming to be a god was quite common among the Roman emperors. In that day, people were permitted to worship other deities in the Roman empire, as long as they also worshipped the emperor as a god. This is what got Christians in trouble in the early centuries of the Church. The reason they were persecuted by the Roman authorities is not that they worshipped Jesus as God, but that they refused to acknowledge the emperor as a god superior to all other gods, including Jesus. The ancient Roman emperors

---

[34] The word "anarchy" means "absence or denial of any authority or established order" (Merriam-Webster, https://www.merriam-webster.com/dictionary/anarchy), (accessed 22 April 2022).

[35] This may be a deliberate attempt on his part to appear as the fulfillment of Malachi's prophecy that the Messiah would make His appearance in the Jewish temple (Malachi 3:1).

[36] Only Jesus can legitimately make this claim (John 1:1, 14; Colossians 2:8–9).

considered themselves to be lord of all. Anyone who refused to worship the emperor as lord was considered a traitor to the state and faced immediately execution. Like the ancient Roman emperors, this man of lawlessness will demand worship as God to the exclusion of all other so-called gods.

It's true that there have been many religious deceivers over the centuries since the time that Jesus walked this earth. But this particular deceiver cannot appear on the scene as long as he is being restrained—much like a dog being restrained by a leash so that he can't break loose to chase a squirrel or, even worse, bite the mailman (2 Thessalonians 2:6–8). Whoever the restrainer[37] is, he is holding back[38] the full expression of evil in the world. This restrainer will prevent the man of lawlessness from coming to power until God's appointed time.[39]

The revealing of this lawless one will occur at just the right time in the outworking of God's plan of the ages. God will deliberately remove the restrainer to allow man's wickedness to reach its zenith in the coming of the "lawless one." But this "false messiah" will meet his demise when the "true Messiah" comes on the scene—Jesus Himself (2 Thessalonians 2:8). You might be inclined to wonder how this man of lawlessness could actually get away with claiming to be God and convince people to believe that it's true? Why wouldn't people just see right through his lies and deception? There are several reasons.

First, even today, we use the word "messiah" in a very different way

---

[37] Some suggestions as to the identity of the "restrainer" include Michael the archangel, the Holy Spirit, and the Church.

[38] In the Greek language, the word translated "restrainer" (*katecho*) literally means "to hold fast, hold back" *(New American Standard Updated Edition Exhaustive Concordance of the Bible).*

[39] In the Greek language, the word translated "time" (*kairos*) literally refers to "a fixed and definite time" (*The Online Bible Thayer's Greek Lexicon and Brown, Driver & Briggs Hebrew Lexicon*).

than the Jews understood the term in Jesus' day. For the Jews, their Messiah would be God's anointed deliverer, foretold by the ancient prophets, who would come to deliver the Jews from their enemies and set up an everlasting kingdom on earth. Their understanding of who the Messiah would be was exclusively Jewish. But even today, the world thinks differently about what it means to be a messiah. According to one modern dictionary's definition, the word "messiah" means "a leader who is believed to have the power to solve the world's problems.[40] In other words, the word "messiah" is more commonly used today of a charismatic leader who steps on the scene of history and promises to deliver people from their problems.

And what does it mean to be a charismatic leader? Jonah Goldberg, a syndicated columnist, author, and commentator, as he quotes German sociologist Max Weber, says that a charismatic leader is someone with a "certain quality of an individual personality, by virtue of which he is set apart from ordinary men and treated as endowed with supernatural, superhuman, or at least specifically exceptional powers or qualities."[41]

When world problems seem overwhelming and out of control, people look for a charismatic leader (a messiah) to fix things. And when someone appears to be accomplishing that, as Weber points out, people see him as different than an ordinary man, even possessing, as Weber says, "supernatural, superhuman, or at least specifically exceptional powers or qualities." So it's not too farfetched to think that this man of lawlessness will be a very charismatic leader who literally wows the world. People will consider him different from other ordinary men, even to the extent that they may think he is the embodiment of God Himself.

Furthermore, this man of lawlessness will demonstrate miraculous powers that will appear to validate his claim. These miraculous powers will

---

[40] https://dictionary.cambridge.org/dictionary/english/messiah (accessed 22 April 2022)
[41] Jonah Goldberg, "Politics Now Defined by Charismatic Leaders," *Ocala Star Banner*, Sunday, August 5, 2018.

convince people to believe that he really is God (2 Thessalonians 2:8–11), or at least someone who possesses god-like powers.[42] The world will see this man as having the ability to do miraculous things that only God (or "a god") could do. However, these supernatural powers are not innately his own but will come directly from Satan himself (2 Thessalonians 2:9). The demonstration of miraculous powers to do things that people will think only God can do, however, is not the only reason that this man will be able to convince people to believe his lie. Paul says that people will be deceived because they "did not receive the love of the truth [...] but took pleasure in wickedness"[43] (2 Thessalonians 2:3–4, 9–12). When people reject the truth, they automatically become susceptible to believing a lie.

Along this same line, the French author Charles-Marie Gustave Le Bon (1841–1931) nails it when he says, "The masses have never thirsted after truth. They turn aside from evidence that is not to their taste, preferring to deify error, if error seduce them. Whoever can supply them with illusions is easily their master; whoever attempts to destroy their illusions is always their victim."[44] This is especially true if the lie allows and encourages people to pursue and practice the things that they find pleasure in doing. A major part of the deception of this man of lawlessness is that he not only will live in total rejection of and contempt for God's moral law, but he will allow for and approve of others doing the same.

The book of Revelation gives us even further insight into this great

---

[42] The Greek word translated "God" (theos) "[...] in the polytheism of the Greeks, denoted 'a god or deity' [...] Hence the word was appropriated by Jews and retained by Christians to denote 'the one true God.'" (Vine's Expository Dictionary of Biblical Words). Hence, in 2 Thessalonians 2:4 the word can be translated either "God" or "a god."

[43] When it says that the people who reject the truth and are taken in by this great deception "take pleasure in wickedness," the Greek word translated "wickedness" (adikia) is the same word used of the "man of lawlessness" coming "with all the deception of wickedness."

[44] Email from Mark Beto, mark.beto@cyberdefenses.com, Mon., July 13, 2020

deception when it describes the same individual whom Paul calls the man of lawlessness as "the beast." Along with blaspheming the name of Almighty God, he will also relentlessly persecute God's people. A second beast is identified later in the book of Revelation as the false prophet (Revelation 16:13; 19:20; 20:10). This second beast will exercise miraculous powers granted to him by Satan. This will convince people all over the world to receive the mark of the beast and to worship his image. In the Olivet Discourse, Jesus expands on this warning when He says that in the last days, "[...] false Christs and false prophets will appear and perform great signs and miracles to deceive even the elect—if that were possible" (Matthew 24:24, NIV). Imagine how persuasive these false messiahs and prophets must be, how compelling their lies, and how breath-taking their miracles are that, if it were possible (which it isn't), they would be able to deceive even God's own people.

You may wonder, if this is not possible, why Jesus would say it at all. I think it's to emphasize how serious this matter is, to underscore how persuasive this deception can be, and to urge those of His followers living on the earth in the last days to pay attention to His warning and take it seriously. I think it is especially a warning directed to those who profess faith in Jesus as Savior, but their faith is not truly "the real deal." While those who have genuine faith in Jesus as Savior ("the elect") will not be deceived, those who profess faith in Christ but whose faith is not genuine will be vulnerable to this deception. Thus Jesus says, "At that time many will fall away and will betray one another and hate one another. Many false prophets will arise and will mislead many" (Matthew 24:10–11). Don't be taken in by this deception, but recognize that this deception is one of the indicators that the coming of Christ is near (Matthew 24:32–34).

So what about you? How easily are you persuaded to believe that something is true, not just because the person speaking to you is so convincing in his presentation, but because you really want to believe it's true? The nineteenth-century Danish philosopher Søren Kierkegaard once said, "There are two ways to be fooled. One is to believe what isn't true; the other is to refuse to believe what is true."[45] Consider the young college student at the beginning of our chapter. Whether we are currently living in the last days or whether the last days are many years in the future, as followers of Jesus, we still face deception that we have to contend with every day. Remember that Satan is a deceiver and "the father of lies" (John 8:44)—the "serpent of old" who deceived Eve in the garden and, through that deception, brought about the fall of man (Genesis 3:1–24; 2 Corinthians 11:3; Revelation 12:9; Romans 5:12). Our only hope of not being deceived is to resist the devil by relying on God's power to take a firm stand against all his schemes and knowing that he will flee from us when we do (James 4:7; Ephesians 6:10–17).

Life becomes challenging as followers of Jesus when we find ourselves caught inextricably between opposing value systems. As a result, we run the risk every day of being led astray by the deceptive lies of the world around us. The world has a way of enticing us to embrace its philosophy and be conformed to its value system, which is totally contrary to God's. Instead of embracing the world's lies, we need to embrace God's truth by presenting ourselves to God as a "living sacrifice" (Romans 12:1). In doing so, we must allow God to transform us by the renewing of our minds as we intentionally give ourselves to Him to do His will. In this way, we will learn to embrace His value system and follow His ways rather than those of the world (Romans 12:2).

We may be inclined to think that all deception comes from some external source, but such is not always the case. In fact, according to Scripture, self-deception may actually be more dangerous because we don't see it coming.

---

[45] Email from Mark Beto, mark.beto@cyberdefenses.com

The Scriptures caution us not to deceive ourselves into pridefully thinking that we're smarter than we really are according to the wisdom of this world (1 Corinthians 3:18). They also warn us not to deceive ourselves into thinking that we have no sin and, therefore, no need of God's forgiveness (1 John 1:7). These represent just two examples of how self-deception can easily sink its teeth into our thinking.

Probably the best way to avoid self-deception is simply to fill our minds with the Word of God. We're told that God's Word "is useful to teach us what is true and to make us realize what is wrong in our lives. It corrects us when we are wrong and teaches us to do what is right" (2 Timothy 3:16, NLT). The Word of God is our only infallible standard for discerning what is true and what is not. As such, it is our best defense against being deceived by Satan or the world or even against deceiving ourselves. In this way, we will be equipped to stand firm and cling to the truth when so many others are embracing a lie. Let the Word of God be your strong foundation and your sure defense!

But that's not all. It's not enough just to know the truth if we don't also love the truth and believe the truth. This is one of the biggest problems both today and throughout the history of the Church. Many who profess to believe lack genuine saving faith. Knowledge alone doesn't save us, nor does it alone protect us from deception. Paul makes this clear when he says that those who fall for this great deception will be those who "[...] did not receive the love of the truth so as to be saved" and "[...] who did not believe the truth but took pleasure in wickedness" (2 Thessalonians 2:10, 12).

If I know that something is true and genuinely believe that it is true, it should make a difference in the way I think and the way I live. But if I don't love the truth that I claim to believe, and I embrace and take pleasure in things that God says do not measure up to His standard of what is right, then I still am vulnerable to being deceived. If I love the things of the world rather than God and His Word, or even just more than I love God and His Word, it still sets me up to be deceived. I will rationalize things that God says are wrong as being ok because it's something I really want. So love God! And love His Word! Then you will not be deceived into believing a lie!

Chapter 5

The Birth Pangs

You will be hearing of wars and rumors of wars. See that you are not frightened for those things must take place, but that is not yet the end. For nation will rise against nation, and kingdom against kingdom, and in various places there will be famines and earthquakes. But all these things are merely the beginning of birth pangs.

Matthew 24:6–8

The woman suddenly awakened out of a deep sleep as she felt shards of pain slicing through her swollen body as if an IUD had just exploded in her gut. As she lay there in agony, clutching her stomach and moaning quietly to herself, just as suddenly as the pain had struck, it began to dissipate and then disappear. Breathing a sigh of relief, she knew that this was just the beginning because she had been through this whole scenario before. The pain would come back again and again and again, with greater intensity and with increasing frequency, until, at last, the ordeal would be over. Awakened at the sound of her moaning, her husband looked at the clock beside their bed. It was 2:00 a.m. "Is it time?" he asked. "Yes," she replied through clenched teeth, "It's time." They quickly threw on their clothes, and he grabbed the suitcase, already packed, sitting by the door. Fortunately, the hospital was only fifteen minutes away, and that was driving at normal speed. He had her there in ten!

As she grimaced in agony when the pain rippled through her body again, after what seemed like an eternity of anguish, the doctor said to her with compassion in his voice, "It won't be long now." And the doctor was right. After one final burst of pain that felt like her insides were being ripped apart, it was over. Suddenly excruciating pain gave way to exhilarating joy as she heard the doctor say, "You have a boy." The pain had been agonizing, but it couldn't even begin to compare with the joy that washed over her as she held her newborn child in her arms. As the ancient psalmist of Israel once said, "Weeping may last through the night, but joy comes with the morning" (Psalm 30:5b, NLT).

This is exactly the picture Jesus has in mind when He uses the metaphor of childbirth to describe some of the traumatic events that will take place on the earth prior to His coming and the birth of His kingdom. He refers to these events as "birth pangs." In fact, Jesus actually describes His coming and the birth of His kingdom as "the regeneration," which literally means "new birth"[46] (Matthew 19:28). Jesus is simply saying that when He comes in the glory and power of His kingdom, the whole world will experience a new birth.

However, just as with a pregnant woman in labor, the birth will be preceded by the anguish of birth pangs. And, if we take the metaphor a step further, as with ordinary birth pangs, the birth pangs that precede the birth of His kingdom will continue to grow in their intensity as the actual day approaches. It's true that there's a sense in which some of the events that Jesus describes as birth pangs have been occurring since the beginning of history. In fact, the apostle Paul even speaks of the entire creation experiencing the pains of childbirth even in his day (Romans 8:19–20).

But Jesus is talking about unprecedented pain and suffering on the earth in the last days leading up to His coming. These painful events are something that His followers living in that day will, if they know what to look for, serve as an indication that the day of His coming is drawing near (Matthew 24:32–35). It's possible that all this may not occur until long after our bones

---

[46]The Greek word translated "regeneration" (*paliggenesia*) literally means "new birth" (*The Online Bible Thayer's Greek Lexicon and Brown, Driver & Briggs Hebrew Lexicon*).

have turned to dust. It's just as possible that we could find ourselves to be the very generation that is still alive on the earth when He comes in the clouds. Either way, we need to look expectantly for the day of His coming and live our lives in a way that reflects the very real possibility that we could be the final generation. So what are these "birth pangs"?

War

Without a doubt, wars have been the plague of mankind, not just from the time of the early disciples but from the dawn of human history. And who can begin to count the untold cost of millions upon millions of human lives, both military and civilian? Just consider the death toll of World War II. According to Wikipedia,

> World War II was the deadliest military conflict in history. An estimated total of 70–85 million people perished, or about 3% of the 1940 world population (est. 2.3 billion). Deaths directly caused by the war (including military and civilian fatalities) are estimated at 50–56 million, with an additional estimated 19–28 million deaths from war-related disease and famine.[47]

Now add to these horrific statistics the incredible death toll on humanity from all the wars ever fought since the beginning of human history, as well as all the wars that have been fought since the end of World War II. The total number of deaths resulting from war is absolutely staggering. Yet, this is nothing compared to what we can expect to happen just before the time when Jesus will come again. Jesus says, "You will be hearing of wars and rumors of wars. [...] For nation will rise against nation, and kingdom against kingdom"

[47]"World War II casualties," https://en.wikipedia.org/wiki/World_War_II_casualties, (accessed 23 April 2022)

(Matthew 24:6a–7). Luke's Gospel adds that along with wars and conflicts between nations, there will also be what he calls "disturbances"[48] (Luke 21:9). By "disturbances," Jesus is saying that along with major wars, there will also be political instability, disorder, revolution, insurrection, and anarchy all over the world.

In the book of Revelation, the apostle John talks about this as he describes a prophetic vision of what is commonly known as "the four horsemen of the apocalypse." The first horseman is seated on a white horse, carrying a bow and wearing a crown upon his head as he goes forth as a conqueror. The second rider is seated on a red horse and is given authority to remove peace from the earth as men become intent on killing one another (Revelation 6:2, 4). These first two horsemen represent God's judgment upon the earth in the last days as He allows the lust for conquest (represented by the first horseman) to remove peace from the earth (represented by the second horseman)[49]. This will bring an escalation of wars, conflicts, rebellions, and anarchy that will engulf the entire planet, bringing untold death and destruction.

The horseman riding the white horse should probably be identified as the future global ruler commonly referred to as the Antichrist,[50] although the apostle John does not specifically identify him as such in this text. A scene like this could easily qualify as a person's worst nightmare, wouldn't you agree?

---

[48]The Greek word translated "disturbances" (*akatasia*) literally means "instability, a state of disorder, disturbance, confusion" (*The Online Bible Thayer's Greek Lexicon and Brown, Driver & Briggs Hebrew Lexicon*), or even "revolution or anarchy" (*Vine's Expository Dictionary of Biblical Words*).

[49]This kind of judgment might be best described as God's "passive" judgment because He does not directly cause these wars but simply removes the restraint and gives men over to their own sinful desires, resulting in men bringing misery and destruction upon themselves. Note Psalm 81:12 and Romans 1:24, 26, 28 where it says, "He gave them over..."

[50] Only the apostle John actually uses the term "antichrist" to refer to this future world leader, although only in his letters—not the book of Revelation. He also indicates that the "spirit of antichrist" was already at work in the world even in his day (1 John 2:18, 22; 2 John chapter 7).

Such will be what Jesus calls the beginning of birth pangs. Just remember that the birth pangs are an indication that Christ's coming is near.

Famine and Disease

What is true for war on our planet is equally true for famine and disease—they, too, have brought great suffering upon the population of our world through human history. That is still true even today. According to David Beasley, head of the World Food Program, "today 270 million people face a famine of biblical proportions in dozens of nations around the world.[51] Even now, as I write this chapter, our world is in the midst of the coronavirus pandemic. As of August 23, 2022, there were 508,916,351 people who had become infected with the COVID-19 virus and 6,241,418 people who had died from it.[52] From Ebola in West Africa to Zika in South America, to MERS in the Middle East, to the current coronavirus pandemic involving more than 200 countries, dangerous outbreaks of disease are on the rise around the world. Even in our day, with all our modern technology, famine and disease are still major problems undermining the well-being of our world.

Yet Jesus says of the last days before His coming that there will be famines in various places all over the world (Matthew 24:7). And Luke's Gospel adds that along with famines there will be plagues" (Luke 21:11). The world has certainly been plagued with famine and epidemic disease repeatedly over the past two thousand years, and that shows little sign of changing in the future. Jesus says that the challenges of war, famine, and disease will not improve in the future but will get worse as the day of His coming draws near.

As John continues to describe his vision of the four horsemen of the apocalypse, he speaks of a black horse whose rider has a pair of scales in

---

[51] David Beasley, opinion author, *USA Today*, December 5, 2020
[52] https://www.worldometers.info/coronavirus/ (accessed 23 April 2022)

his hand. And he hears something that sounds like a voice saying, "A quart of wheat for a denarius, and three quarts of barley for a denarius; and do not damage the oil and the wine" (Revelation 6:6b). This third horseman represents a world being consumed by famine in various locations around the planet. Let's try to understand the magnitude of what John is saying in regard to this third horseman. The pair of scales probably represents rationing that results from worldwide food shortages where people are standing in long lines just to buy what little food is available. These food shortages will drive the price of food up to astronomical highs far greater than many people can afford. In New Testament times, a denarius was the equivalent of one day's wages for the average working man. A quart of wheat or three quarters of barley were barely enough to feed one family for a day and would cost an entire day's wage. And forget about such luxury items as oil and wine. In the last days leading up to the time when Jesus will come again, an entire day's income will be spent just for food, if it's even available.

Now we come to the fourth horsemen in John's vision. John describes what he calls an "ashen horse," which is a pale gray, the color of death,[53] and whose rider's name is, appropriately, "Death." Authority is given to this rider on the ashen horse "over a fourth of the earth to kill with sword and with famine and with pestilence and by the wild beasts of the earth" (Revelation 6:8). Along with famine and war, John also mentions pestilence (disease), along with people being killed by wild animals. Furthermore, all of this horror will encompass 25% of the planet's total landmass of 57,505,694 square miles—this represents more than 14 million square miles.[54] Just to put things

---

[53] *https://dictionary.cambridge.org/* (accessed 23 April 2022)
[54] Some have suggested that the term "earth" refers to earth's population rather than to earth's landmass, but this is not consistent with the meaning of the Greek word (*gee*) translated "earth" in this passage (*The Online Bible Thayer's Greek Lexicon and Brown, Driver & Briggs Hebrew Lexicon*).

in perspective, this is nearly as large as the total area of the North American and European continents.[55] Such will be what Jesus calls the beginning of birth pangs. Just remember that the birth pangs are an indication that Christ's coming is near.

Earthquakes

In 2017 this news report appeared in a prominent national newspaper:

> A powerful earthquake struck Mexico on Tuesday afternoon, toppling buildings, killing children in a school that collapsed, rattling the capital, and sending people flooding into the streets for the second time in just two weeks. Early Wednesday, the director of Mexico's civil protection agency, Luis Felip-Puente, said on Twitter that 216 people had been killed, revising an earlier toll of 248. Ninety-four people were confirmed dead in Mexico City, officials said. Rescuers were frantically digging out people trapped under rubble, including the children buried beneath their school, volunteers at the scene said Tuesday night. At least 21 students were believed to have been killed in the collapse of the school.[56]

Earthquakes have frequently made the earth tremble, historically causing numerous deaths and great devastation. But such earthquakes are nothing like what Jesus says will occur in the last days before His coming and the "birth" of His kingdom. He says to His disciples, "[...] in various places there will be famines and earthquakes" (Matthew 24:7b). This statement by itself

---

[55] For more exact statistics, consult *https://www.whatarethe7continents.com*

[56] Kirk Semple, Paulina Villegas, and Elisabeth Malkin, Mexico Earthquake Kills Hundreds, Trapping Many Under Rubble, New York Times, Sept. 19, 2017, https://www.nytimes.com/2017/09/19/world/americas/mexico-earthquake.html (accessed 23 April 2022)

may not necessarily strike great fear into our hearts since it doesn't sound that different from what the world has experienced in the past. However, the book of Revelation elaborates and provides a better picture of just how catastrophic these earthquakes will be in that future day. In the book of Revelation, John mentions one particular earthquake occurring immediately before the coming of Christ that will rock our entire planet more than any other earthquake in the history of the world. This is not some ordinary earthquake, but what John calls "a great earthquake." It will be of such magnitude and devastation that it will be completely off the seismological charts. You get an idea of the widespread damage and destruction of this earthquake when John says, "Every mountain and island were moved out of their places [....] and the cities of the nations fell" (Revelation 6:14b; 16:19a). What a terrifying prospect for the future of our world! And yet this is only the beginning of birth pangs.

Terrors

Along with war, famine, epidemic disease, and mega earthquakes, according to Luke's account, Jesus also says that there will be "terrors" (Luke 21:10).[57] When he uses the word "terrors," he's not talking here about people just being afraid but of situations or events that evoke sheer terror. You can get a better grasp of what this means when you understand that the definition of the word "terror" is "intense, sharp, overmastering fear."[58] When I think of something happening that would invoke this kind of terror in people, I immediately have visions of innocent men dressed in orange jumpsuits about to have their heads cut off by ISIS or homemade bombs killing and maiming

---

[57] Luke also mentions "great signs in the heavens," which probably refer to what Jesus describes Luke 21:25 as "signs in the sun, moon and stars"; note also greater detail about these "signs" in Matthew 24:29 and Mark 13:24. We will discuss these "great signs in the heavens" in detail in chapter 9.

[58] https://www.merriam-webster.com/dictionary/terror (accessed 23 April 2022)

participants and bystanders at the Boston Marathon or a hail of gunfire in an Orlando night club. I picture evil men driving trucks up on the sidewalk and intentionally killing people by running over them. I picture a lunatic firing an automatic rifle from the thirty-second floor of a hotel in Las Vegas with the intent of killing as many people as possible in a crowded concert below.

But the terrors that will plague the earth just before the coming of Christ and the birth of His kingdom will far exceed anything that we see today. Jesus doesn't specifically describe what these events are that will evoke such terror. But read through the book of Revelation, and you'll discover what some of these terrors may be. Yet these terrors are merely the beginning of birth pangs. Just remember that the birth pangs are an indication that Christ's coming is near.

So how should we respond as followers of Jesus if we find ourselves living on the earth when all these birth pangs begin? It's certainly possible that we could be the final generation on earth who will face a world wracked by global war, worldwide famine, and pandemics. We could be the ones who will see seismic activity in the earth's crust producing earthquakes that are unprecedented in magnitude, causing unprecedented destruction around the world. We could be the ones who experience unimaginable terror gripping our hearts. But even if it turns out that we are not the generation that will see the coming of Christ, the question still remains—how we should respond as followers of Christ to the personal trials that may rock our world right now. What does Jesus say? In the context of all these apocalyptic events that will occur prior to His coming, Jesus simply says, "[...] See that you are not frightened, for those things must take place, but that is not yet the end" (Matthew 24:6b). But how is that even possible when our personal world is falling apart around us?

The ancient psalmist speaks of a time when the people of Jerusalem were seeing their world crashing down around them. In that setting, he writes, "God is our refuge and strength, always ready to help in times of trouble. So we will not fear when earthquakes come and the mountains crumble into the sea. [...] Be still, and know that I am God!" (Psalm 46:1–2, 10, NLT) Again, speaking through the prophet Isaiah, God Himself says to us,

> Do not fear, for I am with you; do not anxiously look about you, for I am your God. I will strengthen you, surely I will help you, surely I will uphold you with My righteous right hand. [...] Do not fear, for I have redeemed you; I have called you by name; you are Mine! When you pass through the waters, I will be with you; and through the rivers, they will not overflow you. When you walk through the fire, you will not be scorched, nor will the flame burn you. For I am the Lord your God, the Holy One of Israel, your Savior.
>
> Isaiah 41:10; 43:1b–3a

This is true whether you're facing the apocalyptic events of the last days before Christ's coming or you're facing the trials of life in this present world.

Not only do we have the promise of God's presence and help, but we know the end of the story. Even if we find ourselves facing the full force of these birth pangs, we know exactly what this means. We know that these birth pangs are announcing that the day of Christ's coming is near—that He is coming to gather us to Himself so that we may be with Him forever in His eternal kingdom (Matthew 24:30–34). Our immediate future may be a little uncertain, but our eternity is sure. And that is the end of the story. I'm not trying to minimize the fact that these things, whether future apocalypse or present trials, can be frightening to experience. But we need not be overwhelmed by fear. When we are afraid, the key is to do what the psalmist did when he said, "I sought the LORD, and He answered me, and delivered me from all my fears" (Psalm 34:4). Jesus says to us, "Peace I leave with you; My peace I give to you; not as the world gives do I give to you. Do not let your heart be troubled, nor let it be fearful" (John 14:27). That's His promise! Believe it!

Chapter 6

The Persecution

Then they will deliver you to tribulation, and will kill you, and you
will be hated by all nations because of My name.

Matthew 24:9

The sky was just beginning to turn pink over the horizon in the early dawn. The local police stealthily surrounded the house where known criminals were gathered in a secret meeting. These people had no regard for the law and knowingly broke it repeatedly. They were hardened, repeat offenders whose criminal activity must be stopped. Since the police had zero tolerance for such behavior, they were about to instigate a raid that would bring these vile criminals to justice. A battering ram forced the door open, and the criminals inside stood wide-eyed in surprise. They always knew the possibility of being discovered in their secret hideout, but no one was expecting it today. Some tried to escape, but others just stood calmly as they were interrogated and then calmly allowed themselves to be handcuffed and taken away. They knew the drill. And they knew what to expect—at least imprisonment and possibly torture and death. Were their criminal activities worth the price they would now have to pay? If you were to ask them, they would answer unquestionably, "Yes." Their crime? Gathering in secret to worship God and to hear from the Word of God in a country where such "religious" activities are against the law.

In many countries around the world, being a Christian is a serious crime, punishable by imprisonment or even death. Although this event just described is fictional, such things occur on a regular basis in countries all around the world where being a Christian is against the law. Persecution of Christians around the world is one of the biggest human rights issues of our time. Of course, it's nothing new. Beginning with the first-century church and continuing through every chapter of church history, it is a harsh reality for many believers today.

According to Open Doors USA,

> While Christian persecution takes many forms, it is defined as any hostility experienced as a result of identification with Jesus Christ. From Sudan to Russia, from Nigeria to North Korea, from Colombia to India, followers of Christianity are targeted for their faith. They are attacked; they are discriminated against at work and at school; they risk sexual violence, torture, arrest and much more.[59]

> The statistics are staggering. Did you know that 309 million Christians in the world today experience high levels of persecution and discrimination for their choice to follow Christ? In North Korea, for example, when Christians are discovered, they, along with their families, are deported to labor camps as political criminals or sometimes even killed right on the spot.[60]

None of this should really surprise us since Jesus Himself told His disciples it would be this way (John 15:18–21). Jesus makes it clear that if the world hates Him, it will most assuredly hate us too. And He indicates that persecution against His followers will increase in the days before His coming. At a time when wars, famines, widespread pandemics, and earthquakes will be throwing the whole world into a panic, Jesus says, "Then [or better, 'at that

---

[59] https://www.opendoorsusa.org/christian-persecution (accessed 23 April 2022)
[60] Joe Baker, "The Countries Where It's Most Dangerous to Be a Christian," *THE GOSPEL COALITION*, Jan. 11, 2018

time'[61]] they will deliver you to tribulation,[62] and will kill you, and you will be hated by all nations because of My name" (Matthew 24:9). Not only will Christians be persecuted for their faith in Jesus, but they will be hated "by all nations." In other words, the persecution that will break out in those days will not just be localized in a few places but will be worldwide. Jesus says that the whole world will hate us, and their hatred will be specifically because we are associated with the name of Christ.

How severe will this persecution be? Severe enough for Jesus to say, "At that time many will fall away [63] and will betray one another and hate one another. Many false prophets will arise and will mislead many" (Matthew 24:10–11). This "falling away" is the very thing that Jesus talks about in the parable of the soils when He speaks of the seed that fell on rocky soil. The picture is that of a farmer throwing his seed at planting time. Some of the seed "fell on the rocky places, where they did not have much soil; and immediately they sprang up, because they had no depth of soil. But when the sun had risen, they were scorched; and because they had no root, they withered away" (Matthew 13:5–6). Jesus later explains the meaning of the parable when He says, "The one on whom seed was sown on the rocky places, this is the man who hears the word and immediately receives it with joy; yet he has no firm root in himself, but is only temporary, and when affliction or persecution arises because of the word, immediately he falls away (Matthew 13:20–21).

Jesus says some will profess faith in Him, but when hard times come,

---

[61] *The Online Bible Thayer's Greek Lexicon and Brown, Driver & Briggs Hebrew Lexicon*

[62] The Greek word translated "tribulation" (*thlipsis*) can be translated "tribulation, trouble, anguish and persecution" (Strong's Greek & Hebrew Dictionary, https://www.logos.com, Lexicon Resource, 2020). In this context, it seems to clearly indicate persecution.

[63]The Greek word translated "fall away" (*skandalizo*) means "to put a stumbling block or impediment in the way, upon which another may trip and fall" and has the idea of "[causing] a person to begin to distrust and desert one whom he ought to trust and obey" (*The Online Bible Thayer's Greek Lexicon and Brown, Driver & Briggs Hebrew Lexicon*).

especially persecution, they will fall away. This is exactly what will happen to many professed followers of Jesus in the last days. Because their faith is not firmly rooted in the gospel, when the price is too great, they will turn their backs on Jesus and walk away. In this case, they will not only abandon the truth of the gospel to escape persecution but many, having turned away from the truth, will be seduced by false prophets and teachers into embracing the lie of the man of lawlessness that we talked about in chapter 4.

This is the apostasy[64] that Paul speaks about in connection with the revealing of the "man of lawlessness" (2 Thessalonians 2:3–4). This lawless one comes with "[...] the deception of wickedness for those who perish, because they did not receive the love of the truth so as to be saved" (2 Thessalonians 2:10). Notice that the ones who embrace this deception of wickedness are not true followers of Jesus but those who "did not receive the love of the truth so as to be saved." Because of the pain of persecution and because of the seductive delusion that will come upon the whole earth in the last days, many professed followers of Jesus will turn away from the faith. More than that, they will betray other followers of Jesus and hate them. Deceived by false prophets, they will become part of the apostasy by believing the great lie promoted by the man of lawlessness.

Jesus says that during this time of persecution and apostasy, "Because lawlessness is increased, most people's love will grow cold" (Matthew 24:12). In chapter 4, we saw that the Bible's definition of lawlessness is not just a person breaking the law but a person holding contempt and disregard for the law, speaking primarily of God's moral law. As we've seen in a previous chapter, lawlessness is "[...] the rejection of the law, or will, of God and the substitution of the will of self." [65] To review, we're talking about a world entirely given over

---

[64]The Greek word translated "apostasy" (*apostasia*) means "a defection, revolt, apostasy" and is used in the New Testament of religious apostasy (*Vine's Dictionary of Biblical Words*).
[65] *Vine's Dictionary of Biblical Words*

to a hedonistic philosophy that shouts—"The only thing that matters in life is me—my pleasure and my happiness" and "Nobody is going to tell me what to do or how to live, not even God!" In such an environment, love cannot flourish—indeed, love cannot even survive in a world where people have no regard for anyone but themselves.

The apostle Paul writes,

> But realize this, that in the last days difficult times will come. For men will be lovers of self, lovers of money, boastful, arrogant, unloving, irreconcilable, malicious gossips, without self-control, brutal, haters of good, treacherous, reckless, conceited, lovers of pleasure rather than lovers of God, holding to a form of godliness, although they have denied its power.
>
> 2 Timothy 3:1–5a

This will be our world under the rule of the man of lawlessness in those final days. Persecution, lawlessness, professed followers of Jesus falling away and being seduced by Satan's lie–it all sounds pretty depressing! But in the midst of all this bad news, there's also good news. At least it will be good news for those followers of Jesus who demonstrate the genuineness of their faith by remaining faithful to Jesus. Yes, says Jesus, there will be those who will fall away, but "[...] the one who endures to the end, he will be saved"[66] (Matthew 24:13).

The idea of enduring to the end is that of holding fast to one's faith during

---

[66]The word translated "saved" here in this verse, in addition to eternal salvation from the wrath of God's judgment (Romans 5:9–10) may have a double meaning that also includes physical deliverance or rescue from persecution at the end of the great tribulation (Jeremiah 30:7; Daniel 12:1). The Greek word "*sozo*" means "to save, to keep safe, to rescue from danger or destruction" (*The Online Bible Thayer's Greek Lexicon and Brown, Driver & Briggs Hebrew Lexicon*).

times of trial for as long as the trial lasts.[67] Don't misunderstand what Jesus is saying here. He's not suggesting for a moment that we are saved by our endurance. What saves us is the gift of God's grace received by faith. But true saving faith is a faith that endures. The faith of those who fall away is not genuine saving faith because it is not a faith that endures. But those who have a genuine faith that endures will never fall away but will endure to the end. This is exactly the apostle Paul's point in writing to the Colossian believers when he talks about believers who "continue in the faith firmly established and steadfast, and not moved away from the hope of the gospel" (Colossians 1:21–23). If our faith in Jesus Christ is the "real deal," then this will be true of us.

Speaking as the Good Shepherd, Jesus says six things about those who are His true sheep—"they hear His voice; He knows them; they follow Him; He gives eternal life to them; they will never perish; and no one will snatch them out of His hand" (paraphrased) (John 10:27–28). In other words, it is not our profession of faith that actually saves us, but our possession of faith—a genuine faith that endures to the end. Paul and Jesus are both talking about the same thing. Regardless of what happens, genuine believers will never fall away from their faith in Jesus. This doesn't mean that genuine believers never experience struggles with doubt and unbelief or even cowardice in the face of pain. They may, in a moment of weakness, deny Jesus outwardly as Peter did and then afterwards repent (Matthew 26:69–75). But a true believer will never inwardly and permanently turn away from Jesus and abandon his faith because genuine faith is a faith that endures. At the end of the day, his faith, though severely battered, will remain intact.

Even with that assurance, however, Paul warns the Corinthian believers to test themselves to be sure that they are "in the faith," allowing for the

---

[67] The Greek word translated "endure" (*hupomeno*) means "to persevere: absolutely and emphatically, under misfortunes and trials to hold fast to one's faith in Christ" (*The Online Bible Thayer's Greek Lexicon and Brown, Driver & Briggs Hebrew Lexicon*).

possibility that they could actually fail the test (2 Corinthians 13:5). He wouldn't be saying this if it were not possible for a person to make a profession of faith without having a genuine faith. As I once heard someone say, "The faith that saves is the faith that works." That's how you can recognize the real thing. If our faith is the real deal, we will not have to worry about failing the test. So what about you? Does your faith pass the test? Can you see the evidence of genuine faith in your actions? Or are you just kidding yourself into thinking your faith is the real deal? Asking yourself these questions will reveal what kind of faith you really have.

Chapter 7

The Abomination

Therefore when you see the ABOMINATION OF DESOLATION which was spoken of through Daniel the prophet, standing in the holy place (let the reader understand), then those who are in Judea must flee to the mountains.

Matthew 24:15–16

The abomination of desolation. What in the world is that? It almost sounds like some dread disease. Maybe some of us would think of the abominable snowman. For most of us, the word "abomination" is not something typically found in normal conversations. The English word "abomination" actually means "something regarded with disgust or hatred"[68] or something that is "vile, shameful, or detestable."[69] Whatever it is, Jesus says that when the "abomination of desolation" stands in the Jewish temple in Jerusalem, it will indicate that His coming and the birth of His kingdom are rapidly approaching.

In the Olivet Discourse, when Jesus says this phrase, He is deliberately using cryptic language undecipherable to the average person. However, He gives a single clue that will enable someone familiar with Old Testament prophecy to know exactly what He is talking about when He refers to the abomination of desolation spoken of by Daniel the prophet. In other words, if you want to know what this abomination of desolation is, you must look to the ancient prophecies of Daniel in the Old Testament for that understanding.

---

[68] https://www.merriam-webster.com/dictionary/abomination, (accessed 24 April 2022)
[69] https://www.dictionary.com/browse/abomination, (accessed 24 April 2022)

Notice, too, that Jesus makes the parenthetical remark, "Let the reader understand." He's telling the reader that there is a cryptic clue here for the reader who knows where to look and what to look for. It becomes pretty obvious, then, that if we are to understand what this abomination of desolation will be in the last days before the coming of Christ and His kingdom, the place to gain that understanding is in the prophecies of Daniel.

What, then, is this thing called the "abomination of desolation" that Daniel the prophet is talking about? Before we take a closer look at the prophecies themselves that contain the phrase, let's first define the meaning of the Hebrew word translated "abomination" that Daniel uses. In the Old Testament, the word "abomination" describes something that is detestable,[70] just like the English word. No surprises here! However, this particular word in the Old Testament is most often specifically used in connection with idolatrous practices, either referring to the idol itself or the idolatrous practices associated with it.[71] The Hebrew word for "desolation" most often refers to devastation resulting from some great disaster."[72] This same word is found in the prophecy of Joel as he describes the consequences of a major locust plague in Israel and employs the metaphor of a wildfire leaving total devastation in its wake (Joel 2:3). Putting these two words together, what Daniel is talking about is some detestable idol or idolatrous practice that is associated with or brings about some horrendous disaster resulting in great devastation. Jesus says that this will occur in the last days before His coming and the birth of His kingdom.

Daniel mentions the abomination of desolation three times in his prophecies. Two of these refer to an event that is still in the future, and the

---

[70] *Thayer's Greek Lexicon*
[71] R. L. Harris, G. L. Archer Jr., & B. K. Waltke (Eds.), *Theological Wordbook of the Old Testament* (Chicago: Moody Press, 1999, electronic edition)
[72] Harris, Archer, & Waltke (Eds.), *Theological Wordbook of the Old Testament*

third refers to an event that has already been fulfilled and is documented in history. By looking at Daniel's prophecy that has already been fulfilled and documented in history, we will have a better idea of what we can still expect to come in the future. Daniel received the prophecy concerning the abomination of desolation in 536 BC when Cyrus the Great, the Persian king who conquered Babylon, was in the third year of his reign over the Persian empire (Daniel 10:1). This prophetic vision reveals the future of the Jewish people as it would interface with future happenings in the Persian empire at that time and in the succeeding Greek empire. Understand that Persia and Greece were the two major civilizations in that part of the world in that day. Daniel is told that there will be three more kings who will succeed King Cyrus. And then a fourth king will amass great wealth and make a failed attempt to conquer Greece (Daniel 11:2).[73] Daniel's prophetic vision goes on to say that after these kings, another mighty king would arise who would rule with great authority. However, his kingdom would be broken up and parceled out toward the "four points of the compass, though not to his own descendants" (Daniel 11:3–4).

Ancient history tells us that this mighty king was Alexander the Great. Between the years 334 to 330 BC, Alexander and his army successfully extended the Greek empire and civilization across Asia Minor (modern

---

[73] The first three kings of Persia in this prophetic vision can be identified from history as Cambyses, Bardiya, and Darius I, who ruled Persia 530–486 BC. King Darius I, who became ruler over the entire Persian Empire in 522 BC, and who ruled in the days of the Jewish prophets Haggai and Zechariah, is not to be confused with Darius the Mede, who was appointed ruler over the Persian province of Babylon in 539 BC by the Persian king, Cyrus the Great (Daniel 5:30). The fourth king who would amass great riches and arouse the whole empire against the realm of Greece is Xerxes I, who ruled Persia 485–464 BC, and who made a failed attempt to invade Greece. Just as a sidenote, King Xerxes I is most likely the Persian king who bore the title "Ahasuerus" in the Old Testament book of Esther (Esther 1:1, et. al.) (Joshua J. Mark, "Achaemenid Kings List & Commentary," March 5, 2020, https://www.worldhistory.org/article/1518/achaemenid-kings-list-commentary/).

Turkey), Syria, Egypt, and all the former territory of the Persian Empire. This would be payback for the failed attempt of the Persian king Xerxes I to conquer Greece nearly 150 years earlier. But tragically, Alexander died in 323 BC at the height of his power with no designated heir to the throne. As a result, the entire Greek empire was divided up among his four generals, just as Daniel prophesied that the kingdom of this mighty man would be "[...] broken up and parceled out toward the four points of the compass, though not to his own descendants..." (Daniel 11:4) At this point, the prophetic vision turns the spotlight on the Seleucid kingdom located in Syria to the north of Israel and the Ptolemaic kingdom located in Egypt to the south of Israel. At the time when the Greek empire was divided, the land of Judea came under the control of the Seleucid kings.

The rest of the prophecy describes the ongoing conflict between two royal dynasties, the Seleucid dynasty in Syria (kings of the north) and the Ptolemaic dynasty in Egypt (kings of the south). If you look at a map of the region, you quickly discover that the Jewish people were caught right in the middle between these two kingdoms. The Jews were alternately ruled either by the Seleucid kings to the north or by the Ptolemaic kings to the south, depending on which kingdom was dominant at the time.

As Daniel's prophecy continues, the focus turns to one of the Seleucid kings—a particularly contemptible person (Daniel 11:21, NIV). This man would desecrate the Jewish temple, put an end to the Jewish sacrifices, and, worst of all, set up in the temple the abomination of desolation (Daniel 11:21, 31). These are the exact words in Daniel's prophetic vision. There it is—Daniel's first reference to the abomination of desolation. This part of Daniel's prophecy would be fulfilled nearly 400 years after he received it by a man named Antiochus IV Epiphanes, a truly contemptible man who became ruler of the Seleucid kingdom to the north of Israel in 175 BC. You'll quickly discover why he was such a "contemptible" man as you read on.

According to the ancient Jewish apocryphal books of 1–2 Maccabees, written in the second century BC, Antiochus IV Epiphanes had an intense hatred for the Jewish people. That hatred extended to the Jewish religion and to their Jewish God. In 168 BC, he suffered a significant defeat in his conflict with the Ptolemaic kingdom to the south of Israel. Subsequently, he took out his frustration on the Jewish people by persecuting them horribly. This included the desecration of the Jewish temple and the discontinuing of the daily sacrifice. He tried to exterminate Judaism altogether, forbidding all Jewish religious practices and commanding all copies of the Jewish Scriptures to be destroyed. But the worst came in 167 BC when he erected a pagan altar upon the Jewish altar of burnt sacrifice in the Jewish temple. Furthermore, he placed a pagan idol of the Greek god Zeus in the temple of God in Jerusalem and required that sacrifices be offered to Zeus rather than to the true God of heaven.

This idol erected in the Jewish temple is actually described in the book of 1 Maccabees as "the abominable idol of desolation upon the altar of God" (1 Maccabees 1:57). You can read the entire account for yourself in the books of 1–2 Maccabees, and you'll see how Antiochus IV Epiphanes perfectly fulfills this ancient prophecy of Daniel (1 Maccabees 1:43–62; 2 Maccabees 6:1–6).

Bear in mind that this is not the abomination of desolation that Jesus says is yet to come in the last days before the birth of His kingdom. We know this to be true because this abomination of desolation had already occurred 200 years before Jesus ever spoke these words. However, what occurred in the past serves as a vivid picture and foreshadowing of that future abomination of desolation yet to come in the last days. And when we look at Antiochus IV Epiphanes and all that he did against the Jewish people, we catch a glimpse of what kind of person will erect this future abomination of desolation that

Jesus describes. As I've already said, Jesus is using cryptic language that only those familiar with the prophecies of Daniel would understand. His reference to the abomination of desolation provides those who understand with clear indicators that the His kingdom is imminent. They will understand that prior to His coming, the people of God will experience a level of persecution unprecedented and unparalleled in all of history.

Returning to Daniel's prophetic vision, the timeline jumps from Antiochus IV Epiphanes across the centuries to the distant future referred to as "the end time; because it is still to come at the appointed time" (Daniel 11:35). Daniel's prophecy begins in his own time in the sixth century BC and looks across more than three centuries to the time of Antiochus IV Epiphanes in the second century BC. Then it takes another giant leap forward into the distant future to something that has not occurred yet, even in our day. It's in this immediate context, as the prophecy comes to a close, that we discover a second reference to the abomination of desolation. What Daniel describes has not yet occurred in history but will occur in the end time (Daniel 12:11). However, this second reference to the abomination of desolation really doesn't add anything to our understanding. Apparently, it will only be understood by those who are present in the future when it occurs.

The final word given to Daniel in this prophetic vision is directed to him personally in the promise that he will enter into rest (his death) and then rise again (his resurrection) to receive his allotted portion (his reward) at the end of the age (Daniel 12:13). Don't miss the fact that the reference to the end of the age takes us right back to the disciples saying to Jesus, "[...] what will be the sign of Your coming, and of the end of the age?" (Matthew 24:3b)

So, where does this leave us? We know that the end of the age when Jesus comes in the power and glory of His kingdom will be preceded by a re-run of what Antiochus IV Epiphanes did nearly 200 years before Jesus ever appeared on the scene of history. But is this everything that Daniel's prophecies tell us about the abomination of desolation? The answer is no. Three years earlier before the prophetic vision we've just been talking about, Daniel received another prophetic message, a portion of which we have already looked at in chapter 2.

We've already seen how this prophecy says that there will be a period of 490 years beginning with the issuing of a decree for the city of Jerusalem to be rebuilt. Remember that at the time of this prophecy, the city of Jerusalem had already been destroyed by the Babylonians. In Daniel's time, the temple was just a pile of rubble. We've seen how this prophecy foretells that during this period of 490 years, Messiah the Prince would come. This was fulfilled in the triumphal entry of Jesus into Jerusalem in AD 33. It also foretells His death, fulfilled on the day of Passover that same year, only days after His entry into the city. And it foretells the subsequent destruction of Jerusalem and the Jewish temple a second time, fulfilled by the Romans in AD 70. However, this only accounts for the first 483 years of the 490 years that will complete God's program. And this is where the last part of Daniel's prophecy comes into the picture. Apparently, the prophetic clock stopped ticking when the Jewish nation rejected Jesus as their Messiah. God temporarily set aside the nation of Israel as His primary instrument to accomplish His purposes in the world.

From this point on, the people of Israel would sit on the sidelines of God's prophetic work until the times of the Gentiles (Luke 21:24) are fulfilled and the fullness of the Gentiles has come in (Romans 11:25). During the interim, God has been primarily accomplishing His work in the world through His Church, consisting of both Jews and Gentiles who believe that Jesus is the true Messiah, Savior, and coming King. This final period of seven years that will bring God's prophetic program to a close has not happened yet.

Remember that Daniel's prophecy speaks about the coming of the Messiah, the Prince. Sadly, Jesus was not the kind of Messiah the Jews were looking for. They wanted and were expecting a powerful military ruler who would overthrow their Roman masters and deliver them from Roman oppression, after which He would rule as king over all the earth. They didn't understand that in AD 33, Jesus had come as a suffering Savior "to finish the transgression, to make an end of sin [...and] to make atonement for iniquity" (Daniel 9:24a) through His death and subsequent resurrection. They didn't understand that only later would He come as a glorious king to complete what He started, which would be "[...] to bring in everlasting righteousness, to seal up vision and prophecy and to anoint the most holy place" (Daniel 9:24b). They just didn't get it, nor did the disciples until after the resurrection. Neither would we if we didn't have a different historical perspective and additional prophetic revelation that they didn't have available to them.

However, Daniel's prophecy goes on to introduce us to another prince (ruler or leader), one who is yet to come, which means that he would arrive on the scene of history at some future time after the destruction of Jerusalem in AD 70. The coming of this other prince will usher in this final seven-year period that will bring human history to a climax in the coming of Jesus and the birth of His kingdom. Daniel writes,

> And he [the prince who is to come] will make a firm covenant with the many for one week for, but in the middle of the week he will put a stop to sacrifice and grain offering; and on the wing of abominations will come one who makes desolate, even until a complete destruction, one that is decreed, is poured out on the one who makes desolate.
>
> Daniel 9:27

According to Daniel's prophecy, this future ruler who will usher in the final seven years of God's prophetic program will make some sort of political or military treaty or agreement[74] with the nation of Israel, supported by a majority but not all of the Jewish people (the many). He will abide by the terms of the treaty for the first three and a half years that the treaty is to be in force but will then break the treaty. He will betray the Jewish people, who thought that he was their friend and ally. Just like Antiochus IV Epiphanes back in the second century BC, he will force the Jewish people at that time to discontinue their regular temple worship, which will center around the practice of offering up animal sacrifices. And then he will do the unthinkable! He will place upon the altar of God his version of the abomination of desolation that was placed in the Jewish temple by Antiochus IV Epiphanes in 167 BC. This is what Daniel's prophecy is talking about when it says, "[...] on the wing of abominations will come one who makes desolate" (Daniel 9:27).

Is it possible that all of this has already taken place, either in conjunction with or immediately after the destruction of Jerusalem in AD 70? Or possibly at some point in history thereafter? There is no historical record either in biblical or secular literature of any of these things happening before or in conjunction with the destruction of Jerusalem in AD 70. Furthermore, there's no way that these things could have happened at some point in history subsequent to the destruction of Jerusalem in AD 70. Here's why! It would require the Jewish people to be living in their own land, having their own government, having possession of Jerusalem, and having their temple in which they could be carrying on the practice of animal sacrifice and grain offering that they had been doing previously since the time of Moses.

---

[74] This is one of the ways the Hebrew word translated "covenant" is used in the Old Testament (*The Online Bible Thayer's Greek Lexicon and Brown, Driver & Briggs Hebrew Lexicon*).

We know from history that when the city of Jerusalem and the temple were completely destroyed in AD 70, all the Jews living in Jerusalem at the time were either slaughtered or taken as slaves. Not long after that, all the Jews living in what became known as Palestine were driven from their homeland and scattered across three continents. The Jewish people did not have a homeland of their own, with their own territory or their own government, until the present-day nation of Israel was founded in 1948 by decree of the United Nations. Even today, the Jews still have no temple where they can reinstate the sacrificial system because the Al-Aqsa Mosque, the third holiest site in Islam, sits on the ancient site of the temple. This means there is no way for this last part of Daniel's prophecy to be fulfilled until the Jewish temple is rebuilt and the Jewish sacrificial system is reinstated, which has not yet happened. All this to say that the fulfillment of this part of Daniel's prophecy is still future, even today.

The final seven years that will complete God's prophetic program for Israel and the world are still future, even from today. And, of course, Jesus makes this same point in the Olivet Discourse when He makes it clear that the appearance of the abomination of desolation spoken of by Daniel the prophet would serve as an indication that the time of His coming and the birth of His kingdom were drawing near (Matthew 24:32–33).

The New Testament gives us additional revelation that describes more clearly what this abomination of desolation really is. We already know, based on what happened in the time of Antiochus IV Epiphanes, that it will be a pagan idol accompanied by some form of idolatrous worship in the very temple of God in Jerusalem. The apostle Paul, however, makes it clear what this will actually look like. As we've already seen in chapter 4, the future man of lawlessness will be someone who "opposes and exalts himself above every so-called god or object of worship, so that he takes his seat in the temple of

God, displaying himself as being God (2 Thessalonians 2:4). I can't imagine anything more blasphemous than a mere man desecrating the temple of the living God by blatantly standing in the holy place and claiming to be God himself.

But there's still more! In the book of Revelation, the apostle John describes this man of lawlessness in a way that represents his true character. John portrays him as a hideous beast rising out of the sea with ten horns and seven heads, with a crown on each of its ten horns and blasphemous names written on each of its seven heads (Revelation 13:1–3). Then John tells of a second beast who will compel the whole world to worship the first beast, convincing people to do so by performing amazing miracles.[75] What John is describing is totally in line with what Jesus says about false messiahs and false prophets coming with great signs and wonders so convincing that, if it were possible, they would deceive even true followers of Jesus (Matthew 24:24). This second beast, who later in the book of Revelation is called "the false prophet" (Revelation 19:20–21), will be responsible for the building of an image of the first beast as an idol—an idol that people will be required to worship or else face execution (Revelation 13:11–15). It seems fairly obvious, at least to me, that this image of the beast is the actual abomination of desolation that Jesus is talking about. It's exactly what is foreshadowed by the image of the pagan Greek god, Zeus, the abominable idol of desolation placed in the Jewish temple by Antiochus IV Epiphanes in 167 BC.

Idolatry is a terrible thing. As we've already seen, it is an abomination to God that ultimately brings destruction upon those who practice it. This is especially true when it rears its ugly head among God's own people, those who claim to be devoted to Him. I'm reminded of how God describes His

---

[75] This talk of beasts with multiple heads belongs to the genre called apocalyptic literature and is filled with vivid symbolism.

people, Israel, when He says through the prophet Jeremiah, "My people have committed two evils: They have forsaken Me, the fountain of living waters, to hew for themselves cisterns, broken cisterns that can hold no water" (Jeremiah 2:13).

In Jeremiah's day, two sources brought fresh water to people living in the land of Israel—natural springs and cisterns. Of course, a natural spring flowing out from filtering rock layers would be the ideal source of fresh, clean water. The alternative would be a cistern; basically, a pit dug out of the rock, plastered with lime. It was used to collect rainwater—what we would call today a reservoir. The water collected in a cistern often became polluted and foul-tasting. Beyond that, a cistern's supply could evaporate during a drought. And a crack in the rock could risk draining all the water out.

This is the metaphor used to demonstrate the utter folly of God's people forsaking Him, "the fountain of living waters," and turning to other gods (idols), "broken cisterns that can hold no water." For us who claim to be followers of Jesus, the application should be obvious. How easy it is for idolatry to gain a foothold in our lives before we even realize what's happening. We tend to think of an idol as a piece of carved wood or stone that a person would bow down to and call his god. If we define idolatry by that definition, it's something we think we'd never do. But idolatry can be much more insidious than that. The truth is that an idol is anything—and I mean anything—that we value and are devoted to more than God. When we engage in idolatry, we are robbing God of the devotion that rightfully belongs to Him alone. Idolatry is anything that receives greater priority in our life than God. It is anything that gives us more satisfaction than we find in Him.

Using that criteria as a definition of idolatry, far more things probably qualify as idols than we ever imagined. We see an example of this in the New

Testament when the apostle Paul says to the Colossians, "Therefore consider the members of your earthly body as dead to immorality, impurity, passion, evil desire, and greed, which amounts to idolatry" (Colossians 3:5). Greed is devotion to the accumulation of wealth and material things, making them our highest priority and looking to them to satisfy our deepest needs and longings. "That is idolatry," says Paul! Our job, our family, and even our ministry, if we have one, can become an idol. When you think of idolatry in these terms, you begin to realize how easily idolatry can sneak under the wire, so to speak, into your life. So, do you have any idols in your life? Whether or not you live to see the coming of the Lord in the future, don't allow any abominable idol of desolation to remain in your life right now in the present.

This would be a good time to take a serious inventory of your life. It would be a good time to identify any broken cisterns that are robbing God of the love and devotion that belong to Him alone. It would be a good time to forsake those broken cisterns and turn back to the One who is the fountain of living waters. He alone can satisfy your deepest longings. And if you do live to see the abominable idol of desolation take its place in the Jewish temple, know that the coming of Christ and the birth of His kingdom are near.

Chapter 8

The Great Tribulation

Then those who are in Judea must flee to the mountains. [...] For there will be a great tribulation, such as has not occurred since the beginning of the world until now, nor ever will.

Matthew 24:16, 21

Have you ever needed to run for your life from some imminent danger? I'm talking about the kind of situation where you don't even have time to pack a suitcase or grab a toothbrush. Just before Hurricane Irma struck South Florida in 2017, tens of thousands evacuated ahead of the storm. Travel on the interstate crept at a snail's pace as thousands of automobiles clogged the highway on their journey north out of harm's way.

Sadly, in some parts of the world, whether due to religious persecution, political oppression, war, or natural disaster, it happens all too often that people must literally run for their lives and get as far away as they can from whatever is threatening their safety. This is exactly the scenario that Jesus gives us as He describes events that will precede His coming and the birth of His kingdom.

In the first part of the Olivet Discourse, Jesus has described some of the things that will happen on the earth in the last days before the birth of His kingdom. He talks about how it all will impact not only His followers but the entire population of our planet. Jesus has just been talking about how deception, war, earthquakes, famine, epidemic disease, lawlessness, apostasy, and persecution will come upon the earth. These will come with ever-increasing intensity leading up to the birth of Christ's kingdom, just as birth pangs of a woman in labor come with ever-increasing intensity until the birth of her child.

In describing what our response to all this should be, He tells us not to be misled nor to be frightened. But not once does He tell people to "run for their lives"—at least not until He mentions the abomination of desolation. It's only at this point Jesus says, "Then [or 'at that time'] those who are in Judea must flee to the mountains" (Matthew 24:16). Notice that Jesus changes the pronoun from "you" (Matthew 24:9, 15) to "those who are in Judea" (Matthew 24:16). This is a crucial distinction because it indicates to me that He's addressing two different audiences. Jesus is speaking directly to His followers when He says, "Then they will deliver you to tribulation, and will kill you, and you will be hated by all nations because of My name" (Matthew 24:9). But when He says, "Then [or 'at that time'] those who are in Judea must flee," He's speaking directly to the Jewish people living in the land of Judea (modern-day Israel) at the time the abomination of desolation appears on the scene.

This is because, at that time, those living in the land of Israel will immediately be in grave danger. At that time, there will be an outpouring of anti-Semitism that, in its scope and intensity, will be unprecedented in all of human history. And those living in the land of Israel at that time will find themselves directly in the line of fire. Of course, persecution of all those who trust in the true God of Israel will continue to intensify all over the world. But that persecution will come down more quickly and with greater intensity upon those living in the land of Israel—especially in Jerusalem. For them, it will be time to get out of Dodge.

The urgency to flee will be so acute that Jesus continues,

> Whoever is on the housetop must not go down to get the things out that are in his house. Whoever is in the field must not turn back to get his cloak. But woe to those who are pregnant and to those who are nursing babies in those days! But pray that your

flight will not be in the winter, or on a Sabbath.

Matthew 24:17–20

In other words, the need for those living in the land of Judea (Israel) to get away as quickly as possible will be so great that there won't even be time for them to pack a bag or grab their coat. Things will get so bad so fast that it will be an especially great hardship on women who are pregnant or nursing mothers with babies.

If all this happens during the winter, that will make it even more difficult to travel quickly out of harm's way because of the greater possibility of inclement weather. About seventy percent of the average rainfall in Israel comes between the months of November and March. And during the months of January and February, it can snow at the higher elevations of Israel's central highlands. This is true in the Golan Heights, but also around Jerusalem, with snowfall sometimes quite heavy."[76] If it happens on the Jewish Sabbath, that, too, will be especially problematic for the Orthodox Jews because their strict adherence to the Mosaic law would limit how far they could travel on the Sabbath. For them, this would make a quick getaway difficult.

You might wonder why Jesus would make a point of giving this warning to the Jews living in the land of Israel during the time just before His coming. As we saw in chapter 3, the people of Israel, the Jewish people, are, and always will be, God's special people—His covenant people. This has been true ever since God made His covenant promise to Abraham—and to His descendants—nearly 4,000 years ago (Genesis 17:7–8). This covenant promise has never been rescinded or revoked in the past, nor can it ever be rescinded or revoked in the future because God's promise to Abraham represents an everlasting covenant.

Though, as a nation, the Jewish people are now living in disobedience and

---

[76] https://weatheronline.com (accessed 28 April 2022)

are under judgment because of their rejection of Jesus as the true Messiah, God's covenant with them remains. As we've already said in the previous chapter, today, God is working His divine program through the Church rather than through the nation of Israel. But this doesn't mean in any way that God is finished with His chosen people. Even today, there is a remnant of the Jewish people who have put their trust in Jesus as the true Messiah, many of whom call themselves messianic Jews. This remnant is what Paul is talking about, even speaking about himself, when he says,

> I say then, God has not rejected His people, has He? May it never be! For I too am an Israelite, a descendant of Abraham, of the tribe of Benjamin. God has not rejected His people [...] there has also come to be at the present time a remnant according to God's gracious choice.
>
> Romans 11:1–2, 5

This remnant of Israel remains today and will until the coming of Christ. This is why Paul can say,

> For I do not want you, brethren, to be uninformed of this mystery [...] that a partial hardening has happened to Israel until the fullness of the Gentiles has come in; and so all Israel will be saved; just as it is written,[77]
>
> "THE DELIVERER WILL COME FROM ZION,
> HE WILL REMOVE UNGODLINESS FROM JACOB."

---

[77] When Paul says, "As it is written," he is giving his own loose paraphrase/summary of Isaiah 59:20–21 based on the Septuagint translation of the Hebrew text, combined with several other Old Testament passages dealing with God's "new covenant" with Israel, specifically Jeremiah 31:31–34; Ezekiel 36:24–33; Zechariah 12:10–13:1.

"THIS IS MY COVENANT WITH THEM,

WHEN I TAKE AWAY THEIR SINS."

Romans 11:25–27

There will be a cut-off point of God's judgment upon Israel, and the entire nation of Israel will come to genuine saving faith in Jesus as their Messiah.

Jesus issues this warning to the people living in Judea (Israel). But it will put all those all around the world who believe in the true God of Israel, both Jews and Christians, on notice that they, too, will need to flee to a place of safety as quickly as possible. Here's why! Jesus says, "For then there will be a great tribulation, such as has not occurred since the beginning of the world until now, nor ever will" (Matthew 24:21). Five hundred years earlier, the prophet Daniel speaks of this same time of great tribulation when he says, "Now at that time [that is, the 'end time,' Daniel chapter 11; Daniel 11:35, 40] [...] there will be a time of distress such as never occurred since there was a nation [referring, of course, to the nation of Israel] until that time" (Daniel 12:1). The prophet Jeremiah likewise speaks of this future time of distress for God's people when he says,

> "For thus says the LORD,
> 'I have heard a sound of terror,
> Of dread, and there is no peace.
> 'Ask now, and see
> If a male can give birth.
> Why do I see every man
> With his hands on his loins, as a woman in childbirth?
> And why have all faces turned pale?
> 'Alas! for that day is great,

105

There is none like it;

And it is the time of Jacob's distress [...]'"

Jeremiah 30:5–7

It seems evident from the descriptions above that Jesus, Daniel, and Jeremiah are all talking about the same future event that will occur in the last days.[78]

So what exactly is this great tribulation or time of distress that will come upon the people of God in the last days? It's important that we interpret this according to the preceding context where Jesus says, "Then [or 'at that time'] they will deliver you to tribulation [...] and will kill you, and you will be hated by all nations because of My name" (Matthew 24:9). When Jesus uses the word "tribulation," He's using it in the sense of intense persecution of God's people.[79] In the preceding context, He's talking about His own followers being persecuted "because of My name." In the second instance, He's saying that the scope of this persecution will expand to include Jewish people everywhere simply because they are Jewish, beginning in the land of Israel and spreading worldwide. This persecution will intensify to a level unparalleled in history. Apparently, there will be a wave of anti-Semitism that launches a persecution of both Jews and Christians such as the world has never seen before.

---

[78] It's noteworthy that the Hebrew word for "distress" (*tsarah*) used by Daniel and Jeremiah has the very same word meaning as the word for "tribulation" (*thlipsis*) in Greek. The Greek word translated "tribulation" (*thlipsis*) means "to have trouble, tribulation, affliction, distress; to suffer from hard circumstances; to be weighed down exceedingly; to be pressed and crushed. It means persecution, affliction, crushing trouble, hard circumstance, terrible suffering" (*Practical Word Studies in the New Testament* [Alpha-Omega Ministries, Inc., 1998. All rights reserved. Database copyright 2014, WORDsearch]).

[79] This same Greek word (*thlipsis*) is translated as "persecution" in Acts 11:19 where it says, "So then those who were scattered because of the persecution [*thlipsis*—persecution] that occurred in connection with Stephen made their way to Phoenicia and Cyprus and Antioch..."

Recalling what happened in 167 BC when Antiochus IV Epiphanes set up the first abomination of desolation in the Jewish temple will clarify what Jesus is talking about. According to our earliest and most reliable source, the books of Maccabees, as we've already seen in chapter 7, Antiochus set up the abominable idol of desolation upon the altar of God in the Jewish temple. He was trying to completely eradicate the Jewish religion that centered around the worship of the true God of Israel. He brutally persecuted those Jews who were faithful followers of the God of Israel. He killed everyone he could while forcing others to flee as fugitives and hide in secret places from the authorities.

Jesus is talking about a persecution very similar to what happened in the time of Antiochus IV Epiphanes. The only significant difference is that the persecution in the last days before the coming of Christ will be far more intense and widespread. It will emanate from Jerusalem and be directed against those living in the land of Judea (Israel). But it will include all Christians and Jews who refuse to worship the image of the beast. This is why Jesus calls it "the great tribulation." The magnitude of this persecution against the people of God will be literally off the charts compared to anything like it that has occurred in the past since the beginning of Israel's history. Both Christians and Jews have been persecuted throughout the centuries in various places all around the globe. But nothing will compare with the persecution that's yet to come in the last days before the coming of Christ. It will be a level of persecution that will be "[...] such as never occurred since there was a nation until that time" (Daniel 12:1).

Of all three accounts of the Olivet Discourse found in the Gospels, the one that probably gives us the most comprehensive picture of this great tribulation, especially as it relates to the city and inhabitants of Jerusalem, is the Gospel of Luke. Luke's account provides an entirely different perspective than the other Gospels. He says,

> When you see Jerusalem being surrounded by armies, you will know that its desolation is near. Then let those who are in Judea flee to the mountains, let those in the city get out, and let those in the country not enter the city. For this is the time of punishment in fulfillment of all that has been written. How dreadful it will be in those days for pregnant women and nursing mothers! There will be great distress in the land and wrath against this people. They will fall by the sword and will be taken as prisoners to all the nations. Jerusalem will be trampled on by the Gentiles until the times of the Gentiles are fulfilled.
>
> Luke 21:20–24 (NIV)

There is no doubt in my mind that Luke's account of these events is a parallel account with the one given in the other synoptic Gospels. Keep in mind that each of the Gospel writers provides his own unique perspective on what Jesus is saying. This is the reason why one Gospel writer may provide details of what Jesus says in the Olivet Discourse that may or may not be included by the others. And don't forget that none of these Gospel accounts of the Olivet Discourse is a word-for-word rendition of Jesus' speech. Rather, it's a summation of what Jesus said in the words of the writer himself with his own God-inspired perspective and emphasis. My point is that Luke's account is somewhat different but complementary, not contradictory, to the other Gospel accounts. I find no indication in the text that Luke's account is talking about anything different from the other Gospels. Luke is simply looking at things through a different lens and with a different emphasis. Instead of focusing on the appearance of the abomination of desolation as Matthew and

Mark do, Luke focuses on the desolation[80] that will come to Jerusalem when it occurs.

Typically in ancient warfare, when an invading army attacked a walled city like Jerusalem, they would simply surround the city, turning the city into a prison from which the inhabitants could not escape. Then they would wait for the people to surrender when they eventually ran out of food. This tactic was called laying siege against the city. In modern times this tactic is called a blockade. If people wanted to escape, they would have to flee while the city was still in the process of being surrounded—otherwise, any possible route of escape would be cut off. This explains why, according to Luke's account, Jesus warns the Jews that when they see the city of Jerusalem being surrounded by armies, it's time to run for their lives.

When the Jews see Jerusalem being surrounded by armies, they need to recognize that "her desolation is near" and that "there will be great distress upon the land and wrath to this people" (Luke 21:20). He's talking about the great persecution (tribulation) that will come to the Jewish people when the "abomination of desolation" appears in the Jewish temple. It's important to note that both Jeremiah and Daniel likewise describe this same time period as a time of "distress." Likewise, Daniel uses similar language in describing this same time period when he says, "[...] on the wing of abominations will come one who makes desolate" (Daniel 9:27).

It's true that this same scenario of Jerusalem being under siege—surrounded by armies, subjected to great devastation, and experiencing great persecution—could describe what the Romans did in AD 70. However, the

---

[80] In the original Greek text the word that Luke uses for "desolation" is the same Greek word (*eremosis*) used in the phrase "abomination of desolation" in the Gospels of Matthew and Mark. As we saw in an earlier footnote, the Greek word for "desolation" means "solitary, deserted," and the corresponding verb carries the force "to lay waste, make desolate" (Morris, *The Gospel of Matthew*, 591, footnote 50).

immediate context does not allow for this to be what Jesus is talking about here in Luke's Gospel. After talking about this great desolation that will come upon Jerusalem and the great persecution (distress) that will come upon the Jewish people, He continues,

> There will be signs in sun and moon and stars, and on the earth dismay among nations, in perplexity at the roaring of the sea and the waves, men fainting from fear and the expectation of the things which are coming upon the world; for the powers of the heavens will be shaken.
>
> Luke 21:25–26

None of these things ever occurred in connection with the destruction of Jerusalem in AD 70. Furthermore, He says, "Then [or 'at that time'] they will see the Son of Man coming in a cloud with power and great glory" (Luke 21:27). The coming of Christ did not occur when Jerusalem was destroyed in AD 70 but is even now still in the future. However, what happened to Jerusalem and the Jewish people in AD 70 may certainly represent a prophetic foreshadowing of the complete fulfillment that will occur at the coming of Jesus Messiah in the power and glory of His kingdom. This would be the same as the "abominable idol of desolation" set up in the Jewish temple by Antiochus IV Epiphanes in 167 BC, being a prophetic foreshadowing of the future abomination of desolation that Jesus is talking about in the Olivet Discourse.

The prophet Zechariah is also describing this future surrounding of Jerusalem by armies and the city's subsequent desolation when he says,

> The burden of the word of the LORD concerning Israel [...]
> Behold, I am going to make Jerusalem a cup that causes reeling to

all the peoples around; and when the siege is against Jerusalem, it will also be against Judah. It will come about in that day that I will make Jerusalem a heavy stone for all the peoples; all who lift it will be severely injured. And all the nations of the earth will be gathered against it. In that day the LORD will defend the inhabitants of Jerusalem [...] And in that day I will set about to destroy all the nations that come against Jerusalem.

Zechariah 12:1–3

Clearly, the outcome of this siege against Jerusalem described by Zechariah never happened in AD 70 either. Instead of the Lord coming to rescue His people, the city of Jerusalem and the Jewish temple were destroyed, and the captured Jews were either enslaved or killed when the city fell to the Romans. Zechariah describes this same siege of Jerusalem again when he says,

Behold, a day is coming for the LORD when the spoil taken from you will be divided among you. For I will gather all the nations against Jerusalem to battle, and the city will be captured, the houses plundered, the women ravished and half of the city exiled, but the rest of the people will not be cut off from the city. Then the LORD will go forth and fight against those nations, as when He fights on a day of battle. And the LORD will be king over all the earth; in that day the LORD will be the only one, and His name the only one.

Zechariah 14:1–3, 9

Once again, elements of Zechariah's prophecy could describe the fall of Jerusalem to the Romans in AD 70, but most assuredly not the entire prophecy. Certainly not the part about the LORD fighting for the Jewish people against their enemies and the part about the LORD being king over all the earth in that day. In AD 70, the outcome was just the opposite. Again, what happened to Jerusalem and the Jewish people in AD 70 may in some ways be a prophetic foreshadowing of the complete fulfillment of Zechariah's prophecy when Jesus comes—but not the fulfillment itself.

Turning once again to Daniel's prophecies, we find an additional description of what this great tribulation will look like. We're told that a future ruler will come upon the scene of history in the last days. This ruler will "[...] speak out against the Most High and wear down the saints of the Highest One" (Daniel 7:25). When Daniel says that this future ruler will wear down the saints, he means that this future king will harass and punish them relentlessly.[81] What a perfect way to describe intense persecution, since in the English language, the word "persecute" literally means "to harass or punish in a manner designed to injure, grieve, or afflict; specifically: to cause to suffer because of belief.[82]

Likewise, the book of Revelation contains a similar prophecy in which the apostle John describes this same future ruler, referring to him as the beast. He will make war with the saints and overcome them. To him, authority will be given for a period of forty-two months over every tribe and people and tongue and nation (Revelation 13:1, 6–8). This future ruler will not only harass and punish the people of God for their religious beliefs through a brutal persecution, but he will actually make war against them and be permitted to defeat them, at least for a time. All of these prophecies of Zechariah, Daniel, and John are in perfect sync with Luke's account of Jerusalem being surrounded by armies and the desolation that will follow in the last days

---

[81] The Hebrew word translated "wear down" (*bela'*) literally means "to wear away, to wear out, to harass constantly" (*The Online Bible Thayer's Greek Lexicon and Brown, Driver & Briggs Hebrew Lexicon*).

[82] *https://www.merriam-webster.com/dictionary/persecute* (accessed 24 April 2022)

before the coming of Christ and the "birth" of His kingdom.

If this evil ruler had his way, he would literally eradicate every one of God's people from the face of the earth. But God is not going to allow this to happen because God Himself has put a limit on how long He will allow the persecution to continue. Jesus makes this clear when He says, "Unless those days had been cut short, no life would have been saved; but for the sake of the elect those days will be cut short" (Matthew 24:22). In other words, if God didn't put a limit on how long this persecution of His people could go on, none of them would survive. But for the sake of the elect (God's people), God has put a leash on this beast so that he can only continue this unprecedented persecution of God's people until God Himself says, "Enough!"

So how does the story end in the final chapter? Definitely not well for this evil ruler who is bent on destroying the people of God. Daniel gives us a vivid description of what will happen; he says,

> Then the court will sit for judgment, and his dominion will be taken away, annihilated and destroyed forever. Then the sovereignty, the dominion and the greatness of all the kingdoms under the whole heaven will be given to the saints of the Highest One; His kingdom will be an everlasting kingdom, and all the dominions will serve and obey Him.
>
> Daniel 7:26–27

Daniel describes a similar scenario in another prophecy that we've already looked at several times when he says, "On the wing of abominations will come one who makes desolate, even until a complete destruction, one that is decreed, is poured out on the one who makes desolate" (Daniel 9:27). In other words, this evil ruler, who is determined to destroy the people of God, will himself be destroyed in the end, along with his evil kingdom. During the time of tribulation that will come upon the people of God in the last days, evil may appear to prevail for a season, but in the end, evil will be defeated and destroyed forever.

Chapter 9

The Day of the Lord

Alas for the day!
For the day of the LORD is near,
And it will come as destruction from the Almighty.

Joel 1:15

Huge black clouds of flying insects could be seen on the horizon blotting out the light of the sun and plunging the land of Israel into semi-darkness. The roar of their wings continued to intensify as they drew closer. It was the one natural disaster that the Jewish people feared above all others—a locust plague. With each locust eating its own weight in food every day, and with each locust swarm containing as many as 40 to 80 million insects, such a plague would quickly devastate the land, leaving famine, starvation, and death in its wake. They would gobble up all the vegetation, devouring the fields of grain that were yet to be harvested, as well as every leaf, flower, fruit, and seed, even tree bark, in a land already in the throes of a prolonged drought. As a result, the land would look like a wildfire had consumed everything in its path. The bare branches left behind would resemble the limbs of skeletons reaching to the sky.[83] The people would tremble with fear at the sight of these millions of insects on the march like a mighty army, knowing the total devastation they would leave behind once they were gone.

It was in the aftermath of just such a locust plague that God raised up the prophet Joel. Not much is known about Joel other than the fact that his prophecy has been preserved among the ancient Jewish Scriptures until

---

[83] "Locust Handbook," New Zealand Digital Library, *https://www.nzdl.org* (accessed 24 April 2022)

this day. Though locust plagues were not all that uncommon in the ancient Middle East, apparently, this particular locust plague was unprecedented in its scope, as Joel describes one swarm of locusts after another, each consuming whatever survived the previous swarm until nothing at all remained (Joel 2:11, 20, 25). In very descriptive language, Joel likens these successive swarms of locusts to an invading army destroying the land and leaving it in ruin (Joel 1:6–7). In fact, the devastation is so great that Joel sees it as a wake-up call and warning from God for the Jewish people to repent and turn back to him (Joel 2:12–13). But Joel also sees this locust plague as a metaphor and prophetic foreshadowing of another far greater and more disastrous apocalyptic future event that Joel refers to as the day of the Lord.

In the Old Testament, the expression day of the Lord is sometimes applied to immediate events relevant to the people of Israel. However, it more often refers in an ultimate sense to a future day when God Himself will intervene in human history to establish His rule on the earth, bringing judgment to the wicked and deliverance to the righteous. With prophetic foresight, Joel says,

> Alas for the day!
> For the day of the LORD is near,
> And it will come as destruction from the Almighty.
> [...] Blow a trumpet in Zion,
> And sound an alarm on My holy mountain!
> Let all the inhabitants of the land tremble,
> For the day of the LORD is coming;
> Surely it is near,
> A day of darkness and gloom,
> A day of clouds and thick darkness.
> [...] There has never been anything like it,

Nor will there be again after it

To the years of many generations.

Joel 1:15; 2:1–2

Joel is not the only prophet in the Old Testament to describe this future day of the Lord with terrifying apocalyptic language. The prophet Isaiah uses almost identical language when he says,

Wail, for the day of the LORD is near!

It will come as destruction from the Almighty.

Therefore all hands will fall limp,

And every man's heart will melt.

They will be terrified,

Pains and anguish will take hold of them;

They will writhe like a woman in labor,

They will look one at another in astonishment,

Their faces aflame.

Behold, the day of the LORD is coming,

Cruel, with fury and burning anger,

To make the land a desolation.

Isaiah 13:6–9

Likewise, the prophet Zephaniah, in very similar language as Joel, describes the day of the Lord as "a day of wrath [...] a day of trouble and distress, a day of destruction and desolation, a day of darkness and gloom, a day of clouds and thick darkness" (Zechariah 1:14–15). As I say, the day of the Lord is not a theme limited to the prophet Joel. It is a theme that appears frequently throughout the Old Testament prophetic books.

The New Testament likewise speaks specifically about the coming day of the Lord in terms that sound reminiscent of the Old Testament prophets. In writing to the Thessalonians about this future day of the Lord, the apostle Paul says,

> Now as to the times and the epochs, brethren, you have no need of anything to be written to you. For you yourselves know full well that the day of the Lord will come just like a thief in the night. While they are saying, "Peace and safety!" then destruction will come upon them suddenly like labor pains upon a woman with child, and they will not escape.
>
> 1 Thessalonians 5:1–3

Sounds very much like the words of the ancient Hebrew prophets, doesn't it?

Although the Scriptures do not indicate when this future day of the Lord will actually occur, Joel's prophecy gives us some pertinent clues as to what we should expect to see happening in our world just before the day of the Lord and where the day of the Lord fits into God's prophetic timetable. We're given the first two clues when Joel says, "The sun will be turned into darkness and the moon into blood before the great and awesome day of the LORD comes" (Joel 2:30–31)

Let's pause for a moment and think about what this means. It seems likely, at least to me, when Joel describes the sun being turned into darkness, that he's talking about a solar eclipse. But what about Joel's description of the moon being turned into blood? That sounds a little crazy! Yet maybe not. There actually is such a thing as a "blood moon" described in scientific literature. According to one writer,

A "blood moon" happens when Earth's moon is in full eclipse. While it has no special astronomical significance, the view in the sky is striking as the usually whitish moon becomes red or ruddy-brown...During a full eclipse...something spectacular happens. The moon is fully in Earth's shadow. At the same time, a little bit of light from Earth's sunrises and sunsets (on the disk of the planet) falls on the surface of the moon. Because the light waves are stretched out, they look red. When this red light strikes the moon's surface, it also appears red.[84]

Both a full solar eclipse, turning the sun into "darkness," and a full lunar eclipse ("blood moon") will appear in the heavens to declare that the day of the Lord is about to commence.

But that's not the only clue that Joel gives us about what to expect before the coming of the day of the Lord. Joel presents the same scenario again, describing it in a slightly different way when he says, "[...] the day of the LORD is near [...] The sun and moon grow dark and the stars lose their brightness" (Joel 3:14–15). Then he continues with an additional clue, saying, "The LORD roars from Zion and utters His voice from Jerusalem, and the heavens and the earth tremble" (Joel 3:16a). Isaiah repeats the very same clues that Joel gives us when he says,

Behold, the day of the LORD is coming [...] For the stars of heaven and their constellations will not flash forth their light; the sun will be dark when it rises and the moon will not shed its light. Therefore I will make the heavens tremble, and the earth will be shaken from its place at the fury of the LORD of hosts in the day of

---

[84] Elizabeth Howell, "What Is a Blood Moon?", 22 January 2019, https://www.space.com (accessed 24 April 2022)

His burning anger.

Isaiah 13:9a–10, 13

It's noteworthy that in these two prophetic passages, the blood moon is not specifically mentioned, but the language still seems to indicate an eclipse of both the sun and the moon occurring simultaneously. Also, both passages add that something is going on that, from the prophet's perspective, causes the stars of heaven to diminish in their brightness or even to disappear from view altogether. But here's the mystery: what could it possibly mean that when the LORD speaks, the heavens and the earth are made to tremble? One might assume that the earth trembling would refer to an earthquake. But what could cause the heavens to tremble? The key passage that I believe explains what this means is another prophecy of Isaiah describing the day of the Lord, which says, "All the stars of the heavens will be dissolved and the sky rolled up like a scroll; all the starry host will fall like withered leaves from the vine, like shriveled figs from the fig tree (Isaiah 34:4, NIV).

It certainly sounds like Isaiah is talking about the same event in which, from the prophet's perspective, the stars appear to be dissolving. Furthermore, if you've ever watched dead leaves or dried-up fruit fall from a tree, then you can understand the metaphor that he's using to describe stars falling out of the sky. But is such a thing even possible? We know scientifically that stars do not fall from the sky. From our knowledge of astronomy, we define stars as huge balls of burning gas that are tens of thousands of light-years away from earth. So how could they fall out of the sky and hit the ground like dried-up figs?

First, in order to understand Isaiah's prediction, we have to remember that the ancient Hebrew prophets did not understand modern astronomy to the extent that we do today with our advanced technology and scientific equipment. And more importantly, these ancient prophets are trying to describe something they've never seen before in language that would have made sense to them at the time. So what phenomenon could Isaiah possibly be describing when he speaks of what appears to be stars falling out of the sky? And what about the sky looking as if it's been rolled up like a scroll? Could this possibly have something to do with the heavens and the earth "trembling"? Is there some kind of reasonable explanation for these phenomena? In my research, I believe that I've found a plausible answer to these questions.

On February 15, 2013, the Chelyabinsk meteor, estimated to be sixty-six feet in diameter, entered Earth's atmosphere, moving at 43,200 miles per hour. Now that's fast! When it struck the atmosphere that surrounds our planet, this meteor exploded in a flash of light that scientists later said was brighter than the sun and visible up to sixty-two miles away. This explosion took place in the upper atmosphere above the city of Chelyabinsk, Russia. When it exploded, it released twenty-six to thirty-three times the energy of the atomic bomb detonated over the Japanese city of Hiroshima, roughly equivalent to the amount of energy released in the former Soviet Union's initial attempt at a thermonuclear device in August 1953. The shock wave caused by this meteor's explosion broke windows and knocked down parts of some 7,200 buildings in six Russian cities and caused some 1,500 people to seek medical attention for injuries, mostly from flying glass.[85] I think that kind of shockwave might qualify as something causing the heavens to "tremble," don't you?

What if what Isaiah describes as a star falling from heaven is really a meteor? What if he is describing a meteor as big or bigger than the meteor that exploded over the city of Chelyabinsk? What if there were dozens or

---

[85] "Chelyabinsk meteor," https://www.en.wikipedia.org/wiki/Chelyabinsk_meteor (accessed 24 April 2022)

even hundreds of these meteors exploding in the upper atmosphere, not only sending out shock waves but peppering the earth with smaller pieces of the meteor?[86] Wouldn't you be inclined to think that all these explosions in the upper atmosphere might make the stars appear to be diminishing or even dissolving, as Isaiah describes it? Furthermore, wouldn't you be inclined to think that they might cause such a tumult in the atmosphere that it could easily be described as the heavens being rolled up as a scroll? All this might sound like an apocalyptic end of the world kind of science fiction movie. But in describing his prophetic vision, Isaiah says in the best way he can describe what he sees that this is exactly what's going to happen in the coming day of the Lord.

But there's still more to understanding these prophecies about the heavens and the earth "trembling." Understanding that a meteor exploding in our upper atmosphere can send out shock waves that are able to shatter windows and known down parts of building would explain the idea of the heavens "trembling." An exploding asteroid can also produce another surprising result. According to an article published by ABC News, a meteor lit up the night sky on January 16, 2018, as it exploded over southeastern Michigan some forty miles northeast of Detroit. This meteor measured only two yards (six feet) or so in diameter and was traveling at a speed of 28,000 miles per hour when it entered earth's atmosphere. In both size and speed, this meteor was nothing compared to the meteor that exploded over the city of Chelyabinsk in Russia, which was more than ten times bigger and traveling at more than twice the speed.

According to this article published by ABC News, "that explosion generated shock waves that traveled down to the ground northeast of Detroit, where residents heard a loud boom and felt the ground beneath them

---

[86] The word "tremble" is the actual word used in the article.

tremble." Again, according to the article, the National Weather Service sent out a tweet that said, "USGS [United States Geological Survey] confirms meteor occurred around 8:10 p.m., causing a magnitude 2.0 earthquake."[87] As crazy as this may sound, it makes perfect sense that huge meteors exploding as they enter earth's atmosphere, just like the one that exploded over the city of Chelyabinsk, would not only send out shock waves into the atmosphere but that these shock waves could cause earthquakes on the ground. And would this not provide a reasonable explanation of the prophetic vision of Joel and Isaiah as they describe the heavens and the earth trembling? I'm not saying that this is what's going to happen, but it certainly falls within the realm of possibility.

However, there is also another possible explanation for these phenomena occurring on the earth and in the heavens. Maybe the ancient prophets of Israel are not describing naturally occurring events at all. Perhaps they are describing a futuristic scene behind their wildest imagination of things never before seen or known in their day.

Could they be using the language of their day to describe a scene of modern warfare using weapons that have only existed in our world for less than a hundred years? Would "blood, fire and columns of smoke" (Joel 2:30) accurately describe the scene of a modern nuclear war? Massive nuclear explosions would likely cast hundreds, even thousands, of tons of debris into the atmosphere. Could that be why "[...] the stars of heaven and their constellations will not flash forth their light; the sun will be dark when it rises and the moon will not shed its light"? (Isaiah 13:10). Could this possibly explain how "the sun will be turned into darkness and the moon into blood before the great and awesome day of the LORD comes"? (Joel 2:31) Could

---

[87] Morgan Wilson, "What you need to know about the meteor that caused seismic shock over Michigan," 17 January 2018, https://abcnews.go.com (accessed 24 April 2022)

multiple nuclear explosions not only cause the sun and moon to grow dark and the stars to lose their brightness but also make the heavens and the earth tremble? (Joel 3:15–16). How might the prophet Isaiah describe the impact of multiple nuclear explosions in the upper atmosphere of earth? Might he say, "All the stars of the heavens will be dissolved and the sky rolled up like a scroll"? (Isaiah 34:4a, NIV). Could multiple nuclear missiles dropping out of the sky to find their targets cause him to say, "All the starry host will fall like withered leaves from the vine, like shriveled figs from the fig tree"? (Isaiah 34:4b, NIV).

We're not talking about science fiction here but possible scenarios in our present modern world. Yet how would such scenes appear to the ancient prophets of Israel? What language would they use to describe such futuristic scenes that would have been totally unfamiliar in their day? Think about it! Whether these prophetic pictures represent natural calamities or a nuclear war, they give us a window into the future of our world as the day of the Lord draws near.

So how do all these prophetic scenes about the day of the Lord fit into God's prophetic timetable? How do they relate to the coming of Christ and the birth of His kingdom on earth? Jesus actually fits the pieces together for us when He says, "But immediately after the tribulation of those days the sun will be darkened, and the moon will not cast its light, and the stars will fall from the sky, and the powers of the heavens will be shaken" (Matthew 24:29). Wow! Did Jesus really say that? Jesus is clearly referencing the very same prophecies regarding the day of the Lord that we've been looking at. He talks about the sun being darkened and the moon not giving its light. He talks about stars falling from the sky and the powers of the heavens being shaken. In Luke's summary account of the Olivet Discourse, Jesus calls these cosmic events affecting the sun, moon, and stars "signs."

By calling these occurrences "signs," Jesus is saying that they are not just random acts of nature with no real significance. Rather, they represent a prophetic message sent from God as a warning to the whole world. They are declaring that God is about to intervene in history and do something of great significance (Luke 21:25).[88] At the coming of Christ, all the ancient prophecies about the day of the Lord will indeed come to pass, just as they were written long ago. When in God's prophetic timetable are all these cosmic events in the heavens supposed to take place? Jesus indicates that all these things that will take place before or in conjunction with His coming will occur "immediately after the tribulation of those days" (Matthew 24:29), referring back, of course, to what He describes as the "great tribulation" (Matthew 24:21).

How do you suppose the people living on the earth at the time will respond when they see all these unprecedented cosmic events taking place in the heavens? We don't have to speculate or try to guess because Jesus tells us exactly how they will respond when He says, "There will be [...] dismay among nations, in perplexity at the roaring of the sea and the waves, men fainting from fear and the expectation of the things which are coming upon the world; for the powers of the heavens will be shaken" (Luke 21:25–26). The first thing He tells us is that these signs in the heavens will cause dismay

---

[88] A "sign" is "something that points to, or represents, something larger or more important than itself... By far the most important use of the word is in reference to the acts of God" (Youngblood, Bruce, and Harrison, "Sign," *Nelson's New Illustrated Bible Dictionary*, Thomas Nelson). According to Dr. David Jeremiah, "The conventional definition of a biblical sign... can be an event, symbol, object, place, or person whose existence or occurrence indicates something important in God's plan of history. There are a number of ways such signs can present themselves, but all express a particular meaning, help us to know or pay attention to, or point to what will be coming (David Jeremiah, *The Book of Signs: 31 Undeniable Prophecies of the Apocalypse*, Thomas Nelson Publishers, 2019). In other words, the purpose of these "signs" is to get people's attention before it's too late. These signs will be a warning of what's about to come in the day of the Lord.

among nations. According to the dictionary, the word "dismay" means "sudden loss of courage or resolution from alarm or fear."[89] Can't you just imagine people literally wringing their hands in a sense of hopelessness as they witness what appears to be the end of the world right before their eyes? And this is not just localized in one spot on the globe. It's clearly affecting the entire planet as nations all around the globe are in "dismay" at these overwhelming catastrophic events.

Not only is there dismay among nations, but people are in perplexity at the roaring of the sea and the waves. The picture is that of people all around the globe who are literally at their wit's end, with no idea of what's happening nor, more importantly, what to do next.[90] The world is not just perplexed over what's happening in the heavens. They're perplexed about the effect all this is having on the oceans as they witness what Jesus describes as the roaring of the sea and the waves. What could this possibly refer to? Here's one possible explanation:

> On March 11, 2011, a magnitude-9 earthquake shook northeastern Japan, unleashing a savage tsunami. The effects of the great earthquake were felt around the world, from Norway's fjords to Antarctica's ice sheet. Tsunami debris has continued to wash up on North American beaches years later...Less than an hour after the earthquake, the first of many tsunami waves hit Japan's coastline. The tsunami waves reached run-up heights (how far the wave surges inland above sea level) of up to 128 feet (39 meters) at Miyako city and traveled inland as far as 6 miles (10 km) in Sendai. The tsunami flooded an estimated area of approximately

---

[89] https://www.merriam-webster.com/dictionary/dismay (accessed 25 April 2022)
[90] In the original Greek text the word translated "perplexity" (*aporia*) means "at a loss for a way" and has the idea of "being at one's wit's end, at a loss how to proceed, without resources" (*Vine's Expository Dictionary of Biblical Words*).

217 square miles (561 square kilometers) in Japan. The waves overtopped and destroyed protective tsunami seawalls at several locations. The massive surge destroyed three-story buildings where peoplehad gathered for safety.[91]

Imagine our world with huge meteors exploding in the atmosphere. Imagine these explosions sending out shock waves in the atmosphere and causing earthquakes on the ground. Imagine some of these meteors making it through the atmosphere intact and crashing into the sea. Or imagine multiple nuclear missiles falling out of the sky, causing massive explosions all around the world that send out shock waves causing the heavens and the earth to tremble. Would it be reasonable to expect that such events might trigger huge tsunamis destroying parts of coastal cities throughout the world?

As we've already seen in the book of Revelation, just before the coming of Christ, there will be a great earthquake of such seismological magnitude and devastation that "[...] every mountain and island were moved out of their places [...] and the cities of the nations fell" (Revelation 6:14; 16:19). It's not difficult to picture a scene where people all around the globe are "fainting from fear and the expectation of the things which are coming upon the world" (Luke 21:26). I can just imagine how people would be

hyperventilating to the point of passing out cold from fear of what's happening and what might be yet to come. They would be wondering if it truly was the end of the world. This description of people fainting from fear is reminiscent of what we saw in the prophecy of Isaiah about the day of the Lord when he says, "Therefore all hands will fall limp, and every man's heart will melt. They will be terrified, pains and anguish will take hold of them; they

---

[91] Becky Oskin, "Japan earthquake & tsunami of 2011: Facts and information," February 25, 2022, htpps://www.livescience.com/39110-japan-2011-earthquake-tsunami-facts.html

will writhe like a woman in labor, they will look another in astonishment, their faces aflame (Isaiah 13:7–8).

In the New Testament, the apostle John describes a similar scene of end-time events and the terror that these things will generate in the hearts of men. He says,

> I looked [...] and there was a great earthquake; and the sun be came black as sackcloth made of hair, and the whole moon became like blood; and the stars of the sky fell to the earth, as a fig tree casts its unripe figs when shaken by a great wind. The sky was split apart like a scroll when it is rolled up, and every mountain and island were moved out of their places.
>
> Revelation 6:12–14

In describing how the world will respond to all this, John continues,

> Then the kings of the earth and the great men and the commanders and the rich and the strong and every slave and freeman hid themselves in the caves and among the rocks of the mountains; and they said to the mountains and to the rocks, "Fall on us and hide us from the presence of Him who sits on the throne, and from the wrath of the Lamb; for the great day of their wrath and who is able to stand?"
>
> Revelation 6:15–17

Just as John describes this as a day of wrath, so Isaiah describes it as a day of fury and burning anger. It seems evident, at least to me, that Joel, Isaiah, Jesus, and John are all talking about this same event using very similar descriptive language.

So what is this significant act of God, this divine intervention into human history, that will indicate that the day of the Lord has officially begun? Jesus tells us when He says, "And then [or 'at that time'] the sign of the Son of Man will appear in the sky, and then [or 'at that time'] all the tribes of the earth will mourn, and they will see the SON OF MAN COMING ON THE CLOUDS OF THE SKY with power and great glory" (Matthew 24:30). The day of the Lord will be none other than the coming of Christ Himself to establish His kingdom on earth. In describing His future coming, Christ uses the same prophetic language as Daniel, who said more than five centuries earlier,

> I kept looking in the night visions,
> And behold, with the clouds of heaven
> One like a Son of Man was coming,
> And He came up to the Ancient of Days
> And was presented before Him.
> And to Him was given dominion,
> Glory and a kingdom,
> That all the peoples, nations and men of every language
> Might serve Him.
> His dominion is an everlasting dominion
> Which will not pass away;
> And His kingdom is one
> Which will not be destroyed.
>
> Daniel 7:13–14

At Christ's coming, the day of the Lord will officially begin. However, the day of the Lord is not a single twenty-four-hour day.[92] Rather, it will be

[92] "Day," Easton's Bible Dictionary, PC Study Bible formatted electronic database, copyright 2003, 2006, Biblesoft, Inc. All rights reserved

an extended period of time beginning with the appearing of Christ but will also include the reign of Christ on earth for a thousand years, ending with the creation of a new heaven and a new earth (2 Peter 3:10–13; Revelation 21:1–4). In that day, we will finally experience the realization of our blessed hope in the glorious appearing of our great God and Savior, Jesus Christ, and all that this entails (Titus 2:13, NIV).

The challenge for those of us who call ourselves followers of Jesus is to be eagerly looking and ready for the day of His appearing. On that day, we and the whole world will see Him coming on the clouds in power and great glory. Is it possible that we have allowed ourselves to become so entangled in the things of this world that this is not really important to us? Maybe not even on our radar at all? At Christ's coming, there will be a special reward for those who love His appearing (2 Timothy 4:8). Do these words describe you?

Chapter 10

The Scattering

Remember the word which you commanded Your servant Moses saying, "If you are unfaithful I will scatter you among the peoples; but if you return to Me and keep My commandments and do them, though those of you who have been scattered were in the most remote part of the heavens, I will gather them from there and will bring them to the place where I have chosen to cause My name to dwell."

Nehemiah 1:8–9

The brutal desert sun beat down on the thousands of people gathered at the oasis of Kadesh-barnea near the border of the ancient land of Canaan. It had been forty long, grueling years that the people of Israel had been wandering around in the wilderness of Sinai—God's judgment on an entire generation for their rebellion and unbelief. And 400 years before that, they had become a nation of slaves serving the Egyptian pharaoh until God sent a rescuer to deliver them. His name was Moses. Now they were about to enter the new homeland that God had promised would belong to them forever. The mantle of leadership would pass from Moses to his successor Joshua who will lead them home. But first, Moses addresses the people one last time before he passes the mantle of leadership. As Moses comes before the nation to speak, the roar of the crowd suddenly quiets. Everyone eagerly awaits the final words of Moses before they move forward to take possession of the land.

This, however, isn't really where the story begins. As we've already seen in chapter 3, Abraham had encountered God hundreds of years earlier, long before Moses was even born. This meeting between Abraham and God would change the course of history for Abraham's descendants, the people of Israel, and the world forever. God's promise was that Abraham's descendants, the people of Israel, would be His special people forever and have ownership of what was in Abraham's day the land of Canaan forever. No conditions. Nothing hidden in the fine print. This was God's unconditional promise to His people. But there is one small caveat in this whole arrangement—at any given time, the actual possession of the land and the state of their relationship with Him will depend upon their faithfulness to Him.

As the people of Israel gather around Moses to hear his final words, he reminds them of all that God has done for them and of all that God expects of them. And then he gives them a warning that would haunt them throughout succeeding generations. He says to them,

> When you become the father of children and children's children and have remained long in the land, and act corruptly, and make an idol in the form of anything, and do that which is evil in the sight of the LORD your God so as to provoke Him to anger, I call heaven and earth to witness against you today, that you will surely perish quickly from the land where you are going over the Jordan to possess it. You shall not live long on it, but will be utterly destroyed. The LORD will scatter you among the peoples, and you will be left[93] few in number among the nations where the LORD drives you.

> Deuteronomy 4:25–27

---

[93] In the Hebrew language, the word translated "left" in the phrase "left few in number" means "to be left over, to be left alive, to survive, remainder, remnant (*The Online Bible Thayer's Greek Lexicon and Brown, Driver & Briggs Hebrew Lexicon*). In Deuteronomy 4:27, this word would best be translated "left as a remnant few in number."

Moses is warning the people of Israel of the dire consequences of forsaking God and turning aside to other gods. They will be scattered among the nations, where most of them will either die or be assimilated into the local cultures. He says that they will be left few in number among the people where they have been scattered. That warning sounds ominous, doesn't it? But don't think for a moment that God has gone back on His word because this warning has a brighter side to it. God promises that, even though He will discipline the nation of Israel when they are unfaithful to Him, He will not totally destroy them as a nation but will leave a remnant of Israel who will survive being in exile.

Moses continues,

> But from there you will seek the LORD your God, and you will find Him if you search for Him with all your heart and all your soul. When you are in distress and all these things have comeupon you, in the latter days you will return to the LORD your God and listen to His voice. For the LORD your God is a compassionate God; He will not fail you nor destroy you nor forget the covenant with your fathers which He swore to them.
>
> Deuteronomy 4:29–31

These who will turn back to the LORD in the latter days will be the remnant of Israel whom God will preserve in the midst of their exile. This remnant will turn back to the LORD in genuine repentance and faith. And it will be this remnant of Israel that will experience the final fulfillment of God's covenant promises in the latter days.

What exactly does Moses mean when he says that the LORD will not forget His covenant that He swore to their fathers? Moses explains,

[When] you return to the LORD your God and obey Him with all your heart and soul according to all that I command you today, you and your sons, then the LORD your God will restore you from captivity, and have compassion on you, and will gather you again from all the peoples where the LORD your God has scattered you. If your outcasts are at the ends of the earth, from there the LORD your God will gather you, and from there He will bring you back.

Deuteronomy 30:2–4

The prophet Micah reiterates this same promise when he says,

And it will come about in the last days[94] that the mountain of the house of the LORD will be established as the chief of the mountains. It will be raised above the hills, and the peoples will stream to it. "In that day," declares the LORD, "I will assemble the lame and gather the outcasts, even those whom I have afflicted. I will make the lame a remnant and the outcasts a strong nation, and the LORD will reign over them in Mount Zion from now on and forever."

Micah 4:1, 6–7

God's promise to Israel is first that there will always be a remnant of His people who will remain from the time of Moses until the coming of

---

[94] The Hebrew word translated "last" (*acharith*) in the phrase "last days" in Micah 4:1 is the same word translated "latter" in the phrase "latter days" in Deuteronomy 4:30. Both Moses and Micah are referring to the same time period. With the exception of one passage in the book of Job, the phrase "latter days" or "last days" is consistently used in Scripture in reference to the final days of human history when God intervenes in history at the coming of the Messiah to establish His kingdom on earth. It is the same time period in the future that Daniel refers to as "the time of the end" or "the end time" and "the end of the age" (Daniel 2:28; 10:14; 11:35, 40; 12:9, 13).

the Messiah to establish His kingdom on earth. But that's not all. God also promises that this remnant of His people will, in the latter days, repent and turn to Him in faith. And then they will be gathered from among the nations where they have been scattered and restored to the land that God had said from the beginning would be their everlasting possession. In spite of Israel's unfaithfulness and disobedience, God will not forsake His covenant with His people nor go back on His promise to Abraham.

Historically, it was in the year 722 BC when the northern kingdom of Israel[95] first experienced the bitter agony of being scattered according to this prophetic warning. The Assyrian army captured and destroyed their capital city of Samaria. The northern kingdom of Israel had been involved in pagan idolatry for many years, and God had been patient with them, sending prophets who faithfully called upon the people to repent. Finally, God acted upon the warning that Moses had given in the book of Deuteronomy. Following the destruction of Samaria, the people of Israel were taken captive into exile and scattered among the nations that made up the Assyrian empire of that day (2 Kings 17:6).

You might think that the southern kingdom of Judah would have watched wide-eyed at what happened to their Israelite brothers to the north and learned a lesson. Apparently, they thought they would escape the same fate as the northern kingdom. It's likely they reasoned that Jerusalem was, after all, the city of God (Psalm 46:4; 87:3). Furthermore, the temple of the Lord, symbolizing God's presence, existed among them. And the false prophets kept assuring the people that, for this reason, they had nothing

---

[95] At this point, in Israel's history the united kingdom of Israel established during the reign of King David had been split in two, with the two southern tribes of Judah and Benjamin being named the kingdom of Judah, and the ten northern tribes being named the kingdom of Israel. You can read more about this in the books of 1–2 Kings and 1–2 Chronicles.

to worry about.[96] As with the northern kingdom, God had sent His true prophets like Isaiah and Jeremiah to call upon His people in Judah to forsake their idolatry and turn back to Him. They persistently refused. Eventually, the southern kingdom of Judah experienced the bitter agony of seeing God's warning fulfilled in 605 BC when the Babylonian army showed up on their doorstep. After the fall of the Assyrian empire, the Babylonian empire had become the greatest superpower of its day. It swept across the ancient Middle East, leaving a path of death and destruction as one kingdom after another fell to the might of the Babylonian war machine.

In 605 BC, the Babylonian army conquered the city of Jerusalem and took captives back to the city of Babylon. When the Jewish people later rebelled against Babylon in a futile attempt to regain their independence, the Babylonian army showed up again less than two decades later. In 586 BC, the Babylonians destroyed the city along with the temple of the Lord. Survivors, except for the poorest of the poor, were taken as captives to live in exile in the city of Babylon. However, unlike the northern kingdom, the southern kingdom of Judah had a special place in God's prophetic program. Because of that, the prophet Jeremiah prophesied that there would be a remnant of Judah who would seek the Lord in the midst of their distress. This remnant would be allowed to return to the land of Israel after living in exile in Babylon for seventy years (Jeremiah 29:10–14). This remnant of Judah would rebuild the temple and eventually the entire city of Jerusalem.

Jeremiah's prophecy was fulfilled in 539 BC when a regime change occurred in Babylon as the city of Babylon was conquered by the Persians. As we've already seen in chapter 2, the former Babylonian empire was absorbed into the mighty Persian empire under the rule of King Cyrus the Great. King Cyrus

---

[96] You can read about this in Jeremiah 6–7.

became God's instrument for rescuing the remnant[97] of God's people from their exile in Babylon. He issued a decree that would permit the Jews to return to the land that God had promised would be theirs as an everlasting possession so that they might rebuild the temple in Jerusalem that had been destroyed nearly fifty years earlier.[98] The vast majority, however, remained as exiles in Babylon, where not only they but their parents and grandparents had built homes, raised families, and actually prospered under Babylonian rule.

For the next five centuries, this remnant of the Jewish people continued to live under the rule of Gentile empires—first, Babylon, then Persia, Greece, and finally, Rome. During this time, the Jewish people no longer had self-rule under their own king. (Hosea 3:4–5) Even King Herod, who ruled in Jesus' day, was not a true king from the royal line of David. Herod was a "client king" appointed by and ruling on behalf of Rome. He wasn't even Jewish![99]

Of all the empires that ruled over the land of Israel, the Roman empire was the most oppressive. And in what seems like a rerun of the Jews' experience with the Babylonians, the Jews rebelled against Roman rule, bringing about the complete destruction of Jerusalem and the Jewish temple for a second time in AD 70.[100] According to the ancient historian Josephus, an eyewitness to what happened, the Romans captured and totally destroyed the city and the temple. The Jews living in Jerusalem were either brutally killed or taken into slavery,[101] marking the end of Israel as a nation. Those few Jews

---

[97] Although Jeremiah doesn't specifically use the word "remnant," Ezra, the scribe, who was one of those who returned, specifically uses the term "remnant" with respect to those Jews whom God brought back to the land of Judah from Babylon (Ezra 9:8, 13–15).

[98] You can read the background for yourself in the books of Ezra, Haggai, and Zechariah.

[99] Herod the Great was an Idumean ("Herod the Great," https://en.wikipedia.org/wiki/Herod_the_Great [accessed 25 April 2022]).

[100] Jesus prophesied that this would happen (Matthew 23:37–39; 24:1–2; Luke 13:34–35). So did Daniel (Daniel 9:26).

[101] "Siege of Jerusalem (AD 70)," htpps://en.wikipedia.org/wiki/Siege of Jerusalem (AD 70) (accessed 25 April 2022)

who survived eventually were scattered again in an exile that spanned three continents. Yet, in 1948, nearly two thousand years later, the modern state of Israel was established by the United Nations. Jews began to emigrate from all around the world to the land that the God of their fathers had said would be their "everlasting possession." In 2021, there were close to 6.9 million Jews living in the state of Israel out of a total world Jewish population of 15.2 million.[102] This clearly represents an amazing miracle of God. Furthermore, the Jews not only retained their unique identity as a people for nearly two millennia, but they actually returned to possess their original homeland (or at least a small part of it).

Yet, even though so many Jews have returned to the land of Israel, because of their continuing unbelief as a nation, according to ancient Hebrew prophecy, they will once again be scattered among the nations in the latter days. Apparently, in the midst of the destruction of Jerusalem and the exile of the Jewish people in his own day, Jeremiah saw a prophetic foreshadowing of a time yet to come. He saw in the distant future that the people of Israel, again back in their land, would be scattered yet again among the nations. He gives a terrifying description of what is to come upon the Jewish people in the latter days when he says,

> "For thus says the LORD,
> 'I have heard a sound of terror,
> Of dread, and there is no peace.
> 'Ask now, and see
> If a male can give birth.
> Why do I see every man
> With his hands on his loins, as a woman in childbirth?

---

[102] https://www.jewishagency.org/jewish-population-5782/ (accessed 25 April 2022)

And why have all faces turned pale?

'Alas! for that day is great,

There is none like it;

And it is the time of Jacob's distress [...].'"

The fierce anger of the LORD will not turn back

Until He has performed and until He has accomplished

The intent of His heart;

In the latter days you will understand this.

Jeremiah 30:5–7, 24

Even though the people of God, both Jews and Christians, have suffered horrible persecution through the centuries, including the death of more than six million Jews in the death camps of Nazi Germany, a tragedy commonly referred to as the Holocaust, yet none of this will compare to what's yet to come. Jeremiah says, "Alas! for that day is great, there is none like it" (Jeremiah 30:7a). The prophet Daniel also describes this same time period as "a time of distress[103] such as never occurred since there was a nation until that time" (Daniel 12:1). Jesus describes it as a time of "great tribulation" (Matthew 24:15). He says that there will be great distress in the land, culminating in death for many of the Jewish people, with survivors of that brutal slaughter being taken captive among the nations, just as in the days of Rome and Babylon (Luke 21:20–24, NIV). Once again, we see the pattern of God scattering His people among the nations because of their persistent rebellion and unbelief.

Does this mean that God will finally give up on the people of Israel and abrogate His covenant regarding their possession of that land? Not at all! As

---

[103] This Hebrew word translated "distress" (*tsarah*) in Jeremiah 30:7 and in Daniel 12:1 is the same Hebrew word used by Moses when he warns the people of Israel what will happen in the "latter days" (Deuteronomy 4:30).

we've already seen, the people of Israel are and always will be God's special people—His covenant people. God's covenant promise has never been rescinded nor revoked, nor can it ever be. That's because God's promise to Abraham represents an everlasting covenant. Yes, there will be a time in the latter days when the Jewish people will experience the time of Jacob's distress. But in that future day, there will also be a remnant of those who, as Moses had said, in their distress will turn back to the LORD in repentance and faith (Deuteronomy 4:24–31).

Yes, the time of Jacob's distress will be bad—the worst experience the Jewish people have had since their birth as a nation, greater than the Inquisition during the Middle Ages and even worse than the Holocaust during World War II. But that is not the end of the story! This time of Jacob's distress won't be the demise of the Jewish people because God will ultimately deliver a remnant of His people. Jeremiah goes on to say,

> "It shall come about on that day," declares the LORD of hosts, "that I will break his yoke from off their neck and will tear off their bonds; and strangers will no longer make them their slaves. But they shall serve the LORD their God and David their king, whom I will raise up for them."

> "Fear not, O Jacob My servant," declares the LORD,
>   "And do not be dismayed, O Israel;
>   For behold, I will save you from afar
>   And your offspring from the land of their captivity.
>   And Jacob will return and will be quiet and at ease,
>   And no one will make him afraid."
>
>   Jeremiah 30:8–10

Knowing God's promise to restore His remnant may provide a reason for hope to the Jewish people when the time of Jacob's distress finally arrives. But it won't make their ordeal any less painful. That's because there's still more to this prophecy of Jeremiah. He says, "'For I am with you,' declares the LORD, 'to save you; for I will destroy completely all the nations where I have scattered you, only I will not destroy you completely. But I will chasten you justly and will by no means leave you unpunished'" (Jeremiah 30:3–11). When the LORD says that He will not destroy the people of Israel completely, He is saying that, in keeping with His covenant promise, He won't totally annihilate[104] them as a people. But He will chasten them as a nation and not allow them to go unpunished for their unfaithfulness. God will punish the wicked among them, but He will also preserve and rescue a righteous remnant who will survive the ordeal.

What exactly does all this mean for the remnant? God says He will not annihilate His people because of their sin in this time of Jacob's distress. But He will exercise corrective discipline upon His people that a remnant might turn their hearts back to Him. Though discipline is painful and unpleasant, it is the way a loving God does what is best for His people in order to bring them back into right relationship with Himself. This is really what the time of Jacob's distress is all about—God using affliction and suffering to turn the hearts of His people back to Him. However, God's discipline always has a dual effect, depending on our response to it. The discipline is a constant, but our response to that discipline is a variable. In the time of Jacob's distress, God's discipline will turn those whose hearts are tender toward Him back to Him in repentance and faith. But that same discipline will turn those whose hearts are hardened toward Him away

---

[104] The Hebrew word translated "destroy completely" (*kalah*) in Jeremiah 30:11 actually means "to annihilate" (*New American Standard Exhaustive Concordance of the Bible*). This is totally in line with the words of Moses in Deuteronomy 4:2.

from Him even more. As I once heard someone say, "The same sun that softens the wax hardens the clay."[105]

This, however, is still not how the story ends. There's more to this story than God's discipline and punishment. There's also deliverance for the righteous remnant of God's people. Those who respond to God's discipline by seeking Him and turning to Him in repentance and faith will be delivered. Jeremiah has just been talking about the latter days, and that's what he's still talking about when he says, "'At that time,' declares the LORD, 'I will be the God of all the families of Israel, and they shall be My people'" (Jeremiah 31:1). What time is He talking about? The latter days. And who is He talking about? All of the tribes of Israel. This includes even the ten northern tribes who were taken into captivity in Assyria, supposedly never to be heard from again. In the last days, when Messiah comes to establish His kingdom on earth, the remnant will include all twelve tribes of Israel. They will be reunited and restored to the land promised to them as an everlasting possession. In that day, the true remnant will return and seek the *Lord* their God, just as Moses said they would (Deuteronomy 4:27–31).

Jeremiah describes Israel's experience in the latter days metaphorically as a second Exodus when God will rescue His people who have been scattered among the nations and restore them to the land of promise. He says to them,

> Thus says the LORD, "The people who survived the sword
> Found grace in the wilderness—
> Israel, when it went to find its rest."
> The LORD appeared to Him from afar, saying,
> "I have loved you with an everlasting love;
> Therefore I have drawn you with lovingkindness.

---

[105] Source unknown

Again I will build you and you will be rebuilt,

O virgin of Israel!

Again you will take up your tambourines,

And go forth to the dances of the merrymakers."

Jeremiah 31:1–4

Jeremiah is reminding them that the people of Israel who survived the sword of pharaoh coming out of Egypt during the time of the Exodus experienced God's grace in the wilderness. In His grace, God promised that in their wilderness journey, He would go with them, and at the end, He would give them rest. Such grace is the tangible expression of His lovingkindness toward them. During Israel's future wilderness experience of being scattered among the nations in the latter days, those who respond to God's discipline with rebellion and unbelief will experience the sword of His justice in receiving the punishment their sins deserve. But the remnant of Israel who responds to God's discipline by seeking Him with repentance and faith will experience His grace just as in the original Exodus.

In that day, they will experience what the psalmist is talking about when he says,

He has not dealt with us according to our sins,

Nor rewarded us according to our iniquities.

For as high as the heavens are above the earth,

So great is His lovingkindness toward those who fear Him.

As far as the east is from the west,

So far has He removed our transgressions from us.

Psalm 103:10–12

Yes, God will discipline His people during the time that they are scattered among the nations in their own wilderness experience. But He will also show

143

His mercy and grace toward the remnant of His people who turn to Him in repentance and faith. He will bring them out from their exile among the nations. He will gather them from the remote parts of the earth.

Jeremiah speaks of how God will express this grace to the remnant of His people when he declares, "Hear the word of the LORD, O nations, and declare in the coastlands afar off, and say, 'He who scattered Israel will gather him and keep him as a shepherd keeps his flock.' For the LORD has ransomed Jacob and redeemed him from the hand of him who was stronger than he" (Jeremiah 31:10–11). The *Lord* will gather together the remnant of His people and restore them to the land that He had promised to Abraham and his descendants as an everlasting possession.

The prophet Ezekiel was a contemporary of Jeremiah living among the exiles in Babylon. He also speaks of this future time of God's discipline for His people and His future gathering of the remnant of Israel. He says,

> "As I live," declares the Lord GOD, "surely with a mighty hand and with an outstretched arm and with wrath poured out, I shall be king over you. I will bring you out from the peoples and gather you from the lands where you are scattered, with a mighty hand and with an outstretched arm and with wrath poured out; and I will bring you into the wilderness of the peoples, and there I will enter into judgment with you face to face. As I entered into judgment with your fathers in the wilderness of the land of Egypt, so I will enter into judgment with you," declares the Lord GOD.
>
> Ezekiel 20:33–36

Using the same metaphor as Jeremiah, Ezekiel draws a point of comparison with the time when Moses brought the people of Israel out of Egypt into the wilderness of Sinai on their journey to take possession of the land God had promised them. It's possible that the wilderness of the peoples is an actual geographical location. But I'm more inclined to think that it's a metaphor of Israel's exile when they will be scattered among the nations of the earth in the latter days. For God's people living among the Gentile nations during the time of Jacob's distress this will indeed be like living in a desolate wilderness. As Barnes explains, "In contrasts to the literal 'wilderness of Egypt' (Ezekiel 20:36), 'the wilderness of the people' is their spiritual wilderness period of trial, discipline and purification, while exiled among the nations."[106] Here the *Lord* will judge His people just as He did in the wilderness before He bought them into the land He had promised them.

As the prophecy continues, the metaphor changes to that of a shepherd with his sheep when the *Lord* says to His people,

> I will make you pass under the rod, and I will bring you into the
> bond of the covenant; and I will purge from you the rebels and
> those who transgress against Me; I will bring them out of the land
> where they sojourn, but they will not enter the land of Israel. Thus
> you will know that I am the LORD.
>
> Ezekiel 20:37–38

In explaining this metaphor, one writer says, "The idiom derives from the custom of a shepherd standing at the entrance of the fold and using his rod to count, examine, and sort his sheep."[107] As the sheep pass under the rod, God will bring His true sheep (the remnant) into the bond of the covenant. But He will purge from them the rebels and transgressors, who are not His true

---

[106] Albert Barnes, *Barnes' Notes*, Electronic Database Copyright 1997, 2003, 2005, 2006 by Biblesoft, Inc.
[107] Daniel I. Block, "The Book of Ezekiel Chapters 1–24," *New International Commentary* (W. B. Eerdmans publishing Co., 1997, WORDsearch Corp., 2010)

sheep at all.

In the Gospel of John, Jesus uses a similar metaphor of distinguishing between those who are His true sheep and those who are not. In keeping with the Old Testament, Jesus describes Himself as "the true Shepherd." And to those Jews who don't believe Him, He says, "You do not believe because you are not My sheep. My sheep hear my voice, and I know them, and they follow Me" (John 10:26–27). In like manner, in Ezekiel's prophecy, God is distinguishing between those named among His people who are His true sheep and those who are not. Those who are described as rebels and transgressors will be purged out to face God's just punishment. But His true sheep, those who respond to His chastening by seeking Him in repentance and faith, will be brought into what he calls "the bond of the covenant."

In Ezekiel's day, a covenant was a legally-binding, contractual agreement between two parties in which one or both parties were legally bound to abide by the stipulations contained in the agreement. By using this metaphor of a binding contractual agreement with His people, God is telling them that He will enter into a covenant agreement with them that He is absolutely and unconditionally bound to fulfill. Jeremiah defines for us more precisely the terms of this covenant when he says,

> "Behold, days are coming," declares the Lord, "when I will make a new covenant with the house of Israel and with the house of Judah, not like the covenant which I made with their fathers in the day I took them by the hand to bring them out of the land of Egypt, My covenant which they broke, although I was a husband to them," declares the Lord. "But this is the covenant which I will make with the house of Israel after those days," declares the Lord, "I will put My law with in them and on their heart I will write it; and I will

be their God, and they shall be My people. They will not teach again, each man his neighbor and each man his brother, saying, 'Know the Lord,' for they will all know Me, from the least of them to the greatest of them," declares the Lord, "for I will forgive their iniquity, and their sin I will remember no more."

Jeremiah 31:31–34

In the day of the Messiah's coming, God will replace the old covenant that He had made with Israel based on the principle of law with a new covenant based on the principle of grace. And this new covenant will provide for an entirely new relationship between God and His people. And so will come to pass the words of the apostle Paul, written more than five hundred years later when he says, "And so all Israel will be saved; just as it is written, 'THE DELIVERER WILL COME FROM ZION, HE WILL REMOVE UNGODLINESS FROM JACOB. THIS IS MY COVENANT WITH THEM, WHEN I TAKE AWAY THEIR SINS'" (Romans 11:26–27). Isaiah sums it up so well when he says, "And it will be said in that day, 'Behold, this is our God for whom we have waited that He might save us. This is the Lord for whom we have waited; let us rejoice and be glad in His salvation'" (Isaiah 25:9).

Chapter 11

The Great Escape

[...] there will be a time of distress such as never occurred since there was a nation until that time; and at that time your people, everyone who is found written in the book, will be rescued.

Daniel 12:1b

The date was May 26, 1940. The beach was more crowded with soldiers than the New York City subway at rush hour. More than 300,000 Belgian, British, and French troops were completely surrounded on three sides by the German army with no way of escape. Only twenty nautical miles across the Strait of Dover was safety, but these desperate troops had no way to get there. Their rescue would require nothing less than a miracle. And then it came— what the history books call "The Miracle of Dunkirk."

On that day, British naval vessels, along with hundreds of private citizens in privately owned boats ranging from large yachts and fishing vessels to smaller pleasure craft and tiny dinghies, crossed the English Channel with one single objective in mind. They were going to rescue as many of these soldiers trapped on the beach at Dunkirk as possible. On the first day, they managed to rescue less than 8,000 troops. But by the eighth day of crossing the English Channel, again and again, a total of 338,226 troops had escaped and been brought to safety.[108] Without "The Miracle of Dunkirk," the Allied forces might very well have lost World War II barely after it had begun. Yet, there is a greater danger and a more impressive rescue in store for God's people before the coming of Christ.

---

[108] "Dunkirk Evacuation," https://en.wikipedia.org/wiki/Dunkirk_evacuation (accessed 24 April 2022)

The prophet Jeremiah lived through one of the most challenging and difficult periods in the history of the nation of Israel. He witnessed the Babylonian war machine plow through the land of Judah, as well as the surrounding nations, bringing a swath of death and destruction everywhere they went. He witnessed the destruction of Jerusalem and the Jewish temple in 586 BC, and he saw the vast majority of the Jewish people taken into exile in the land of Babylon. Yet, as we saw in chapter ten, even with all that he endured in his lifetime, as he looked through his prophetic lens, he saw something far worse in the future. What he saw was something that would come upon the people of Israel in the "the latter days" that he calls "the time of Jacob's distress." Yet in the midst of this prophecy of judgment, there is also a promise of deliverance. He says, "For thus says the LORD [...] 'Alas! for that day is great, there is none like it [...], but he will be saved from it. The fierce anger of the LORD will not turn back until He has performed and until He has accomplished the intent of His heart; in the latter days you will understand this'" (Jeremiah 30:5, 7, 24). As we've already seen, God's intent is not to destroy His people but to discipline them so that they will turn back to Him in repentance and faith.

As we've already seen in chapter 10, Moses spoke about the very same thing eight hundred years before the time of Jeremiah. He warned the people about turning away from Him to serve other gods as they stood on the brink of entering the promised land. He said that if they chose to forsake Him, they would be scattered among the nations, and only a small remnant of the nation would survive. But then he said, "When you are in distress and all these things have come upon you, in the latter days you will return to the LORD your God and listen to His voice" (Deuteronomy 4:30).

Jeremiah is not the only prophet who speaks of this coming time of distress for the people of Israel in the distant future. Daniel the prophet, who lived more than eight hundred years after Moses, and about a hundred years after Jeremiah, clearly describes this same event. Speaking of something that will occur in what he calls the "end time" when he says, "And there will be a time of distress such as never occurred since there was a nation until that time; and at that time your people, everyone who is found written in the book, will be rescued[109] (Daniel 12:1).

It's important to note that Daniel is very specific about who will escape from this future time of distress. This rescue will not include all of the Jewish people living in that day, but only those whose names are found written "in the book." Daniel is likely talking about God's "book of life," which is mentioned a number of times in both the Old and Testaments.[110] Apparently, this book contains the names of all the true saints of God through the ages.[111] Only the true remnant of God's people—those with a genuine faith relationship with Him—will be rescued in that future day. Furthermore, he indicates that this rescue will occur at the same time as the resurrection of the righteous.[112]

Like Jeremiah and Daniel before Him, Jesus says that prior to His coming, there will be a time of intense persecution targeting not only the people of Israel but all of His own followers. It will be a persecution greater in magnitude than anything that has ever occurred in the past or will ever occur in the future. In fact, it will be so severe that if this persecution were not cut

---

[109] The Hebrew word translated "rescued" (*malat*) means "to slip away, to escape, to be delivered" (*The Online Bible Thayer's Greek Lexicon and Brown, Driver & Briggs Hebrew Lexicon*).

[110] Psalm 69:28; Philippians 4:3; Revelation 13:8; 17:8; 20:12, 15; 21:27

[111] The idea of "the book" is derived from the custom of the ancients of keeping genealogical records (Nehemiah 7:5, 64; 12:22–23) and of enrolling citizens for various purposes (Jeremiah 22:30; Ezekiel 13:9). So God is represented as having a record of all who are under His special care and guardianship...In the New Testament it is the record of the righteous who are to inherit eternal life (Philippians 4:3; Revelation 3:5; 13:8; 17:8; 21:27) ("Book of Life," *International Standard Bible Encyclopedia, Electronic Database Copyright 1996, 2003, 2006 by Biblesoft, Inc.*).

[112] For a detailed discussion of the resurrection, see chapter 15.

short, Jesus says, no one would survive. But for the sake of God's elect—those who have a genuine faith relationship with Him—it will be cut short, and they will be rescued out of it (Matthew 24:21–22).

According to the prophet Zechariah, there will be a great spiritual awakening among the Jewish remnant who survive this time of Jacob's distress. It will occur at a time when the armies of Israel's enemies have invaded the land of Judah (Israel) and have the city of Jerusalem surrounded. "And in that day [says the LORD] I will set about to destroy all the nations that come against Jerusalem" (Zechariah 12:9). Along with this promise of rescue from Israel's enemies, the *Lord* continues,

> [In that day] I will pour out on the house of David and on the inhabitants of Jerusalem, the Spirit of grace and of supplication, so that they will look on Me whom they have pierced; and they will mourn for Him, as one mourns for an only son, and they will weep bitterly over Him like the bitter weeping over a firstborn. In that day there will be great mourning in Jerusalem, like the mourning of Hadadrimmon in the plain of Megiddo. In that day a fountain will be opened for the house of David and for the inhabitants of Jerusalem, for sin and for impurity.
>
> Zechariah 12:10–11; 13:1

As Anthony R. Petterson explains, "[...] it is God's Spirit being poured out here to produce 'grace and pleas for mercy' among God's people—signs of repentance."[113]

There can be no doubt about the genuineness of Israel's repentance. It seems pretty evident in their great sorrow over realizing how they as a nation

[113] Anthony R. Petersen, "Zechariah," *ESV Expository Commentary*, Vol. vii, (Wheaton, IL: Crossway, 2018)

had been so wrong in not only rejecting but killing their true Messiah. Zechariah's prophecy uses two very emotionally charged metaphors to highlight the depths of grief in their repentance as they come to realize what they've done. The first metaphor compares their grief to the tragic loss of a firstborn son. The second metaphor compares their grief to how the people of Judah felt when godly King Josiah died in battle near the ancient village of Hadadrimmon (2 Chronicles 35:20–27). They realized with overwhelming sorrow that with Josiah's death would come the death of their nation. As the Babylonian war machine was plowing across the face of the ancient Middle East, uprooting one kingdom after another, they knew that the time would come when the Babylonians would be at the gates of Jerusalem. In that day, their kingdom would be no more. Such will be the depth of grief experienced by the remnant of Israel in that day.

While it's evident that the remnant of Israel responded to this outpouring of God's Spirit with a repentant heart, it's also evident that they responded with a believing heart. In doing so, they demonstrate how repentance and faith go hand in hand. Although most translations have the *Lord* saying, "They will look *on Me* whom they have pierced," I believe a better translation would be, "They will look *toward Me* whom they have pierced."[114] As Alfred Barnes explains it, the idea is that of looking to or toward their Messiah "with trustful hope and longing."[115] This same expression of faith is seen in Hezekiah's prayer as recorded in the book of 2 Chronicles. As the army of Israel faced a seemingly unbeatable enemy, Hezekiah prayed, "O our God [...] we are powerless before this great multitude who are coming against us; nor do we know what to do, but our eyes are on You" (2 Chronicles 20:12).

---

[114] This is an equally valid translation of the original Hebrew. The Hebrew word translated "on me" (*'el*) can also be translated "toward (of direction, not necessarily physical motion)" (*The Online Bible Thayer's Greek Lexicon and Brown, Driver & Briggs Hebrew Lexicon*).
[115] Alfred Barnes, *Barnes' Notes*

The eyes of Hezekiah and the Israeli army were focused on the *Lord* as they looked toward Him in faith, trusting Him to rescue them from this superior enemy force.

In the same way, the believing remnant of Israel will be looking in faith toward the *Lord* to rescue them out of a time of distress so intense that, as Jesus said, without divine intervention, no one would survive (Matthew 24:22). Furthermore, with great sorrow, they will recognize Jesus as their true Messiah—the only One who can save them. They will recognize that their Messiah is the same Jesus "whom they had pierced" when the Jewish leaders had Him crucified in AD 33. At last, the Jewish people will acknowledge Jesus as their true and only Messiah.

While Zechariah focuses on the spiritual awakening of Israel in that day, the prophet Joel indicates that this spiritual awakening is not limited to the people of Israel but encompasses the people of the entire world. After addressing serious issues in his own day, Joel looks forward through his prophetic lens to see things that will happen as the final day of the Lord approaches. In his prophetic glimpse into the future, he sees a worldwide spiritual awakening that includes not only the people of Israel but all of mankind.

Joel describes what will be happening in that future day like this:
It will come about after this
That I will pour out My Spirit on all mankind;
And your sons and daughters will prophesy,
Your old men will dream dreams,
Your young men will see visions.
Even on the male and female servants
I will pour out My Spirit in those days.

I will display wonders in the sky and on the earth,

Blood, fire and columns of smoke.

The sun will be turned into darkness

And the moon into blood

Before the great and awesome day of the LORD comes.

And it will come about that whoever calls on the name

of the LORD

Will be delivered;

For on Mount Zion and in Jerusalem

There will be those who escape,

As the LORD has said,

Even among the survivors whom the LORD calls.

Joel 2:28–31

Apparently, this outpouring of God's Spirit upon all mankind, both Jew and Gentile, represents God offering yet another opportunity for not only the Jewish people—but the whole world—to turn to Him in repentance and faith. It's true that the *Lord* is speaking directly to the people of Israel in this prophecy. However, the text is clear that this outpouring of the Spirit encompasses the entire population of the planet, both Jew and Gentile alike. Furthermore, the promise is given that whoever calls upon the name of the Lord, whether Jew or Gentile, will be delivered [i.e., rescued].[116]

So what exactly does it mean to call on the name of the *Lord*? According to Vine, "To call on God's name is to summon His aid [...] Calling in this sense

---

[116] As already seen in footnote 109, the Hebrew word translated "deliver" (*malat*) means "to escape, slip away." The most common use of this word is to express the idea of escaping from any kind of danger (*Vine's Expository Dictionary of Biblical Words*). This word also means "to release or rescue" (New Exhaustive Strong's Numbers and Concordance with Expanded Greek-Hebrew Dictionary, Copyright 1994, 2003, 2006 Biblesoft Inc. and International Bible Translators, Inc.). It is the same Hebrew word translated "rescue" in Daniel 12:1.

constitutes a prayer prompted by recognized need and directed to One who is able and willing to respond."[117] To call on the name of the Lord is an expression of humble faith that looks to God alone to meet a particular need. It is calling on God to do for them what they humbly acknowledge they cannot do for themselves. In this case, it is depending on God to rescue them not only from the persecution of the great tribulation but from the wrath of God that will fall upon a rebellious and unbelieving world in the day of the Lord.

That God would do a work of His Spirit in our world in the last days to turn the hearts of men and women, both Jew and Gentile, to Himself is entirely consistent with the teaching of the Old Testament. There God reveals His love for the people of all nations and His passion for the people of all nations to experience His grace and mercy—not His wrath and judgment. The prophet Isaiah speaks of this as the *Lord* Himself declares, "Turn to Me and be saved, all the ends of the earth; for I am God, and there is no other" (Isaiah 45:22). That will continue to be His message and His heart even as the day of the Lord approaches and Jesus comes to establish His kingdom on earth.

This same passion that God has for the salvation of all mankind, both Jew and Gentile, is also clearly expressed in the New Testament when the apostle Paul says, "This is good and acceptable in the sight of God our Savior who desires all men to be saved and to come to the knowledge of the truth" (1 Timothy 2:3–4). In fact, God doesn't just desire to see all men saved, but seeing this happen would bring Him great delight and pleasure.[118] It's significant that Paul even quotes directly from the prophecy of Joel with

---

[117] *Vine's Expository Dictionary of Biblical Words*
[118] The Greek word translated "desire" (*thelo*) essentially includes the idea of loving or liking to do something; to be fond of doing something; and in imitation of the Hebrew word "haphetz" (Psalm 40:8) can mean "to take delight, have pleasure in something" (*The Online Bible Thayer's Greek Lexicon and Brown, Driver & Briggs Hebrew Lexicon*).

emphasis upon the fact that God's gift of salvation is available to all, both Jew and Gentile, and always has been. In writing to the believers in Rome who were from both Jewish and Gentile backgrounds, Paul says, "For there is no distinction between Jew and Greek; for the same Lord is Lord of all, abounding in riches for all who call on Him; for whoever will call on the name of the Lord will be saved" (Romans 10:12–13).[119]

The apostle Peter, speaking in reference to the coming day of the Lord, expresses this same desire that God has for the salvation of all men, both Jew and Gentile alike, when he says, "The Lord is not slow about His promise, as some count slowness, but is patient toward you, not wishing for any to perish but for all to come to repentance" (2 Peter 3:9). Yet, while God is patient in extending His grace to the world, His patience will not last forever. Peter makes this clear when he says, "But the day of the Lord will come" (2 Peter 3:10). When God's grace toward sinners is rejected, there is nothing left but judgment. As Jesus says, "Whoever believes in the Son has eternal life, but whoever rejects[120] the Son will not see life, for God's wrath remains on him" (John 3:36, NIV).

Calling upon the name of the Lord is an expression of faith toward God and dependence upon His grace. But it is also an expression of repentance from sin because you really can't have one without the other. Merrill F. Unger makes this clear when he says that repentance is "[...] a fundamental and thorough change in the hearts of men from sin and toward God. Although faith alone is the condition for salvation,...there can be no saving faith without

---

[119] These words of Paul here translated "wish" (*boulomai*) likewise can convey the idea of affection or desire (*The Online Bible Thayer's Greek Lexicon and Brown, Driver & Briggs Hebrew Lexicon*).

[120] The Greek word translated "reject" (*apeithoo*) means "not to allow oneself to be persuaded; not to comply with; to refuse or withold belief" (*The Online Bible Thayer's Greek Lexicon and Brown, Driver & Briggs Hebrew Lexicon*).

true repentance."[121] Augustus Strong agrees when he says, "Since repentance and faith are but different sides or aspects of the same act of turning, faith is as inseparable from repentance as repentance is from faith. That must be an unreal faith where there is no repentance, just as that must be an unreal repentance where there is no faith."[122] For all those, whether Jew or Gentile, who call upon the Lord in that future day, God will provide a way of escape. And so the prophet Joel says, "For on Mount Zion and in Jerusalem there will be those who escape, as the LORD has said, even among the survivors[123] whom the LORD calls." (Joel 2:32).

When will this awesome rescue of God's people take place? At the end of the great tribulation when Jesus comes to establish His kingdom on earth! The prophet Zechariah makes this clear as he describes this great escape of God's people when he says,

> You will flee by my mountain valley, for it will extend to Azel. You will flee as you fled from the earthquake in the days of Uzziah king of Judah. Then the LORD my God will come, and all the holy ones with Him!
>
> In that day there will be no light; the luminaries will dwindle. For it will be a unique day which is known to the Lord, neither day nor night, but it will come about that at evening time there will be light. And the LORD will be king over all the earth; in that day the LORD will be the only one, and His name the only one.
>
> Zechariah 14:5–7, 9

---

[121] "Repentance," *The New Unger's Bible Dictionary (Originally published by Moody Press of Chicago, Illinois. Copyright © 1988)*

[122] Augustus Hopkins Strong, *Systematic Theology* (Philadelphia, PA, The Judson Press, 1907)

[123] The Hebrew word translated "survivors" (*sarid*) means "a survivor, a remnant" (*The Online Bible Thayer's Greek Lexicon and Brown, Driver & Briggs Hebrew Lexicon*). Note also Isaiah 11:11; Jeremiah 31:7; Micah 4:7.

Now compare these words of Zechariah to the words of Jesus when He says,

> But immediately after the tribulation of those days THE SUN WILL BE DARKENED, AND THE MOON WILL NOT GIVE ITS LIGHT, AND THE STARS WILL FALL from the sky, and the powers of the heavens will be shaken. And then the sign of the Son of Man will appear in the sky, and then all the tribes of the earth will mourn, and they will see the SON OF MAN COMING ON THE CLOUDS OF THE SKY with power and great glory. And He will send forth His angels with A GREAT TRUMPET and THEY WILL GATHER TOGETHER His elect from the four winds, from one end of the sky to the other.
>
> Matthew 24:29–31

What a glorious day that will be! This is the wonderful hope of God's people who will be living on the earth in that future day when Jesus comes in the glory and power of His kingdom. As incredible as the "Miracle of Dunkirk" may have been at the beginning of World War II, this rescue for all of God's people from the intense persecution of the great tribulation will be far greater. In that day, our King will not only be coming to rescue us but to receive us to Himself so that we may live and reign with Him forever in His eternal kingdom.[124]

---

[124] We will be talking more about this great rescue at the coming of Christ in chapter 14.

Chapter 12

The Bride

Let us rejoice and be glad and give the glory to Him, for the marriage of the Lamb has come and His bride has made herself ready.

Revelation 19:7

Most people, I think, love a love story, especially one with a happy ending. And one of the classic love stories of all time, nearly three thousand years old, is recorded in the Bible. The story of Hosea is actually a true story (not an allegory or a fable). The story begins with two young lovers—Hosea and the lovely Gomer—getting married. Hosea served as a prophet proclaiming the *Lord's* message to the people of the northern kingdom of Israel.[125] His assignment was to call the people of Israel in the northern kingdom to repent of their idolatry or face the judgment of God. In obedience to God's explicit instruction, Hosea married a woman whom the *Lord* told him would break his heart by becoming an adulterous woman. Their marriage would become, as God intended, a living object lesson of the *Lord's* relationship with His people.

During the course of their marriage, Hosea and Gomer had three beautiful children—two sons and a daughter. Each child, again in obedience to God's explicit instruction, was given a prophetic name that sent a message to the people of Israel. Their first child, a son, was to be named Jezreel because the valley of Jezreel would mark the beginning of the end for the northern

---

[125] As we've already seen in chapter 10, in 930 BC the united kingdom of Israel, founded by King David in 1010 BC, experienced a rebellion of the ten northern tribes of Israel, leaving only the two southern tribes of Judah and Benjamin remaining under the rule of David's grandson, King Rehoboam. The northern kingdom retained the name, kingdom of Israel, while the southern kingdom became the kingdom of Judah.

kingdom of Israel."[126] Their second child, a daughter, was to be named Lo-ruhamma, which in Hebrew means "No mercy." God would withdraw His mercy and deal with His people in disciplinary judgment. Their third child was another son, whom Hosea was instructed to name Lo-ammi, which means in Hebrew "Not my people," as God would temporarily disown His people—and scatter them among the nations until they turned back to Him in repentance and faith.[127]

Hosea's happy love story quickly turns sour when he discovers that his wife has been committing adultery, not just once but multiple times. When she continues in her adulterous behavior despite the pain she is causing her husband, Hosea's heart is broken. Hosea could have had her stoned to death according to the Jewish law of that day. Apparently, Hosea decides instead to divorce her and send her out of his home because she will not turn away from her adulterous ways. He knows that she will have to learn the hard way that living on her own and pursuing her lovers will not lead to true happiness. Instead, it will lead to poverty and pain because she will no longer be able to rely on her husband's provision and protection. One can only imagine the heartbreak for Hosea, knowing how much he loves his wife and yet also knowing that she does not return that love.

Yet it's because of his love for her that he divorces her and sends her out on her own. He is divorcing her not for the sake of retribution but reconciliation. His actions are not intended to be punitive but restorative, not destructive but disciplinary. In our day, we would call this tough love. He sends his wife

---

[126] In the valley of Jezreel, the northern kingdom of Israel was defeated by the invading Assyrian army. This battle marked the beginning of the end for the northern kingdom, which was conquered by the Assyrians in 722 BC. The capital city of Samaria was totally destroyed, and the people of the northern kingdom were taken into exile in Assyria, never to be heard from again as they became assimilated within the Assyrian empire.

[127] As we've already seen in chapter 10, this is exactly what Moses said would happen hundreds of years earlier back in the time of the Exodus (Deuteronomy 4:25–31).

away so that, in the end, he may get her back as the faithful and loving wife she once had been. It's not clear how much time passes, but eventually, Hosea learns that his wife has not done well living on her own. She has fallen on hard times, and things have gotten so bad for her that she has been sold into slavery. Then the *Lord* tells Hosea to go and show his continuing love for his wife in spite of the pain and sorrow that she has caused him. Because of his great love for her, he buys her out of slavery and restores her as his wife (Hosea 3:1–3). What an amazing love story.

As beautiful as this love story is, Hosea's story, by God's design, masterfully illustrates one far greater. I'm talking about the relentless redeeming love God has for His chosen people. The story of Hosea's redeeming love for his wife begins in the seventh century BC, but the story of God's redeeming love for His chosen people has its roots in an encounter between God and a man named Abraham long before the time of Hosea in the second millennium BC. In that encounter between God and Abraham, as we've already seen previously in earlier chapters, God made a covenant promise to Abraham and to Abraham's descendants, the people of Israel, that He would be their God forever and that the land of Canaan would belong to Abraham and his descendants, the people of Israel, forever. Abraham's brush with God that day and the promise he received from God would change not only his own life but the lives of His future descendants, the people of Israel, and ultimately the world forever.

As we've seen in previous chapters, this covenant promise has never been rescinded or revoked, nor can it ever be, since God's promise to Abraham represents an everlasting covenant. For this reason, the promise of God to Abraham is irrevocable, just as Paul says of the people of Israel in the New Testament, "From the standpoint of God's choice they are beloved for the sake of the fathers; for the gifts and the calling of God are irrevocable" (Romans 11:28–29). Paul is saying that because of His promise to Abraham, Isaac, and

Jacob (the fathers), God cannot and will not ever change His mind about the special covenant relationship that He has with the people of Israel.

Now fast forward in your thinking from the time of Abraham to the time of the Exodus some 400 years later. God delivered His people, Israel, under the leadership of Moses from slavery in Egypt. He delivered them from Egypt with the intent of bringing them into the land that He had promised them, the land of Canaan, which He had promised Abraham would be their everlasting possession. Three months into their journey on their way to this land, the *Lord* brought them to the mountain of Sinai. There He appeared to the people from the top of the mountain and entered into another covenant with Israel, in which He said to them,

> You yourselves have seen what I did to Egypt, and how I carried you on eagles' wings and brought you to myself. Now if you obey me fully and keep my covenant, then out of all nations you will be my treasured possession. Although all the earth is mine, you will be for me a kingdom of priests and a holy nation.
>
> Exodus 19:4–6a (NIV)

This is probably the time that Jeremiah is referring to when he says, "Thus says the LORD, 'The people who survived the sword found grace in the wilderness—Israel, when it went to find its rest.' The LORD appeared to him from far, saying, 'I have loved you with an everlasting love'" (Jeremiah 31:2–3a).

The *Lord* is declaring His special love for His people as He brings them through the desert to the land of promise. His love for them is a deeply emotional love that involves a passionate longing and desire for them.[128]

---

[128] "Basically this Hebrew verb is equivalent to the English 'to love' in the sense of having a strong emotional attachment to and desire either to possess or to be in the presence of the object" (*Vine's Expository Dictionary of Biblical Words*).

The *Lord* does not just love His people, but He is passionately head over heels in love with them. Now that's quite a statement! But there's even more. Because of His passionate love for Israel, He goes on to say, "Therefore I have drawn you with lovingkindness" (Jeremiah 31:3b). This is the language of a lover seeking to win the heart of his beloved.[129] The *Lord* not only loves His people but by showing His love for them, He hopes to win their love in return.

Centuries later, in the time of Jeremiah, a time when Israel had forsaken the *Lord* to worship idols, the *Lord* reminisces of those earlier days in Israel's history. In this context, He says to them, "I remember the devotion[130] of your youth, how as a bride you loved[131] me and followed me through the desert, through a land not sown" (Jeremiah 2:2, NIV). Here is the first clear reference to the covenant made at Sinai between the *Lord* and His people, Israel, being likened to a marriage covenant. The *Lord* Himself refers to Israel as His bride and remembers how much she loved Him in those early days after they had entered into the marriage covenant. He remembers her passionate affection and loving devotion to Him in those early days. Sadly, this love that Israel had for the *Lord* at the beginning was not destined to last, nor was the marriage, as the people of Israel became guilty of spiritual adultery in forsaking the *Lord* to engage in the worship of idols. And this is exactly what we've already seen in the book of Hosea.

We're going to see the *Lord* doing precisely the same thing in His relationship with the people of Israel as Hosea did with his adulterous wife,

---

[129] The Hebrew word here translated "I have 'drawn' you" (*mashak*) means "to draw in the sense of 'to entice, allure, woo.'" Harris, Archer, & Waltke (Eds.), *Theological Wordbook of the Old Testament*.

[130] The Hebrew word here for Israel's initial "devotion" (*hesed*) to the *Lord* is the same word translated "lovingkindness" (*chesed*) in reference to the *Lord*'s love for Israel in Jeremiah 31:3.

[131] The Hebrew word here for Israel's initial love for the *Lord* (*ahab*) is the same word used of the *Lord*'s love for the people of Israel in Jeremiah 31:3.

Gomer. And we'll see that He does it with precisely the same intent, not to hurt Israel but to win back her love. As one commentator explains it,

> This judgment upon Israel designed to win back her love is portrayed as the *Lord* issues to Israel, His unfaithful wife, a certificate of divorce and sends her out of His home. We see this when, speaking through His prophet, the *Lord* says to the people of Israel, "Rebuke your mother, rebuke her, for she is not my wife, and I am not her husband. This is the legal language of the ancient Near East. This is the language of a husband officially declaring that the marriage is over, and that his wife should pack her bags and leave.[132]

At first, I struggled with the idea that the *Lord* would actually divorce the nation of Israel, declaring that she is no longer His wife and He is no longer her husband. It seemed to me counterintuitive that the same God who says, "I hate divorce" (Malachi 2:16), would divorce Israel for her spiritual adultery in worshipping other gods. Then I remembered the words of Jesus in the Sermon on the Mount when He said, "It has been said, 'Anyone who divorces his wife must give her a certificate of divorce.' But I tell you that anyone who divorces his wife, except for marital unfaithfulness, causes her to become an adulteress, and anyone who marries the divorced woman commits adultery" (Matthew 5:31–32, NIV). He's referring, of course, to the teaching of the rabbis regarding what the Mosaic law teaches about divorce. Jesus doesn't contradict this statement about a man giving his wife a certificate of divorce

---

[132] At first it might appear to be a little confusing as to who is speaking in this chapter when he keeps saying, "I will," until we get to verses 13, 16, and 21 where the phrase, "declares the LORD," appears three times. It seems evident that the *Lord* is speaking to Israel (not Hosea speaking to Gomer) throughout the entire chapter.

but simply goes on to add an exception clause that changes everything. Although it is true that God hates divorce, Jesus makes it clear that divorce is permissible in the case of sexual immorality. And this is exactly what Israel is guilty of doing.

I might still question whether nor not this passage in the book of Hosea is actually saying that the *Lord* divorced Israel for her spiritual adultery if it were not for two other passages in the Old Testament that make it clear that this is exactly what the *Lord* did. Remember in the book of Jeremiah how the *Lord* reminisces about the earlier days of their marriage in the wilderness when Israel was devoted to Him with steadfast love? We come across this statement where the *Lord* says, "I gave faithless Israel her certificate of divorce and sent her away because of all her adulteries" (Jeremiah 3:8a, NIV). Yes, it really does say that God divorced Israel and sent her away.

This idea of God divorcing His people is really metaphorical language referring to the coming invasion by the Assyrian army in 722 BC when the people of the northern kingdom of Israel would be taken into exile to live in Assyria. Later, in the book of Isaiah, we're told how the people of Judah watched as the people of the northern kingdom were taken into exile, and yet they continued in their own flagrant idol worship just as the northern kingdom had done. A little more than a hundred years later, the *Lord* did the very same thing with the southern kingdom of Judah that He did with the northern kingdom of Israel. Again the language of divorce is used to describe what happened. Isaiah says to them, "This is what the LORD says: 'Where is your mother's certificate of divorce with which I sent her away? [...] Because of your transgressions your mother was sent away'" (Isaiah 50:1, NIV). He's referring here to the invasion of the Babylonian army in 586 BC when the people of the southern kingdom were taken into exile in Babylon.

So there you have it. Because of their blatant, unrepentant sin, the *Lord* divorced the people of Israel, both the northern and southern kingdoms. Clearly, it broke the heart of God to divorce His unrepentant idolatrous people, just as it did Hosea's in divorcing his wife, Gomer. But this isn't the end of the story. Like Hosea, the *Lord* did not divorce His people because He was finished with them. Indeed, His covenant promise to Abraham would render such action on the part of God impossible. His promise to Abraham's descendants, the people of Israel, was that He would be their God, and they would be His people forever.

So how do we explain the divorce? Very simply, like Hosea, He divorced His wife (the people of Israel) out of tough love to bring them to repentance for their flagrant adultery in worshipping other gods. However, as in the case of Hosea with Gomer, God's intent was not punitive but disciplinary, not to destroy His people but to deliver them from the bondage of their sin. God's intent was always to bring His people back to Himself as a loyal, loving, and devoted wife. He knew that once life became really difficult for Israel, she would think to herself, "[...] I will go back to my husband as at first, for then I was better off than now" (Hosea 2:1–13, esp. v. 7b, NIV).

The final chapter of the story of God's redeeming love for His people, Israel, brings us to the beautiful and joyful ending of what otherwise would have been a tragic story of monumental proportion. Turning His focus to the latter days and the coming of the Messiah when He will restore the remnant of Israel to Himself, the *Lord* says of His wayward people, Israel,

> Therefore, behold, I will allure her, bring her into the wilderness and speak kindly to her. I will betroth you to Me forever; yes, I will betroth you to Me in righteousness and in justice, in lovingkindness and in compassion, and I will betroth you to Me in faithfulness.

Then you will know the LORD.

Hosea 2:14, 19–20

Remember it was in the wilderness of Sinai that the *Lord* entered into a marriage covenant with Israel, and, according to the prophecy of Jeremiah, even in the midst of the rampant idolatry of His people, He could still look back and say with great delight, "I remember the devotion of your youth, how as a bride you loved me and followed me through the desert, through a land not sown" (Jeremiah 2:2b, NIV). Now He's saying that He will bring the people of Israel back to the wilderness where their love relationship began and where they entered into the covenant of marriage. It's possible that He will literally bring her back to the wilderness of Sinai. However, it appears more likely that He is speaking metaphorically of bringing Israel back to the time when they first fell in love and entered into the marriage covenant.

There He will allure her and speak kindly to her (literally, "speak to her heart"[133]). Another translation says, "[...] I will win her back once again. I will lead her into the desert and speak tenderly to her there" (Hosea 2:14, NLT). This is clearly the language of courtship and romance. In other words, after having divorced His people for their spiritual adultery, now He will seek to win their heart and their love once again. In spite of Israel's sin, the *Lord* will seek to court them and win them back as His beloved bride.

But this is only part of the story! Not only will the *Lord* seek to win back their love, but He adds, "I will betroth you to Me forever; yes, I will betroth you to Me in righteousness and in justice, in lovingkindness and in compassion, and I will betroth you to Me in faithfulness. Then you will know the LORD" (Hosea 2:19–20). To understand what this means, you have to

---

[133] New Exhaustive Strong's Numbers and Concordance with Expanded Greek-Hebrew Dictionary

understand that in the Jewish culture of that day, wedding customs were very different than they are in our culture today. According to one messianic Jewish Bible teacher, Glenn Kay, in that day, a couple didn't just go off and get married. It all started with the betrothal. He says,

> [A couple] would appear together under the Huppah—or canopy—and in public they would express their intention of becoming betrothed or engaged. From ancient times the wedding canopy has been a symbol of a new household being planned [...] While under the Huppah the couple participated in a ceremony in which some items were exchanged—such as rings, and a cup of wine was shared to seal the betrothal vows. After the ceremony the couple was considered to have entered into the betrothal agreement [...] During this time the couple was considered married—yet did not have sexual relations—and continued to live separately until the end of the betrothal."[134]

When the *Lord* says to Israel, "I will betroth you to me forever," He's saying that their relationship will go back to the beginning, and they will start all over again as in the beginning when He first entered into the marriage covenant with Israel in the wilderness of Sinai. But this time will be different because He says, "I will betroth you to Me forever." This time it will be a new covenant, as the *Lord* makes clear when He says through the prophet Jeremiah,

> "Behold, days are coming," declares the LORD, "when I will make a new covenant with the house of Israel and with the house of Judah,

---

[134] Glen Kay, "Jewish Wedding Customs and the Bride of the Messiah" (htpps://www.messianicfellowship.50webs.com/wedding)

not like the covenant which I made with their fathers in the day I took them by the hand to bring them out of the land of Egypt, My covenant which they broke, although I was a husband to them," declares the LORD.

Jeremiah 31:31–32

So how is this new covenant to be different from the old one? The *Lord* continues,

"But this is the covenant which I will make with the house of Israel after those days," declares the LORD, "I will put My law within them and on their heart I will write it; and I will be their God, and they shall be My people. They will not teach again, each man his neighbor and each man his brother, saying, 'Know the LORD,' for they will all know Me, from the least of them to the greatest of them," declares the LORD, "for I will forgive their iniquity, and their sin I will remember no more."

Jeremiah 31:33–34

In that future day of Christ's coming to establish His kingdom on earth, He will fulfill the promise to His people that He will not only forgive all their sins, but He will restore them to Himself as His wife forever with a new covenant very different in every way from the old one. And so will be fulfilled the prophecy of Isaiah when he says, "[...] as the bridegroom rejoices over the bride, So your God will rejoice over you" (Isaiah 62:5). What a beautiful and joyous ending to an otherwise tragic story! A new bride. A new covenant. A new marriage that will last forever. What a glorious future our God has in store for His chosen people, Israel.

While this metaphor of Israel being the bride or the wife of Yahweh is seen clearly in the Old Testament, the same metaphor is also used in the New Testament in relation to the Church. As Jesus teaches the disciples about His future coming, He says to them, "[...] I will come again and receive you to Myself, that where I am you may be also" (John 14:3b). You may not immediately see the connection between these words and the marriage metaphor, but read on, and it will become clear. The backstory begins following the Passover meal on the eve of Christ's crucifixion. Judas has already left, and Jesus says to His remaining disciples, "Little children, I am with you a little while longer. You will seek Me; and as I said to the Jews, now I also say to you, 'Where I am going, you cannot come'" (John 13:33).

This is not the first time that Jesus has told the disciples that He would be going away and they would not be able to follow. There are three other incidents recorded in the Gospel of John when Jesus told them He would be going away (John 7:34; 8:21; 12:8, 35). Because of their expectation that Jesus would usher in the promised messianic kingdom very soon, this time, it really rocked their boat (an appropriate metaphor since four of the disciples were former fishermen). Imagine what must have been going through the minds of the disciples as they tried to digest what Jesus had just told them. They must have been thinking, "How can this be?" "What does this mean?" "Where are You going?" "Why can't we come with You?" They are bewildered, confused, anxious, and afraid. All of their expectations, misguided though they were, had just been dashed to the ground.

How do we know that this was the reaction of the disciples to Jesus' words? Because of Jesus' response to their questions. He says to them, "Do not let your hearts be troubled. Trust in God; trust also in me" (John 14:1, NLT). This indicates that they were indeed perplexed, confused, anxious, and afraid[135] over the implications of what He had just told them. Furthermore, another way of translating the words "Do not let your hearts be troubled" would be, "Do not keep on letting your hearts be troubled,"[136] indicating that this was already the case. Jesus can see that the disciples are not taking His words well. So He simply says to them, "You're going to have to trust God on this! And you're going to have to trust Me!" What the disciples need to understand is that their expectation isn't wrong—just the timing of it. They are not wrong in believing that He is the Messiah, nor are they wrong in thinking that He will come to Israel as their promised King to establish the kingdom of God on earth. The problem is that their timing is off, as He's been trying to tell them all along.

When you stop to think about it, the disciples are very much like us, aren't they? We often do the very same thing. When God's plans don't seem to match up with our own—when God's actions don't line up with our expectations—when God's timing doesn't line up with when we want to see things happen or expect to see things happen—our typical response is to get stressed out. We become agitated, confused, anxious, and afraid. But if we're listening, we'll hear that still small voice of God's Spirit within us saying, "Just trust Me on this!" And that's exactly what Jesus is asking the disciples to do here. It's in this context that Jesus provides a prophetic promise designed to dispel their fear, their anxiety, and their confusion and to settle their troubled hearts. And maybe ours too!

Jesus says, "In My Father's house are many dwelling places; if it were not so, I would have told you; for I go to prepare a place for you. If I go and

---

[135] The Greek word translated "trouble" (*tarasso*) means "to cause one inward commotion, take away his calmness of mind, disturb his equanimity; to disquiet, make restless...to stir up...to trouble...to render anxious or distressed, to perplex" (*The Online Bible Thayer's Greek Lexicon and Brown, Driver & Briggs Hebrew Lexicon*).

[136] The Greek grammar is a present tense verb, which indicates ongoing, continuous action.

prepare a place for you, I will come again and receive you to Myself, that where I am, there you may be also" (John 14:2–3). At first glance, what Jesus is saying here may seem a little confusing. What is Jesus talking about when He speaks of the Father's house and says that in the Father's house are many rooms? What does He mean when He says that He's leaving to prepare a place for them (and us)? What does He mean when He says that He's coming back so that they (and we) will never be separated from Him again?

Actually, what Jesus is saying here makes perfect sense if we understand it in light of this same metaphor of marriage that we see with Israel in the Old Testament. As we've already explained, according to the Jewish custom of that day, a couple would become betrothed to one another in a special ceremony. During the betrothal period, which typically lasted about a year, the bride would continue to live in her own father's house and prepare her dress for the wedding. During that time, the bridegroom would return to his own father's house, where he would prepare a place where they could spend the rest of their lives together as husband and wife. If there was not enough room in his father's house, the solution to that problem was not typically to build another house but to enlarge his father's house by adding another room. When the preparations were complete, the bridegroom would come back for his bride and bring her to their new home in his father's house.

Does this give you a clearer picture of what Jesus is saying to His disciples and to us as the Church? As the Church of Jesus Christ, we are His bride, and He is our bridegroom. The moment we put our trust in Christ and enter into a saving relationship with Him, we are betrothed to Him as His bride. To understand the picture fully, we must see it in light of the parable in the Gospel of Luke, where Jesus says, "A nobleman went to a distant country to receive a kingdom for himself, and then return" (Luke 19:12). This lines up exactly with what Daniel sees in a prophetic vision when he says,

I kept looking in the night visions,

And behold, with the clouds heaven

One like a Son of Man was coming,

And He came up to the Ancient of Days

And was presented before Him.

And to Him was given dominion,

Glory and a kingdom,

That all the peoples, nations and men of every language

Might serve Him.

His dominion is an everlasting dominion

Which will not pass away;

And His kingdom is one

Which will not be destroyed.

Daniel 7:13–14

Jesus did not return to heaven to prepare for us a place to live with Him in there. On the contrary, He returned to heaven to receive a kingdom from His Father[137] that He is preparing for us on earth. When He returns and brings that kingdom to earth, He will receive us to Himself as His bride so that we may live with Him there (in His Father's House) forever.[138] Do you see how all this fits together as He compares His coming to the gathering of His elect with a bridegroom coming to receive his bride?

As I mentioned earlier, the disciples didn't get it wrong that Jesus was indeed the Messiah who would most assuredly establish the messianic

---

[137] See chapter 13

[138] Don't misunderstand. I'm not suggesting that, as believers, we won't go to heaven to be with Jesus when we die (see chapter 15). What I'm saying is that dying and going to heaven is not what Jesus is talking about in this chapter. He's talking about His future coming to establish the kingdom of God on this earth, where we will live with Him as His bride forever in His Father's house.

kingdom of God on earth. What they got wrong was the timing of when this would take place. They had no idea that Jesus would go away to heaven and then come back again in the distant future to establish His kingdom on the earth. When Jesus says that He must go away to prepare a place for them in the Father's house, it has nothing to do with heaven but represents the kingdom that He will establish on the earth at His coming.

The preparations are all that remain to be accomplished before He comes back to establish that kingdom at the end of the age. The disciples needed to understand that Jesus is not abandoning them any more than the bridegroom is abandoning his bride when he goes away to prepare a place for them to live as husband and wife. In the meantime, they, and we, must wait for that future day when the time is right and the preparations are complete. That's when Jesus, our glorious Bridegroom, will return. And so Jesus continues, "If I go and prepare a place for you, I will come again and receive you to Myself, that where I am, there you may be also" (John 14:3). He is not coming back as the Bridegroom to take us back to heaven, but to take us as His bride to live with Him forever in His everlasting kingdom on earth.

This brings us back again to the metaphor of the Jewish marriage. Mr. Kay explains,

> The final step in the wedding process is called—Nissuin—the word comes from the Hebrew verb—hsn (nasa)—which means—"to carry." This is a graphic description—as the bride would be waiting for her groom to come—to carry her off to her new home. The period of the betrothal—was a time of great anticipation—as the bride waited for the arrival of her betrothed. One of the unique features of the Biblical Jewish wedding was the time of the groom's arrival—it was to be a surprise. The bride...knew the approximate

timing, but the exact hour or day was uncertain. It was the father of the groom who would give the final approval for the marriage to begin. Since the time of his arrival was a surprise, the bride and her bridal party were always to be ready...It was customary for one of the groom's party to go ahead of the bridegroom, leading the way to the bride's house, and shout—"Behold, the bridegroom comes!" This would be followed by the sounding of the shofar (trumpet). At the sounding of the shofar the entire wedding processional would go through the streets of the city to the bride's house. The groomsmen would again set up the huppah. Again the couple would say a blessing over the cup of wine. The ceremony finalized the promises and vows.[139]

It's fitting, in light of this metaphor of marriage, that Jesus would say, "If I go and prepare a place for you, I will come again and receive you to Myself, that where I am, there you may be also" (John 14:3). This is exactly what a Jewish bridegroom would do with his bride at the end of the betrothal period. And just in case there's any doubt that Jesus is using the metaphor of marriage in reference to His future coming to establish His kingdom, it's important to note that the language here is the very same language used in that day for a bridegroom coming to take (receive) his bride as his wife. We see this in the case of Joseph and Mary (Matthew 1:20).[140] The angel is telling Joseph not to be afraid to cut short the betrothal period and consummate the marriage by taking (receiving) his bride into his home to be his wife.

---

[139] Glen Kay, "Jewish Wedding Customs and the Bride of the Messiah"

[140] In describing the use of the Greek word translated "receive" (*paralambano*), Vine writes, "Besides its meaning, 'to receive,' [*paralambano*] denotes 'to take to (or with) oneself,' of 'taking' a wife, e.g., Matthew 1:20, 24; of 'taking' a person or persons with one" (*Vine's Expository Dictionary of Biblical Words*).

This is also the same word used of Christ coming to gather His elect when He says, "Then there will be two men in the field; one will be taken [received] and one will be left. Two women will be grinding at the mill; one will be taken [received] and one will be left" (Matthew 24:40–41). He will be coming as the Bridegroom for His bride to take (receive) her as His wife so that she will be with Him forever in His everlasting kingdom. All of this will occur at the coming of Christ when He sends forth His angels with a great trumpet (sound) to gather His elect (Matthew 24:30–31). From that time on, we will live and reign forever with our glorious Bridegroom in the kingdom that He has prepared for us as His bride.

In that future day, God's promise to Israel will be fulfilled as He said through Hosea the prophet, "I will betroth you to Me forever; yes, I will betroth you to Me in righteousness and in justice, in loving kindness and in compassion, and I will betroth you to Me in faithfulness. Then you will know the LORD" (Hosea 2:19–20). In that future day, God's promise to the Church will be fulfilled as Jesus said, "[...] I will come again and receive you to Myself, that where I am, there you may be also" (John 14:3). Or as Paul says so beautifully, "We will be caught up together meet the Lord in the air, and so we shall always be with the Lord" (1 Thessalonians 4:17). And in that glorious day, all of God's redeemed people through the ages, both Jew and Gentile, both Israel and the Church, will live with Him forever as His one and only bride in the glorious and everlasting kingdom in which Christ shall reign forever and ever.

But wait! I almost left out the best part. In a Jewish wedding, after the bridegroom came for his bride to take her back to his father's house, there would always be a time of joyful celebration. Again, Glenn Kay says,

The pinnacle of this joyful celebration was the marriage supper. It was much more than just a sit-down dinner for all the guests. It included seven full days of food, music, dance and celebration... After the festivities the husband was free to bring his bride to their new home to live together as husband and wife in the full covenant of marriage.[141]

According to Jewish custom, no wedding would be complete without the marriage feast. And so too with Christ and His bride. In describing another of his prophetic visions in the book of Revelation, John says,

Then I heard something like the voice of a great multitude and like the sound of many waters and like the sound of mighty peals of thunder, saying, "Hallelujah! For the Lord our God, the Almighty, reigns. Let us rejoice and be glad and give the glory to Him, for the marriage of the Lamb has come and His bride has made herself ready." It was given to her to clothe herself in fine linen, bright *and* clean; for the fine linen is the righteous acts of the saints. Then he said to me, "Write, 'Blessed are those who are invited to the marriage supper of the Lamb.'" And he said to me, "These are the true words of God."

Revelation 19:6–9

I suppose the idea of a marriage supper when Christ comes to receive His bride could be taken literally, but it strikes me as being more likely the continuation of the marriage metaphor rather than a literal sit-down dinner when Christ comes to receive us as His bride. If this is the case, then the marriage supper would simply represent a joyful celebration in His glorious

---

[141] Glen Kay, "Jewish Wedding Customs and the Bride of the Messiah"

kingdom that will last not just for seven days but for all eternity. There will be no end to the joyful celebration of all that Christ has done for us as we live forever with our glorious King as His beloved bride in His everlasting kingdom. To Him be glory and praise forever!

As followers of Christ, whether Jew or Gentile, we need to see ourselves for who we truly are as the bride of Christ. And we need to understand that we are all currently in the betrothal period waiting for our glorious Bridegroom to come and take us home with Him as His wife. And just as the bride and bridegroom would live together as husband and wife in the home that he had prepared for her in his father's house, so Christ will take us home that we may be with Him in the home that He has prepared for us in His everlasting kingdom. In that day, the words of Isaiah's prophecy will come to pass, which says, "As the bridegroom rejoices over the bride, So your God will rejoice over you" (Isaiah 62:5).

It's important to note that in promising the disciples that He will come again, He gives no indication of when this will happen. When Jesus originally spoke these words to the disciples, they apparently expected Him to come back immediately. After His death and resurrection, one of the first things they asked Jesus was, "Lord, is it at this time You are restoring the kingdom to Israel?" (Acts 1:6) It's important to note that Jesus doesn't really answer their question. He does not give them a simple yes or no answer, which is what they must have expected. Instead, Jesus says to the disciples, "It is not for you to know times or epochs which the Father has fixed by His own authority; but you will receive power when the Holy Spirit has come upon you; and you shall be My witnesses both in Jerusalem, and in all Judea and Samaria, and even to the remotest part of the earth" (Acts 1:7–8). The point that Jesus is making here is that it isn't important for us to know the exact time of His coming. What matters is that we complete the work that He has given us to do as we faithfully wait for His return.

Yes, we have been waiting a long time for our glorious Bridegroom to return. The betrothal period has gone on far longer than we ever thought it would. And still, we have no idea how long we must wait until His return. But we have His promise to us as the people of God that when the time is right, He will come again for us as His bride. Just as the Scriptures say of Christ's first coming—"But when the right time came, God sent his Son..." (Galatians 4:4, NLT), so also when He comes for His bride, it will be at just the right time. It may seem that we've been waiting far too long, but when our Bridegroom finally appears, it will be at just the right time in the unfolding of God's plan of redemption.

The Savior is coming. That promise has not changed, nor has the One who made the promise. As the Scripture encourages us,

> Let us hold fast the confession of our hope without wavering, for He who promised is faithful. Therefore, do not throw away your confidence, which has a great reward. For you have need of endurance, so that when you have done the will of God, you may receive what was promised.
>
> FOR YET IN A VERY LITTLE WHILE,
> He who is coming will come, and will not delay.
>
> Hebrews 10:23, 35–37

Come, Lord Jesus! Come!

Chapter 13

The Coronation

Then the seventh angel sounded; and there were loud voices in heaven, saying, "The kingdom of the world has become the kingdom of our Lord and of His Christ; and He will reign forever and ever."

Revelation 11:15

June 2, 1953—the significance of the date was lost on me as an eight-year-old. But in London, England, it was coronation day for Queen Elizabeth II, her formal crowning as monarch of the United Kingdom.

One historical account of this grand event records:

A thousand dignitaries and guests attended the coronation at London's Westminster Abbey, and hundreds of millions listened on radio and for the first time watched the proceedings on live television...The ceremony at Westminster was one of pomp and pageantry...In the procession through the streets of London that followed, Elizabeth and her husband were joined by representatives from the more than 40 member states of the Commonwealth, including heads of state, sultans, and prime ministers. British troops like the Yeomen of the Guard were joined by a great variety of Commonwealth troops, including police from the Solomon Islands, Malaysians in white uniforms and green sarongs, Pakistanis in puggaree headdresses, Canadian Mounties, and New Zealanders and Australians in wide-brimmed hats. After the parade, Elizabeth stood with her family on the Buckingham

Palace balcony and waved to the crowd as jet planes of the Royal
Air Force flew across the Mall in tight formation.[142]

As grand and magnificent as Queen Elizabeth's coronation was over
six decades ago, it pales into insignificance when compared with another
coronation yet future. This coronation will impact not just a single nation
but the entire world, not just for a lifetime but forever. I'm talking about
the coronation of Jesus Christ (Messiah) as King of kings and Lord of lords.
From that day forward, He will rule over the nations and alter the destiny of
our planet forever.

Many of the ancient Hebrew prophets spoke of the future reign of the
Messiah when He would establish a new world order and rule over all the
nations of the earth. Speaking of the Messiah, the prophet Zechariah says,

> He will speak peace to the nations; and His dominion will be from
> sea to sea, and from the River to the ends of the earth. [...] Then the
> LORD, my God, will come, and all the holy ones with Him! [...]
> And the LORD will be king over all the earth; in that day the LORD
> will be the only one, and His name the only one.
>
> Zechariah 9:10b; 14:5b, 9

The prophet Isaiah likewise prophesies of the future kingdom reign of
Messiah when he says, "There will be no end to the increase of His government
or of peace, on the throne of David and over his kingdom, to establish it and
to uphold it with justice and righteousness from then on and forevermore
(Isaiah 9:7).

While many of the ancient Hebrew prophets speak of Messiah's reign,

---

[142] Coronation of Queen Elizabeth II (https://www.history.com/this-day-in-history/coro-
nation-of-queen-elizabeth-ii) (accessed 26 April 2022)

only one of the prophets actually describes His coronation as King—Daniel. Think for a moment what you would expect to see if God removed the veil between heaven and earth, and you could see with your own eyes what heaven is like. If you are envisioning God sitting on a throne surrounded by an innumerable company of angels, you would be right. It was in the first year of Belshazzar, king of ancient Babylon, in the mid-sixth century BC, when God pulled back the veil between heaven and earth for the prophet Daniel in a dream as he lay upon his bed. Actually, the dream involved a series of visions, one of which gave Daniel a clear and unhindered view of the very throne room of God.

Here's how Daniel describes what he saw:

> I was looking in my visions at night [...] I kept looking until thrones were set up, and the Ancient of Days took His seat; His vesture was like white snow and the hair of His head like pure wool. His throne was ablaze with flames, its wheels were a burning fire. A river of fire was flowing and coming out from before Him; thousands upon thousands were attending Him, and myriads upon myriads were standing before Him [...].
>
> Daniel 7:9–10

Notice that Daniel not only sees in his vision of the heavenly throne room God Himself seated upon His throne, but many thrones around the throne of God. Think in terms of the President of the United States seated at the head of a huge conference table with chairs set up all around the table for the members of his Cabinet. That's the setup Daniel is describing here.

The psalmist tells us that there are angels who make up the assembly of the holy ones who sit on thrones surrounding the throne of God. He paints a picture of this for us when he says,

The heavens will praise Your wonders, O LORD; Your faithfulness also in the assembly of the holy ones. For who in the skies is comparable to the LORD? Who among the sons of the mighty is like the LORD, a God greatly feared in the council of the holy ones, and awesome above all those who are around Him?

Psalm 89:5–7

Likewise, in the book of Revelation, the apostle John has a vision of heaven and the heavenly throne room of God; he speaks of this same assembly of holy ones when he says, "Immediately I was in the Spirit; and behold, a throne was standing in heaven, and One sitting on the throne. Around the throne were twenty-four thrones; and upon the thrones I saw twenty-four elders sitting, clothed in white garments, and golden crowns on their heads (Revelation 4:2, 4).

This assembly of the holy ones consisting of twenty-four elders wearing golden crowns on their heads seated on their own thrones surrounding God's throne are apparently angelic rulers of the highest order who sit in the very presence of God. At the center of this assembly of the holy ones, Daniel sees the Ancient of Days seated on the throne from which He rules heaven and earth. There He is, dressed in white, with hair as white as pure wool. His throne emanates such brilliant light that Daniel describes it as being ablaze with flames with a river of fire flowing and coming out from before Him. Imagine what a breathtaking sight this would have been.

The name "Ancient of Days" is only used of God three times in the entirety of Scripture, and they are all in this passage describing Daniel's vision of the heavenly throne room. It is a name for God that highlights He is the God of eternity. As the ancient psalmist declares, "Before the mountains were born or You gave birth to the earth and the world, even from everlasting to everlasting, You are God" (Psalm 90:2). In other words, there has never been a time when God did not exist, nor will there ever be a time when God will cease to exist. By His very nature, God is timeless. He lives outside of time and is totally unrestricted by time. He is indeed the Ancient of Days.

But there's still more. If you pictured God surrounded by an innumerable company of angels, you got that right too! In describing his vision of heaven, Daniel says, "Thousands upon thousands were attending Him, and myriads upon myriads were standing before Him" (Daniel 7:10). He's talking, of course, about the same picture the psalmist describes when he says, "Bless the LORD, you His angels, mighty in strength, who perform His word, obeying the voice of His word! Bless the LORD, all you His hosts, you who serve Him, doing His will" (Psalm 103:20–21). How many angels would constitute thousands upon thousands and myriads upon myriads? According to the dictionary, "A myriad...is technically the number ten thousand...More generally, a myriad may be an indefinitely large number of things."[143] In other words, more than Daniel could ever hope to count. What an awesome spectacle.

But all of this is just a description of the setting for the event that is about to take place. Are you ready? Daniel is about to have a front-row seat at the coronation of the King of kings, who will establish His kingdom rule over the nations of earth forever. In describing his vision, Daniel continues, "I kept looking in the night visions, and behold, with the clouds of heaven One like a Son of Man was coming, and He came up to the Ancient of Days and was presented before Him" (Daniel 7:13). Daniel is describing someone coming on the clouds of heaven who appears to be human but yet is clearly much more than human. It is no coincidence that in the Gospel of Matthew, Jesus refers to Himself thirty-one times as the "Son of man," clearly identifying

---

[143] Myriad (https://en.wikipedia.org/wiki/Myriad) (accessed 26 April 2022)

Himself as the Messiah foretold by the ancient Hebrew prophets. It should not surprise us that Jesus describes His future coming as King to establish His messianic kingdom on earth using the very same language as Daniel's prophecy.

As Jesus speaks of that future day, He says,

> But immediately after the tribulation of those days THE SUN WILL BE DARKENED, AND THE MOON WILL NOT GIVE ITS LIGHT, AND THE STARS WILL FALL from the sky, and the powers of the heavens will be shaken. And then the sign of the Son of Man will appear in the sky, and then all the tribes of the earth will mourn, and they will see the SON OF MAN COMING ON THE CLOUDS OF THE SKY with power and great glory.
>
> Matthew 24:29–30

Yet, before Jesus can establish His kingdom on earth, something else must happen first. Queen Elizabeth did not become queen of the United Kingdom with the power and authority to rule until first she had been coronated as queen by the Archbishop of Canterbury. And King Jesus will not become the King of all the earth until first He is coronated as king by God the Father. In describing what he sees in this vision, Daniel continues, "And to Him was given dominion, glory and a kingdom, that all the peoples, nations and men of every language might serve Him. His dominion is an everlasting dominion which will not pass away; and His kingdom is one which will not be destroyed" (Daniel 7:14). In reading Daniel's account of this vision, we become eyewitnesses to the coronation of Jesus Christ (Messiah) as God appoints Him King over all the earth. The psalmist speaks of the same event when he says,

For the Lord declares, "I have placed my chosen king on the throne in Jerusalem, on my holy mountain." The king proclaims the LORD's decree: "The LORD said to me, 'You are my son. Today I have become your Father. Only ask, and I will give you the nations as your inheritance, the whole earth as your possession.'"

Psalm 2:6–8 (NLT)

After His coronation in heaven, Jesus will come to earth to claim His inheritance and to establish His rule over our planet and all the nations of the earth forever. None of this has happened yet, but it will all come to pass at God's appointed time in human history. Jesus speaks of this very thing Himself in a parable intended to clarify for His disciples the timeline between His coming as Savior to make atonement for sin and His coming as King to establish His messianic kingdom upon the earth. What they needed to understand is that His coronation had not yet taken place.

In a few days, it would be Passover week, beginning with the triumphal entry of Jesus into Jerusalem. Jesus would be acclaimed the Messiah by His followers along the way. But it would all end with His crucifixion and burial, plunging His disciples into confusion and despair. The disciples apparently expected that Jesus would declare Himself as Israel's Messiah/King during the Passover and that the kingdom age would immediately be upon them. Jesus tried to warn them that the time for His kingdom to be established on earth had not yet come. What they didn't understand is that He could not establish His kingdom until His coronation as King.

It's in this context that Luke's Gospel tells us, "While they were listening to these things, Jesus went on to tell a parable, because He was near Jerusalem, and they supposed that the kingdom of God was going to appear immediately. So He said, 'A nobleman went to a distant country to receive a kingdom for himself, and then return'" (Luke 19:11–12). Jesus is telling them that He must return to heaven for His coronation as King and to receive His authority from the Father. And then He will come in power and great glory to establish His kingdom on the earth. The disciples understood bits and pieces of the ancient messianic prophecies, but they didn't have the whole picture. Jesus is trying to help them (and us) to get the big picture of how all the prophecies fit together.

After the resurrection, the disciples were still expecting the kingdom of God to come to earth immediately. The book of Acts tells us that after the resurrection, Jesus met with the disciples and taught them about the kingdom of God. He did so for a period of forty days until the day of His ascension back to the Father in heaven (Acts 1:1–3). Yet, the disciples still wanted to know, "Lord, is it at this time You are restoring the kingdom to Israel?" (Acts 1:4) The disciples still didn't understand that the whole interim period in which the gospel would be proclaimed to the nations was yet to come before the end of the age and the birth of Christ's kingdom on earth. Jesus had already told them this in the Olivet Discourse (Acts 1:7–8; cp. Matthew 24:14). Yet, even after the resurrection, they still just didn't get it. Of course, we need to cut the disciples some slack since we have the benefit from our vantage point of history and with the completed revelation of the entire written Word of God to understand the bigger picture that the disciples in Jesus' day didn't have. In that, we are richly blessed!

Yes, Daniel is the only prophet in the Old Testament to give us a front-row seat at the coronation of King Messiah. In the same way, John is the only apostle in the New Testament to give us that same front-row seat. In the book of Revelation, John records visions from God, providing a panoramic view of the final days of human history. One of those visions involves seven angels, each one blowing a trumpet in succession. And each trumpet is followed by a particular event that will occur during those final days. John writes,

Then the seventh angel sounded; and there were loud voices in heaven, saying, "The kingdom of the world has become the kingdom of our Lord and of His Christ; and He will reign forever and ever." And the twenty-four elders, who sit on their thrones before God, fell on their faces and worshiped God, saying, "We give You thanks, O Lord God, the Almighty, who are and who were, because You have taken Your great power and have begun to reign."

Revelation 11:15–17

This sounding of the seventh and last trumpet announces the coronation of Jesus over the kingdom of this world. This comes directly out of the Old Testament, where it was customary practice for a trumpet to sound announcing the coronation of a new king in Israel. We see it in the coronation of David's son, Solomon, in the year 970 BC. The chronicler of 1 Kings writes,

So Zadok the priest, Nathan the prophet, Benaiah the son of Jehoiada, the Cherethites, and the Pelethites went down and had Solomon ride on King David's mule, and brought him to Gihon. Zadok the priest then took the horn of oil from the tent and anointed Solomon. Then they blew the trumpet, and all the people said, "Long live King Solomon!" All the people went up after him, and the people were playing on flutes and rejoicing with great joy, so that the earth shook at their noise.

1 Kings 1:38–40

In like manner, the sounding of the seventh trumpet in John's vision will indicate that Jesus has been crowned as King with full authority to rule over the nations of earth.

191

Daniel sees the Son of Man appearing before God the Father, surrounded by the assembly of the holy ones, to receive the kingdom that is His promised inheritance. But John gets to see the excitement and overwhelming response of the assembly of the holy ones when with the sounding of the trumpet, Jesus is crowned as King of the earth, with full authority to rule the nations. The book of Revelation gives us the rest of the story. Only after the coronation is it the time appointed by the Father for Jesus to reign on the earth as King of kings and Lord of lords. Only then will Jesus be vested with full authority to rule over the nations.

Finally, the words spoken in The Lord's Prayer will come to pass—"Your kingdom come. Your will be done, on earth as it is in heaven" (Matthew 6:10). At last, our blessed hope will no longer be something that we eagerly look for in the future. It will be something that we will experience as a present reality. May we, along with John, again cry out with eager anticipation, "Come, Lord Jesus" (Revelation 22:20).

Chapter 14

The Gathering

And He will send forth His angels with A GREAT TRUMPET and THEY WILL GATHER TOGETHER His elect from the four winds, from one end of the sky to the other.

Matthew 24:31

It will be a time when the world is filled with chaos, a time when everyone in the world is terrified, not just as they see horrific devastation and loss of life all around the globe, but as they wonder if this could actually be the end of the world. It will begin with wars and conflicts around the globe, accompanied by famines, pandemics, and earthquakes that have brought unprecedented death and destruction to the planet. The final battle of earth's armies will launch a tidal wave of death and destruction, bringing loss of life to fully a third of earth's population. After hundreds of seismic events causing death and destruction around the globe, one great earthquake will rip the very fabric of the earth's crust with such unprecedented violence that all the major cities around the globe will be destroyed.

At that time, the earth will be plunged into darkness by a total eclipse of the sun and an unusual phenomenon called a blood moon, which is a total lunar eclipse that turns the entire surface of the moon to the color of blood. Asteroids penetrating earth's atmosphere will give the appearance of stars falling from the sky. Some will explode in midair, sending out shock waves that literally shake the atmosphere above and the earth below. Others will be landing in the oceans, causing gigantic tsunamis that result in even more death and devastation around the globe. How much worse could it possibly get? Everywhere around the globe, people will be wondering if mankind, and even the planet itself, can survive. Then, in the midst of all this chaos and devastation, suddenly, it will seem as if the entire sky is being ripped apart. As people look up at the sky with fear and amazement over this incredible phenomenon, they will see Jesus Christ "[...] coming on the clouds of the sky with power and great glory" (Matthew 24:30).

For those of us who are the people of God, it will signal our day of redemption (Luke 21:28), but for an unbelieving and rebellious world, it will signal their day of judgment. While we who are the people of God will look up with heads held high, rejoicing that the King is coming, the people of this world will be crawling into caves and holes in the ground, terrified that the day of God's wrath has finally come (Revelation 6:15–17). Even as the trumpet is still sounding in heaven to announce the coronation of the King, Jesus will already be descending out of heaven on the clouds of the sky. And the first thing He will do even before His feet touch the ground will be to "send out His angels to gather together His elect from the four corners of the earth" (Matthew 24:30). In describing His coming in this way, Jesus is deliberately using the language of the ancient Hebrew prophets. He wants to make sure there is no mistaking the fact that His coming fulfills the messianic prophecies of the Old Testament.

The prophet Isaiah, living nearly eight hundred years before the first coming of Christ, declared,

> Now in that day the remnant of Israel, and those of the house of Jacob who have escaped, will never again rely on the one who struck them, but will truly rely on the LORD, the Holy One of Israel. A remnant will return, the remnant of Jacob, to the mighty God. For though your people, O Israel, may be like the sand of the sea, only a remnant within them will return; a destruction is

determined, overflowing with righteousness. Then a shoot will spring from the stem of Jesse, and a branch from his roots will bear fruit. And He will lift up a standard for the nations and assemble the banished ones of Israel, and will gather the dispersed of Judah from the four corners of the earth.

Isaiah 10:20–22; 11:1, 12

Likewise, the prophet Zephaniah, living seven hundred years before the first coming of Christ, declared, "'At that time I will gather you; at that time I will bring you home. I will give you honor and praise among all the peoples of the earth when I restore your fortunes before your very eyes,' says the Lord" (Zephaniah 3:20, NIV).

According to prophecies such as these, the day will come when the *Lord* will gather His people who had been scattered among the peoples of the earth. At last, they will come home to the land that God had promised long ago to Abraham and his descendants as their everlasting possession. In that day, the Jewish people will be able to breathe a sigh of relief and say to themselves, "Home at last!" The time of Jacob's distress will give way to the time of the Messiah's deliverance when He comes to gather the remnant of His people and bring them home to their own land.

Even though Jesus is fulfilling the ancient prophecies at His coming, strangely, He does not refer to those gathered by the angels at His coming as the remnant of Israel or the dispersed of Judah, or the banished ones of Israel as the prophets do. Rather, He describes them as His elect. Why the change in terminology? And who are the elect? In the original language of the New Testament, the word "elect" simply means "chosen ones," and more specifically, those "chosen by God to obtain salvation through Christ..." God's holy and beloved followers.[144] Could He still be talking about the remnant of Israel? Or is He talking about someone else? Could He possibly be talking about the remnant of Israel and someone else too? The prophet Isaiah answers these questions when he says, "'The Lord GOD, who gathers the dispersed of Israel, declares, 'Yet others I will gather to them, to those already gathered'" (Isaiah 56:8). Who are these "others" to be gathered along with the remnant of Israel? It would appear that they are Gentiles who have put their trust in the God of Israel.

In the New Testament, Jesus affirms the same thing about others being included in God's plan of salvation along with the Jewish remnant. Using the metaphor of a shepherd and his sheep, Jesus says,

> I am the good shepherd, and I know My own and My own know
> Me, even as the Father knows Me and I know the Father; and I lay
> down My life for the sheep. I have other sheep, which are not of
> this fold; I must bring them also, and they will hear My voice; and
> they will become one flock with one shepherd.
>
> John 10:14–16

So who are these other sheep that Jesus is talking about? And what does He mean when He says that these other sheep will become one flock along with the remnant of Israel? I would agree with The FaithLife Study Bible when it says that Jesus is "alluding to the Gentiles and the ultimate universal scope of salvation via Christ's atoning death."[145] Jesus is looking ahead to the birth of the Church, which was yet future at the time, and which would include both Jewish and Gentile believers together as God's elect people.

---

[144] *Practical Word Studies in The New Testament*
[145] D. Barry Bomar, et. Al, *Faithlife Study Bible* (Bellingham, WA: Logos Bible Software, 2012)

The apostle Paul further explains how bringing Jewish and Gentile believers together as one people of God has been God's plan all along. Speaking to a primarily Gentile group of believers in the Ephesian church, he says,

> But now in Christ Jesus you who formerly were far off have been brought near by the blood of Christ. For He Himself is our peace, who made both groups [that is, Jewish and Gentile believers] into one and broke down the barrier of the dividing wall, by abolishing in His flesh the enmity, which is the Law of commandments contained in ordinances, so that in Himself He might make the two into one new man, thus establishing peace, and might reconcile them both [that is, Jewish and Gentile believers] in one body to God through the cross, by it having put to death the enmity.
>
> Ephesians 2:13–16

Both Jewish and Gentile believers, whom Paul describes collectively now as "one body" in Christ, and whom Jesus describes as "one flock with one shepherd," will participate in this great gathering of His elect as the Good Shepherd comes to gather His sheep.

In writing to the Thessalonian believers, the apostle Paul provides an account of Christ's coming that parallels the account provided by Jesus in the Olivet Discourse as recorded in the Gospels of Matthew, Mark, and Luke. It's important to note, however, the similarities and differences between these two accounts. Both Jesus and Paul are describing the same event, but each from a perspective and with an emphasis that is uniquely their own. Together, these two accounts of Christ's coming not only complement one another, but together they provide a more complete description of what His coming will look like than either one standing alone.

In the Olivet Discourse, Jesus describes His coming when He says,

> But immediately after the tribulation of those days THE SUN WILL
> BE DARKENED, AND THE MOON WILL NOT GIVE ITS LIGHT,
> AND THE STARS WILL FALL from the sky, and the powers of the
> heavens will be shaken. And then the sign of the Son of Man will
> appear in the sky, and then all the tribes of the earth will mourn,
> and they will see the SON OF MAN COMING ON THE CLOUDS
> OF THE SKY with power and great glory. And He will send forth
> His angels with A GREAT TRUMPET and THEY WILL GATHER
> TOGETHER His elect from the four winds, from one end of the
> sky to the other.
>
> Matthew 24:29–31

In writing to the Thessalonian believers, Paul describes this same event
when he says,

> For the Lord Himself will descend from heaven with a shout, with
> the voice of the archangel and with the trumpet of God, and the
> dead in Christ will rise first. Then we who are alive and remain will
> be caught up together with them in the clouds to meet the Lord in
> the air, and so we shall always be with the Lord.
>
> 1 Thessalonians 4:16–17

It's important to note that Paul prefaces what He says about the coming
of Christ with the words, "For this we say to you by the word of the Lord"
(1 Thessalonians 4:15). Paul wants to make it perfectly clear that what he's
about to say doesn't represent his own opinion or speculation but comes
directly from the Lord Jesus Christ Himself. Of course, Paul is not suggesting

here that he was hiding behind one of the gnarly olive trees on the Mount of Olives, listening as Jesus was teaching the disciples about His future coming. At that point in time, Paul was not yet even a believer. Nor is Paul saying that his source is one of the four Gospel accounts of Jesus' life and teaching. At that time, none of the Gospels had even been written.[146]

It's possible that Paul means what he's about to say came by direct revelation from Jesus Himself. It's also possible that the content of his teaching came directly from the teaching of Jesus, as it had been passed on through His apostles before the Gospels were ever written. This teaching of the apostles (Acts 2:42) was then incorporated into the Gospel accounts at a later date (Luke 1:1–4). The point that Paul is making here is that his teaching about the coming of Christ did not originate with him but with Jesus Christ Himself.

In the Olivet Discourse, Jesus describes Himself as coming on the clouds of the sky, which identifies Him with an ancient messianic prophecy of Daniel (Daniel 7:13). Paul, on the other hand, describes Christ's coming by simply saying, "The Lord will descend from heaven," without reference to this prophecy of Daniel. A reference to this ancient Hebrew prophecy would not have meant a great deal to his primarily non-Jewish audience.

Jesus says that when He comes, He will send forth His angels with a loud trumpet blast.[147] Paul adds to this by saying that the sounding of the trumpet will also be accompanied by a shout and the voice of the archangel. Vincent says,

---

[146] Appendix 8: Chronological Order of the Books of the New Testament, https://bible-study.org.nz/chronological-order-of-new-testament/ (accessed 28 April 2022)

[147] A better translation would be "loud trumpet sound" (ESV, NIV) or "great sound of a trumpet" (NKJV). Jesus is talking about the sound that a trumpet makes, not the size of the trumpet.

The blowing of trumpets was anciently the signal for the host of Israel on their march through the desert. It summoned to war, and proclaimed public festivals, and marked the beginning of months...Hence the symbolism of the New Testament. Jehovah's people shall be summoned before their king by the sound of the trumpet.[148]

This sounding of the trumpet is probably intended to announce the coming of the King and to summon His people to meet Him in the air, as Vincent suggests. However, I think that it announces not only the coming of the King[149] but also the coronation of the King that immediately precedes His coming, as seen in the book of Revelation.

As John describes his vision of seven angels blowing seven trumpets, each announcing a significant end that will occur in the last days, he says,

Then the seventh angel sounded; and there were loud voices in heaven, saying, "The kingdom of the world has become the kingdom of our Lord and of His Christ; and He will reign forever and ever." And the twenty-four elders, who sit on their thrones before God, fell on their faces and worshiped God, saying, "We give You thanks, O Lord God, the Almighty, who are and who were, because You have taken Your great power and have begun to reign.

Revelation 11:15–17

---

[148] *Vincent's Word Studies in the New Testament* (Electronic Database. Copyright 1997, 2003, 2005, 2006 by Biblesoft, Inc.)

[149] Trumpets were always blown on the accession of an Israelite king (1 Kings 1:34) (Craig S. Keener, *Bible Background Commentary—New Testament* [Intervarsity Press, 1993]).

This seems to indicate that as the last of these seven trumpets sounds to announce His coronation, Jesus will immediately descend from heaven to earth with His holy angels. The sounding of the trumpet will serve the dual purpose of announcing both the coronation of Jesus as King and the coming of Jesus to gather His people. At the same time, the archangel[150] , likely the commanding officer of the angelic hosts, will issue the order[151] for the angels to move out and begin gathering together God's elect. The shout may very well be a "hoorah!" from the angelic hosts as they go. It's hard to imagine how excited the angels will be when that command finally comes.

According to Paul's account of Christ's coming, when the trumpet sounds, those who have died as believers in Christ will immediately be raised from the dead in new resurrection bodies[152] in what the book of Revelation calls the first resurrection (Revelation 20:4–6). You may be wondering why Paul includes the resurrection of the dead at the time of Christ's coming when Jesus doesn't mention it at all in the Olivet discourse. Since this is a major difference between these two accounts, it would certainly be a reasonable question to consider. I would suggest that the reason Paul includes the resurrection and Jesus does not is that Jesus and Paul are each addressing different audiences with different concerns.

In the Olivet Discourse, Jesus is speaking to the disciples and addressing their concern about when His coming will occur and how they will know when the time is near. Jesus responds to this question by describing key events that will indicate that His coming is near. He wants them to have hope knowing that at the end of the great tribulation, He will come to

---

[150] This was probably the archangel Michael, who can be seen commanding the angelic army as they move out to do battle in the heavenly realms (Revelation 12:7–9).

[151] The Greek word translated "shout" (*keleusma*) means "a call, summons, shout of command" (Vine's Expository Dictionary of Biblical Words).

[152] This is likely "the first resurrection" (Revelation 20:5). We'll talk more about this in chapter 15.

gather together His elect as the ancient prophets foretold. In that regard, the subject of the resurrection would not necessarily be relevant. In writing to the Thessalonian believers, Paul is speaking to former pagans and addressing their concern about believers in their midst who had already died. Will they get to participate in Christ's coming, or will they somehow miss out? In light of this concern, it makes perfect sense that Paul would include the resurrection of the dead with respect to the coming of Christ.

In the Olivet Discourse, Jesus says that His purpose in sending forth the angels is for them to gather together His elect from every nook and cranny of the planet. He's using a metaphor of a mother hen gathering her chicks beneath her wings to care for them and protect them from danger.[153] We see the significance of this metaphor even more clearly when Jesus says to the Jewish people gathered in the temple, "Jerusalem, Jerusalem, who kills the prophets and stones those who are sent to her! How often I wanted to gather[154] your children together, the way a hen gathers her chicks under her wings, and you were unwilling" (Matthew 23:37). As Paul addresses the matter of Christ's coming in writing to the Thessalonians, he uses the very same metaphor of a hen gathering her chicks that Jesus does, and actually, the very same word in the original Greek text, when he says, "Now we request you, brethren, with regard to the coming[155] of our Lord Jesus and

---

[153] This Greek word translated "gather together" (*episunago*) is used "of a hen and her chickens (Matthew 23:37); and of the Lord's would-be protecting care of the people of Jerusalem, id, and Luke 13:34; of the 'gathering' together of the elect, Matthew 24:31; Mark 13:7" (Vine's Expository Dictionary of Biblical Words).

[154] This is the same Greek word for "gather together" (*episunago*) used of Christ's gathering together of the elect in Matthew 24:31.

[155] The Greek word for "coming" (*parousia*) is the word that Paul consistently uses throughout the Thessalonian epistles for the coming of Christ (1 Thessalonians 2:19; 3:13; 4:15; 5:23; 2 Thessalonians 2:1, 8). This is also word used to describe "the visit of a king or dignitary to a city—a visit arranged in order to show the visitor's magnificence to the people" (see chapter 3, footnote 24).

our gathering together[156] to Him" (2 Thessalonians 2:1).

This metaphor of a mother hen and her chicks actually comes directly out of the Old Testament, where the psalmist says, "He who dwells in the shelter of the Most High will rest in the shadow of the Almighty. He will cover you with his feathers, and under his wings you will find refuge" (Psalm 91:1, 4a, NIV). In sending forth the angels to gather together His people to Himself, He's doing so to bring them into His presence not only to care for them but also to rescue them and protect them from danger. Bear in mind that the people of God have been enduring unimaginable persecution—what Jesus calls "the great tribulation" (Matthew 24:21). Jesus describes the intensity of this persecution when He says, "Unless those days had been cut short, no life would have been saved; but for the sake of the elect those days will be cut short" (Matthew 24:22).

Paul describes this gathering together of God's people at Christ's coming with even greater emphasis on the idea of rescue and protection when he says that we "[...] will be caught up together with them [resurrected saints] in the clouds to meet the Lord in the air, and so we shall always be with the Lord" (1 Thessalonians 4:17). When Paul says that we will be caught up in the clouds, the word that Paul uses in the original Greek text means "to seize, catch up [or] snatch away."[157] This particular Greek word is often used to mean "snatch away" in the sense of rescue from danger.[158] It's the same word used in the book of Jude of believers being encouraged to rescue other believers who are in danger of becoming ensnared in false teaching. Jude says, "[...] have mercy on some, who are doubting; save others, snatching them out of the fire; and

---

[156] When Paul speaks of "our gathering together to Him (Christ)," again it is the Greek word translated "gather together" (*episunago*) in Matthew 24:31 when Jesus speaks of sending His angels to "gather together His elect."

[157] *New American Standard Exhaustive Concordance of the Bible*

[158] *The Online Bible Thayer's Greek Lexicon and Brown, Driver & Briggs Hebrew Lexicon*

on some have mercy with fear, hating even the garment polluted by the flesh" (Jude 23–24).

Jesus is not only coming to gather us together to Himself so that we may be with Him, but He is also coming to snatch us out of harm's way from a world that hates us. Jesus develops this same theme of rescue at His coming further on in the Olivet discourse as He draws an analogy between the days that precede His coming and the days of Noah. He says,

> For the coming of the Son of Man will be just like the days of Noah. For as in those days before the flood they were eating and drinking, marrying and giving in marriage until the day that Noah entered the ark, and they did not understand until the flood came and took them all away; so will the coming of the Son of Man be.
>
> Matthew 24:37–39

Imagine what it must have been like when the flood came upon the earth. Torrential rains were falling from above even as springs of water were gushing out of the ground below, quickly engulfing the entire earth with water deep enough and rising high enough to cover the peaks of the highest mountains. There's no way of knowing what the human population of earth was at the time, but whatever the number, everyone living on the earth died as a result of the flood. The only exception was one man by the name of Noah, and his family, who alone escaped the swirling waters that would drag the rest of the human race to a watery grave. God sent His judgment upon the earth in the form of a worldwide flood that would engulf the planet because a flood of wickedness and evil had already engulfed the planet, threatening God's future plans for the human race and even their very survival. The flood was sudden, devastating, and deadly, with only eight survivors (Genesis 6–7). So in what way are the days of Noah analogous to the day of Christ's coming? At His coming, Christ will appear just as suddenly and unexpectedly as the flood that came upon a rebellious and unbelieving world in the days of Noah.

Jesus will be showing up to rescue His people when there will be "[...] dismay among nations, in perplexity at the roaring of the sea and the waves, men fainting from fear and the expectation of the things which are coming upon the world; for the powers of the heavens will be shaken" (Luke 21:25–26). It's in this context that Jesus says in language very similar to that of Paul, "Then there will be two men in the field; one will be taken[159] and one will be left. Two women will be grinding at the mill; one will be taken and one will be left" (Matthew 24:40–41). When the flood came, Noah and his family were taken into the ark where they would be safe. The wicked were left to be swept away by the flood to meet their death (Genesis 7:13–24). In the same way, at Christ's coming, the people of God will be taken (caught up) to meet the Lord in the air as He descends through the clouds. But the wicked will be left behind to face His judgment and wrath.

It's important to note that the word in the original text translated as "taken" is the same word translated as the word "receive" in the Gospel of John when Jesus says to His disciples, "If I go and prepare a place for you, I will come again and receive you [take you] unto Myself, that where I am, there you may be also" (John 14:3). Being "taken," being "received," being "caught up," and being "gathered" are all different ways of saying the same thing. Think about it! We don't have to wait to meet the Lord until His feet touch the ground—we will be taken up directly from the earth into the clouds to meet Him in the air. And so shall we ever be with the Lord! Such is our eternal destiny—our glorious hope in Christ!

---

[159] The Greek word translated "take" means "to take to oneself, to join to oneself, an associate, a companion" (*The Online Bible Thayer's Greek Lexicon and Brown, Driver & Briggs Hebrew Lexicon*). It also denotes "to take to or with oneself," and us used of a man 'taking a wife'" (*Vine's Expository Dictionary of Biblical Words*).

You may be wondering why we would be caught up in the clouds to meet the Lord in the air only to come back down with Him as He continues His descent to earth. Wouldn't it be simpler for us just to meet Him when His feet touch down on earth? This is certainly a reasonable question, and it deserves a reasonable answer. Although the text itself doesn't give us an answer, the meaning and usage of the word translated "meet" in the culture of that day provides an important clue. As one commentator explains it,

> In secular Greek the word (apantēsis) was a technical term for meeting a visiting dignitary. A delegation honored the visitor by going outside the city and meeting him and his entourage on the road. Together the entire party would then proceed back into the city with great pomp and fanfare.[160]

Keep in mind that we are talking about Christ's *parousia*,[161] a word that we have seen in the culture of that day was used to describe the arrival of a king or dignitary to a city in a way that would display his magnificence to the people. We will be caught up in the clouds to meet the Lord in the air so that we can welcome Him as our King even as He welcomes us into His presence. Then we will all descend with Him the rest of the way on the final leg of His journey from heaven to earth as He comes to establish His kingdom.

The prophet Zechariah was privileged to see this glorious event taking place through his prophetic lens. He says, "Then the LORD, my God, will come, and all the holy ones[162] with Him. And the LORD will be king over

---

[160] Michael Martin, "1 & 2 Thessalonians," *New American Commentary*, E. Ray Clendenen, General Editor, (Nashville TN: Broadman & Holman Publishers, 1995)

[161] Note footnote 155 in this chapter

[162] In the Old Testament, the term "holy ones" (*qadoshim*) sometimes refers to the angels (Deuteronomy 33:2; Job 5:1; 15:15; Psalm 89:5, 7; Daniel 4:17), and it sometimes refers to God's people [the saints] (Psalm 16:3; 34:9; 106:16). In Zechariah 14:5, it probably refers to

all the earth; in that day the LORD will be the only one, and His name the only one" (Zechariah 14:5b, 9). Likewise, the apostle Paul makes reference to this coming of the Lord accompanied by all His saints when he says, "May the Lord cause you to increase and abound in love for one another, and for all people, just as we also *do* for you; so that He may establish your hearts without blame in holiness before our God and Father at the coming[163] of our Lord Jesus with all His saints" (1 Thessalonians 3:12–13).

The whole world will be looking as we descend through the clouds with our glorious King, sharing in His glory as He comes to establish His kingdom on the earth. This is the fulfillment of God's promise expressed through the apostle Paul when he says, "When Christ, who is our life, is revealed, then you also will be revealed with Him in glory" (Colossians 3:4). What an amazing day that will be! I can imagine that this will be a scene similar to the ancient practice in the Roman Empire known as the "Roman Triumph," when a conquering general would march into the city of Rome with great fanfare, surrounded by his loyal army, to celebrate his victory. A modern example would be the ticker-tape parade as our victorious troops returning from World War II marched through the streets of New York City.

Think what it will be like when we hear the trumpet sound, not only announcing that Jesus is King but summoning us into His presence to meet Him in the air and to share in the celebration of His victory. We will welcome Him to our planet, even as He welcomes us into His presence to join His royal entourage. Then we will descend to earth with Him to declare His victory over the former ruler of this world (John 12:31; 16:11). In that day, Jesus will be presented to the people of earth as the One crowned in heaven

---

both since the New Testament indicates that both the angels (Matthew 24:31; 25:31; Mark 13:27; 2 Thessalonians 1:7), and the saints of God (1 Thessalonians 3:13) will accompany Christ when He comes to establish His messianic kingdom on earth.

[163] Again, the Greek word here is *parousia*; see footnote 155.

to rule over the kingdom of this world (Revelation 11:15). And we will share in His glory as we reign with Him in His glorious kingdom forever. Whether we are privileged to live until the day of Christ's coming, or we die and join those who will be raised from the dead in that day, the final outcome will be the same. Our redemption will be complete as we enter into glory and reign with Christ forever in His eternal kingdom. In that day, we, too, will say to Him, "We give thanks to you, Lord God Almighty, the One who is and who was, because you have taken your great power and have begun to reign" (Revelation 11:17, NIV). This is our hope! This is our future! This is our destiny!

Chapter 15

The Rising

For the Lord Himself will descend from heaven with a shout, with the voice of the archangel and with the trumpet of God, and the dead in Christ will rise...

1 Thessalonians 4:16

The funeral home was especially busy that Thursday afternoon, with people finding their seats in two separate chapels for the services that would soon begin. In many ways, the two groups of people looked the same: people talking in low tones as an organ playing "Nearer My God to Thee" is piped through the sound system; a coffin smothered with flowers holding a lifeless body garishly made up with cosmetics in a futile attempt to mask the look of death; family members sitting on the front row with the sound of quiet sobbing and an occasional sniffle. But that's where the similarities end. The inescapable difference in the mood of the two gatherings becomes obvious. In one chapel, the prevailing spirit is one of overpowering sorrow to the point of despair. In the other, overwhelming peace even in the midst of sorrow. What is the difference between these two groups and the prevailing spirit that emanates from them? One group has hope beyond this life, not only for the deceased but for themselves—a hope based on confidence in the promises of God that this life is not all there is. The other group does not.

Throughout the Scriptures, the brevity and tenuousness of this present life are highlighted to encourage us to live on earth with eternity's values in view. James reminds us of this when he says, "You do not know what your life will be like tomorrow. You are just a vapor that appears for a little while and then vanishes away" (James 4:14). If you have ever observed mist rising from a lake in early morning and then seen that mist quickly melt away in the warmth of the sun, then you understand what James is talking about. Life in this present world, even at its best, is like that—here for a moment and then gone.

Moses echoes the same truth when he says, "Seventy years are given to us! Some even live to eighty. But even the best years are filled with pain and trouble; soon they disappear, and we fly away" (Psalm 90:10, NLT). Likewise, David picks up the same theme in one of the psalms when he says,

> LORD, remind me how brief my time on earth will be. Remind me that my days are numbered—how fleeting my life is. You have made my life no longer than the width of my hand. My entire lifetime is just a moment to you; at best, each of us is but a breath. We are merely moving shadows, and all our busy rushing ends in nothing.
>
> Psalm 39:4–6a (NLT)

If all we can expect is a life that is here for a little while and then quickly gone with no prospect of anything beyond it, that would be reason for despair. But David's words don't end there; he continues, "And so, Lord, where do I put my hope? My only hope is in you" (Psalm 39:7, NLT). Hope is the game-changer when we are staring death in the face.

This is the hope that Paul is talking about when he says to the Thessalonian church, "But we do not want you to be uninformed, brethren, about those who are asleep, so that you will not grieve as do the rest who have no hope" (1 Thessalonians 4:13). Of course, Paul is not suggesting that in death, we have literally just fallen asleep. He's using a common Scriptural euphemism for death,[164] much the same as when we say that a person has passed away. Somehow saying that a person has fallen asleep or passed away sounds less grim than saying that person is dead. We also say a person's body is laid to rest. But that's our physical body—not us! Physical death is nothing more than the separation of our spirit from the body (James 2:26). Each of us is a spiritual being or living soul (Genesis 2:7) dwelling in a material body, for which Paul uses the metaphor of an earthly tent (2 Corinthians 5:1). Paul makes it clear that we do not cease to exist as a person when our earthly tent wears out and dies. On the contrary, the real person who dwells within this material body is immortal and can never die, even when the body does.

So, where will we be as followers of Christ when we no longer possess a material body? Paul answers this question for us. He says that when we are at home in the body, we are absent from the Lord, but that his personal preference is to be absent from the body and to be at home with the Lord (2 Corinthians 5:6–8). Again, speaking in reference to his own imminent death, Paul says, "For me, to live is Christ and to die is gain" (Philippians 1:21). He adds that faced with the choice of living or dying, he would prefer to depart and be with Christ, which he says is the "far better" choice of the two (Philippians 1:23). So where is Jesus now? In heaven! And where will we be as followers of Christ when we die and no longer possess a material body? Where Jesus is! But don't make the mistake of thinking that we're going to be in heaven living as disembodied spirits for all eternity. Heaven is a temporary abode, and living as a disembodied spirit is a temporary state. Even that is going to change at the coming of Christ.

Returning to the subject of grieving over the death of someone we love, it's important for us to understand that Paul is not suggesting for a moment that there is no place for grief when someone whom we love has died. I know

---

[164] The use of sleep as a metaphor for death is also found in the Old Testament (Isaiah 26:19).

from personal experience how painful it is to see death snatch away someone I loved dearly. Apparently, these Thessalonian believers were grieving over the death of some of their own, whether friends or members of their own family. Grief is a normal response. This is true whether we're talking about first-century Greek culture or twenty-first-century American culture. As we're going to see, death does not have the final word for believers, but it does bring about a separation between us and those we love—we grieve because we miss them dearly. Paul does not tell these Thessalonian believers not to grieve at all but not to grieve in the same manner as those who have no hope beyond the grave.

You must understand that these Thessalonian believers had been saved out of raw paganism, and their understanding of death was largely shaped by their pagan roots. Writing about how pagans viewed death in the world of Paul's day, William Barclay says, "In the face of death the pagan world stood in despair. They met it with grim resignation and bleak hopelessness...On their tombstones grim epitaphs were carved. 'I was not; I became; I am not; I care not.'"[165] Because the pagan world in that day had such a bleak concept of death, their grief was naturally enshrouded in an ethos of despair. Sadly, even in our world today, those who have no understanding of the biblical truth about death have the same comfortless perspective. But such should not be the case for those of us who have faith in Christ and confidence in the promises of God. Yes, we grieve, but not as the rest of the world who have no real hope beyond the grave.

Of course, not all hope is the same. There's a kind of hope embraced by the pop culture of our day that is nothing more than wishful thinking that rests upon pure fantasy. Paul is not comforting these Thessalonian believers with fantastical wishing. He uses the word "hope" as it is used throughout

---

[165] William Barclay, *Daily Study Bible*, Westminster John Knox Press, 1956

the New Testament—it means "a favorable and confident expectation and anticipation of good for the future."[166] What he's talking about is the kind of hope found in the book of Hebrews—"This hope we have as an anchor of the soul, a hope both sure and steadfast" (Hebrews 6:19). Paul speaks of a hope that reaches beyond the grave like an anchor, keeping us from drifting into despair by keeping us firmly attached to the promises of God and His faithfulness to fulfill those promises (Hebrews 10:23; 35–36). It's the difference between wishing that something will happen and having a certainty that something will happen because our hope is firmly anchored in the promise of someone whom we truly believe can be trusted to do what he's promised to do.

So what is this hope that we have in the face of death that Paul discloses? It is the hope of a future bodily resurrection from the dead. When God originally created man, the book of Genesis tells us, "The LORD God formed man of dust from the ground, and breathed into his nostrils the breath of life; and man became a living being" (Genesis 2:7). We were created to live in a material body in a material world, and death is only a temporary interruption that will change at the resurrection.

Jesus speaks of this future resurrection in the Gospel of John when He says,

> Truly, truly, I say to you, an hour is coming and now is, when the dead will hear the voice of the Son of God, and those who hear will live. Do not marvel at this; for an hour is coming, in which all who are in the tombs will hear His voice, and will come forth; those who did the good deeds to a resurrection of life, those who committed the evil deeds to a resurrection of judgment.
>
> John 5:25, 28–29

---

[166] *Vine's Expository Dictionary of Biblical Words*

The prophet Daniel also speaks of this same future resurrection of life in connection with God's rescue of His people out of the great tribulation; he says,

> There will be a time of distress such as never occurred since there was a nation until that time; and at that time your people, everyone who is found written in the book, will be rescued. Many of those who sleep in the dust of the ground will awake, these to everlasting life, but the others to disgrace and everlasting contempt.
>
> Daniel 12:1b–2

The day is coming for all the true people of God that He will raise us from the dead. This will include not just the Church but all the true people of God who have lived throughout the ages. In that day, He will give us a brand new body that can never die again so that we may live in the presence of our Savior forever. When our hope is firmly anchored in this promise of future resurrection, we no longer have to fear death because we know that death is only temporary. And furthermore, we know that we will be in the presence of our Savior in heaven until that day when our body will be resurrected from the dead. It is this hope that sustains us in the midst of our grief.

The apostle Paul describes the day of Christ's coming to gather together His elect when he says,

> For the Lord Himself will descend from heaven with a shout, with the voice of the archangel and with the trumpet of God, and the dead in Christ will rise first. Then we who are alive and remain will be caught up together with them in the clouds to meet the Lord in the air, and so we shall always be with the Lord.
>
> 1 Thessalonians 4:16–17

It is this hope of bodily resurrection at the coming of Christ that gives us confidence as we face our own mortality.

Apparently, in Paul's day, some in the church at Corinth were confused about the whole subject of bodily resurrection, and some even denied the resurrection altogether. This confusion is understandable in light of the cultural beliefs of the ancient Greek world, which made believing in physical, bodily resurrection from the dead a hard pill to swallow. The prevailing Greek philosophy taught that spirit is good and matter is evil. Based on this premise, physical death seemed a welcome release of the spirit from the encumbrance of the flesh. Needless to say, the idea of a physical resurrection of the body was something they would not embrace easily. People in that day were looking for redemption from the body, not redemption of the body. As William Barclay puts it, "For the Greek, immortality lay precisely in getting rid of the body. For him, the resurrection of the body was unthinkable."[167] Greek philosophers would have considered a physical resurrection of the body not a blessing but a curse. And because the Corinthian believers lived in that culture with this prevailing mindset, some of them still struggled with the idea of an actual resurrection of the body.

In writing to them, Paul makes it clear that the center point and cornerstone of the gospel message from the very beginning have always been and will always be the death, burial, and resurrection of Christ. And all of this was in direct fulfillment of the ancient prophecies of the Old Testament, just as Jesus Himself had said (1 Corinthians 15:1–4; Luke 24:45–46). As Randy Alcorn explains, "The physical resurrection of Jesus Christ is the cornerstone of redemption—for both mankind and the whole earth. Indeed, without Christ's resurrection and what it means—an eternal future for fully restored

---

[167] William Barclay, *Daily Study Bible*

human beings dwelling on a fully restored Earth—there is no Christianity.[168] But our hope of future resurrection is worthless unless its reality is valid.

So how can we be sure that the message of Christ's resurrection really is true and not just a fable or a myth? The answer is a simple one: the abundance of eyewitnesses who actually saw Jesus alive and personally interacted with Him after He had been dead in the tomb for thirty-six hours. We discover that all four Gospels record numerous appearances of Jesus risen from the dead (Matthew 28:1–10; Mark 16:1–14; Luke 24:1–48; John 20:1–29). Likewise, in the book of Acts, Luke, the historian, says, "To these [that is, the disciples] He [Jesus] also presented Himself alive after His suffering, by many convincing proofs, appearing to them over a period of forty days and speaking of the things concerning the kingdom of God" (Acts 1:3).

Paul responds to this issue of whether or not Jesus truly rose from the dead by providing a list of eyewitnesses who saw Jesus alive after He had died on the cross and been buried in the tomb for some thirty-six hours. The list, many of whom he mentions by name, numbers more than five hundred people. It includes some who were not even followers of Christ until the risen Christ appeared to them. Most of these people were still living at the time and available to tell their story if called upon to do so (1 Corinthians 15:5–9). In any court of law, eyewitness testimony is the most powerful and compelling form of evidence that exists. Imagine a defense attorney in a court of law calling more than five hundred eyewitnesses to testify on behalf of his client. I think his client would stand a good chance of being exonerated. Don't you?

But Paul doesn't just make a case by providing evidence for the resurrection of Christ. He goes on to build a case for the bodily resurrection of believers as well. He points out that if there is no resurrection of the

---

[168] Randy Alcorn, *Heaven* (Wheaton, IL: Tyndale House Publishers, Copyright 2004 by Eternal Perspective Ministries)

dead, then it would be impossible for Christ Himself to have been raised from the dead. Furthermore, if Christ has not been raised from the dead, then six things would be true: 1) Paul's preaching is in vain; 2) our faith is in vain;[169] 3) Paul is a liar; 4) our faith is worthless because we are still in our sins; 5) those who have already died have perished;[170] and 6) and if our hope in Christ does not extend beyond this present earthly life, then we deserve to be pitied for our foolishness in embracing such an empty hope (1 Corinthians 15:12–19). If you want a guarantee that our hope of resurrection is not an "empty" hope, you have it in the resurrection of Jesus Christ.

Using an agricultural metaphor familiar to the people of His day, Paul affirms that Christ's resurrection guarantees our resurrection. He says that in His own resurrection, Christ has become "the first fruits of those who are asleep" (1 Corinthians 15:20). In the Old Testament, the first fruits (Leviticus 23:9–14) were the first sheaves of ripened grain from the harvest that would be offered to the Lord. The first fruits served as the guarantee of the full harvest yet to come. When Paul says that Christ is "the first fruits of those who are asleep," he's saying that, just as the first fruits of grain guaranteed a future harvest, so the resurrection of Christ guarantees a future harvest of souls—those who will also be raised from the dead. The resurrection of Christ confirms His victory over sin and death and displays the pattern of resurrection life that will one day be ours. And when will this happen? Paul

---

[169] The Greek word translated "vain" (*kenos*) means "empty...metaphorically, of endeavors, labors, acts, which result in nothing, vain, fruitless, without effort" (*The Online Bible Thayer's Greek Lexicon and Brown, Driver & Briggs Hebrew Lexicon*). It would be like coming to a cookie jar expecting to find some cookies inside, but the cookie jar is empty. What good is an "empty" cookie jar? So likewise, what good is an "empty" faith?
[170] The Greek word translated "perish" (*apollumi*) means "to perish, to be lost, ruined, destroyed" (*The Online Bible Thayer's Greek Lexicon and Brown, Driver & Briggs Hebrew Lexicon*).

answers, "But each in his own order: Christ the first fruits, after that those who are Christ's at His coming" (1 Corinthians 15:23).

Knowing that we have a secure hope of a future resurrection should bring us great comfort and assurance in the face of our own mortality. But this raises another question for us as well as the Corinthian believers. Paul anticipates the question, "But someone will say, How are the dead raised? And with what kind of body do they come?" (1 Corinthians 15:35). Keep in mind that Paul is writing to people who, in the prevailing philosophy of the day, find the whole idea of a bodily resurrection after death peculiar. The question that he raises, of course, is a rhetorical one that he intends to answer.

Using the same agricultural metaphor that he employed earlier to describe Christ's resurrection as the first fruits of a greater harvest of souls yet to come (1 Corinthians 15:23), Paul launches into his answer to this powerful question. He points out that when a farmer plants his seed, he expects the harvest to follow in due time. He also understands that the seed he plants in the ground must itself die before the new plant can sprout. Furthermore, the plant that sprouts looks very different from the seed from which it germinated (1 Corinthians 15:36–38).

Our present mortal body is like that seed planted in the ground. In due time it will emerge, not looking like the seed that was planted but as a brand-new stalk of grain. The seed that was planted and died will come forth as something entirely new and different than what it was before. Right now, we live in a mortal body made of flesh and blood that will die and be buried in the ground or, in some cases, simply cremated. But in the resurrection, that same body will come forth out of the grave or out of the ashes as something entirely new and different than before. Why should this be so difficult to accept, since even in the natural world, as Paul points out, different species of animals have different kinds of flesh? The flesh of a human being is far different from that of an animal, a bird, or a fish (1 Corinthians 15:39). If these things are apparent in the natural realm, why should we be surprised that this same principle holds true in the spiritual realm?

Changing metaphors, Paul introduces something new about our future resurrection body–he points out the differences in glory (i.e., radiance or brilliance) that we see in the sun, the moon, and the stars. Each has its own level of brilliance, and each is different from the other, with one displaying greater brilliance than another. The brilliance of the sun is far greater than that of the moon, which merely reflects the light of the sun. And the brilliance of the stars in faraway galaxies varies from one star to another. Likewise, our future resurrection body will be far different and better than our present mortal body that will return to the dust (or ashes) from whence it came (1 Corinthians 15:40–49). Our future resurrection body will be far more glorious than our present body, reflecting the glory of God in a way that our present body is not equipped to do.

Coming back to the metaphor of the seed and the harvest, Paul says, "It [our present mortal body] is sown a perishable body, it is raised an imperishable body; it is sown in dishonor, it is raised in glory; it is sown in weakness, it is raised in power; it is sown a natural body, it is raised a spiritual body" (1 Corinthians 15:42–44).

The first thing we discover about our future resurrection body is that, unlike our present body, it will be an imperishable body. This means that it will "not [be] liable to corruption or decay; indestructible; enduring." The body that we have now is far from indestructible. It will most certainly not endure forever. On the contrary, the body that we have now gradually wears out in a process of decay that accelerates as we grow older. Eventually, our body ceases to function, resulting in death. Unlike our present body, our future resurrection body will never wear out but will last forever.

The second thing we discover about our future resurrection body is that it will be raised in glory. We were originally created in the image of God (Genesis 1:27) so that we might reflect God's own glory (Isaiah 43:7). My personal definition or description of God's glory is that it is "the radiant beauty of God's own infinite perfection." Sadly, although we still possess the image of God in our present mortal body, because of sin, we are no longer capable of reflecting God's glory as we were created to do (Romans 3:23). Even though the Spirit of God is at work in our hearts as followers of Christ so that we increasingly reflect more and more of His glory (2 Corinthians 3:18), only when we receive our future resurrection body, will we be able to reflect His glory fully as God intended from the beginning.

Actually, this is not the first time in the Bible that the promise of receiving a glorious new body at the resurrection is given in Scripture. Even the prophet Daniel in the Old Testament talks about this same promise of a new glorified body for those who awake to everlasting life (Daniel 12:2). Using the same metaphor of the heavenly bodies that Paul does, Daniel says, "Those who have insight will shine brightly like the brightness of the expanse of heaven, and those who lead the many to righteousness, like the stars forever and ever" (Daniel 12:3). Jesus uses a similar metaphor when He says, "Then THE RIGHTEOUS WILL SHINE FORTH AS THE SUN in the kingdom of their Father" (Matthew 13:43a), possibly even alluding to the words of Daniel. Now that's something to look forward to! How awesome to think that we will be raised from the dead with an indestructible body that will live forever. How much more awesome to think that we will receive an indestructible and glorious body that will allow us to reflect perfectly and fully the exquisite beauty of the magnificent glory of our glorious God.

The third thing we discover about our future resurrection body is that it will be unimaginably powerful. As Paul says, while our present mortal body is sown in weakness, it will be raised in power.[171] Think about that! While the body we have now is relatively weak and limited in what it can do, our new resurrection body will have incredible strength. It will have the ability to do the kinds of things that in our present world would be labeled as miracles. Apparently, things we consider miraculous today will be considered quite ordinary in our future resurrection bodies.

Finally, we discover that our future resurrection body will no longer be a natural body but a spiritual body. At first glance, we might be tempted to think that the contrast here is between a material body (natural body) and an immaterial body (spiritual body). But this is not the case. Let me explain. Or rather, let Paul explain. Paul points out that our present natural body is one that we have inherited from Adam, an "earthy" body, or literally, a body "made of earth."[172] This is completely in line with the book of Genesis when it says, "Then the LORD God formed man of dust from the ground, and breathed into his nostrils the breath of life; and man became a living being" (Genesis 2:7). Our future resurrection body will not be a body made of the same material, nor will it be a body that is immaterial, but it will be a body made of new material. Our new body will not be made out of the dust from the ground as Adam's was. Apparently, our new body will be like that of the angels since Jesus says of those raised from the dead that "[...] they cannot even die anymore, because they are like angels, and are sons of God, being sons of the resurrection" (Luke 20:36). As one writer points out, "Spiritual body does not mean a non-material body but, from the analogies, a physical one

---

[171] The Greek word translated "weakness" (*astheneia*) means "lack of strength, weakness, infirmity," while the Greek word translated "power" (*dunamis*) means "strength, ability, power." In fact, the Greek word here for "power" is the word used throughout the New Testament for "the power of performing miracles" (*The Online Bible Thayer's Greek Lexicon and Brown, Driver & Briggs Hebrew Lexicon*).

[172] The Greek word translated "earthy" (*choikos*) is used to describe a body "made of earth" (*The Online Bible Thayer's Greek Lexicon and Brown, Driver & Briggs Hebrew Lexicon*).

similar to the present natural body organizationally, but radically different in that it will be imperishable, glorious and powerful, fit to live eternally with God. There is continuity, but there is also change."[173]

Our new resurrection body will be indestructible, never able to wear out or decay, lasting throughout all eternity. It will be glorious, reflecting the radiant beauty of God Himself. It will have amazing strength, probably what we would consider super-human strength, enabling us to do things that in our present body would be thought miraculous. And it will be spiritual in nature, not immaterial, but a body like that of the angels. It will be made of spiritual stuff rather than formed from the dust of the ground like Adam's. All in all, our future resurrection body will be incredibly better and more glorious than anything we could ever imagine, perfectly suited for eternity.

Of course, all of this explains what glorious transformation will occur in the bodies of those who will be raised from the dead at Christ's coming. But what about those who are still alive in their natural mortal bodies? What will happen to them? As mortal beings in natural bodies, there is no way that we can inherit the kingdom of God (1 Corinthians 15:50). It would be totally impossible because eventually, our mortal bodies would grow old and die. A mortal body subject to decay and death is simply not suited for living in an eternal kingdom that will never end (Daniel 7:13–14; Isaiah 9:6–7). Fortunately, God has already addressed this problem.

In answering this question, Paul lets us in on a little secret—he tells us that at the resurrection, the natural mortal body of believers still living will be instantly transformed into something entirely new. It will be changed into the same kind of immortal body that those who have died will receive at the resurrection (1 Corinthians 15:51–53). If we're still alive in our natural

---

[173] *NASB Study Bible*, Kenneth Barker, general editor (Grand Rapids, MI: Lockman Foundation, 1999)

bodies at the coming of Christ, we get to skip the dying part altogether! There's no way Paul could make this any plainer when he says, "Behold, I tell you a mystery; we will not all sleep, but we will all be changed; [...] the dead will be raised imperishable, and we will be changed. For this perishable must put on the imperishable, and this mortal must put on immortality" (1 Corinthians 15:51–53). This is not just something that may happen or should happen or even will happen in that future day, but something that must happen because there simply is no other way for a person to live forever in God's eternal kingdom.[174] The bottom line is that at the coming of Christ, all of God's elect, both those who are raised from the dead and those who are still alive when He comes, will receive the same indestructible, immortal, glorious, powerful, spiritual body that will enable us to live and thrive in God's eternal kingdom forever.

What's even more amazing is that this brand-new body will be just like Christ's own glorious resurrection body. In writing to the Philippian believers, Paul reminds us: "But our citizenship is in heaven. And we eagerly await a Savior from there, the Lord Jesus Christ, who, by the power that enables him to bring everything under his control, will transform[175] our lowly bodies so that they will be like his glorious body" (Philippians 3:20–21, NIV). Although we continue to live in this present dark world, for now, this world

---

[174] The Greek word translated "must" (*dei*) means "it is necessary" (*The Online Bible Thayer's Greek Lexicon and Brown, Driver & Briggs Hebrew Lexicon*).

[175] The Greek word translated "transform" (*metaschematizo*) means "to change one's outward appearance (*Practical Word Studies in the New Testament*). It's the same Greek word used of Jesus' transfiguration recorded in the Gospel of Matthew where it says, "[...] Jesus took Peter and the two brothers, James and John, and led them up a high mountain to be alone. As the men watched, Jesus' appearance was transformed so that his face shone like the sun, and his clothes became as white as light" (Matthew 17:1–2, NLT). It's an entirely different word than the one Paul uses when he says, "Behold, I tell you a mystery; we will not all sleep, but we will all be changed" (1 Corinthians 15:51). There the Greek word translated "change" (*alasso*) literally means "to cause one thing to cease and another to take it's place" (*The Online Bible Thayer's Greek Lexicon and Brown, Driver & Briggs Hebrew Lexicon*).

is not our true home because, through Christ, we have become citizens of His heavenly kingdom. Many of the people living in ancient Philippi were actually citizens of Rome, even though most had never been to Rome. In the same way, we are actually citizens of Christ's kingdom, now still in heaven, though we still currently live in this world. But all this will change when Christ comes to establish His kingdom on earth.

I'm sorry to say that Paul is not telling us here that we will necessarily experience all the same supernatural powers that Jesus had after the resurrection. He's not necessarily telling us that we will be able to appear and disappear at will, as Jesus did after the resurrection when He suddenly showed up in a locked room where the disciples had gathered (Luke 24:36). Or when He suddenly disappeared from sight with the two disciples in Emmaus (Luke 24:31; John 20:19). Nor is he necessarily saying that we will be able to defy gravity as Jesus did after the resurrection when He ascended into the sky from the Mount of Olives and disappeared in the clouds (Acts 1:9).

What Paul is saying is that the outward appearance of our new body, unlike that of our present natural body, will reflect the visible glory of God, just like the resurrection body of Jesus. The apostle John speaks of it as well when he says, "Beloved, now we are children of God, and it has not appeared as yet what we will be. We know that when He appears, we will be like Him, because we will see just as He is" (1 John 3:2). In other words, our new body will, in appearance, look just like His, though not necessarily implying that we will possess all the same supernatural powers that His does. Nevertheless, our new bodies will be the perfect creation that God had in mind for us from the beginning, and they will equip us to experience perfect fellowship with our God throughout all eternity. Isn't that really what it's all about? And that is truly something we can look forward to!

The amazing thing about all this is not just what is going to happen at Christ's return but how quickly it will come about. Remember that we're talking about millions of believers, both resurrected saints going all the way back to Adam and those saints still alive on the earth at His coming. Yet the resurrection of believers who have died and the transformation of believers who are still living on the earth in mortal bodies at the coming of Christ will take place so quickly that Paul describes it as taking place in a moment,[176] in the twinkling of an eye.

When is this all going to happen? Of course, we know that it will happen at the coming of Christ. But where does all this fit into God's overall prophetic plan for human history? We discover an important clue when it says that it will happen at the last trumpet (1 Corinthians 15:52). This isn't the first time that a trumpet has been mentioned in connection with the coming of Christ. Jesus says that at His coming will be there will the sound of a great trumpet (Matthew 24:31). And Paul says in writing to the Thessalonian believers that Christ's coming will be accompanied by the sound of the trumpet of God (1 Thessalonians 4:16). However, this reference in 1 Corinthians is the only place in Scripture that this trumpet sound at Christ's coming is called the last trumpet.

In the book of Revelation, John describes a vision of seven angels sounding seven trumpets, each announcing a particular event that will take place during the great tribulation. These trumpet blasts lead up to a grand crescendo as the last of the seven trumpets sounds. John writes, "Then the seventh angel sounded; and there were loud voices in heaven, saying, 'The kingdom of the world has become the kingdom of our Lord and of His Christ; and He will

---

[176] The Greek word here translated "moment" (*atomos*) literally means something that is "indivisble" (*Vine's Expository Dictionary of Biblical Words*). In other words, we're talking about the smallest possible measurement of time—so small that it cannot be divided into anything smaller.

reign forever and ever'" (Revelation 11:15). This last trumpet announces the coronation of the King, followed by His coming to gather His people so that they may be with Him in His kingdom forever. How many last trumpets can there be? When the last trumpet sounds, then it has to be the last one, or else it wouldn't be the last trumpet. It doesn't matter how many trumpets there are, whether seven or seventy; there can still only be one last trumpet.

Paul appears to be talking about the same thing that John actually saw in his vision decades later. Furthermore, there is no more room for another so-called last trumpet after the coming of Christ to establish His kingdom on earth. Paul clearly indicates that when the dead are raised at the coming of Christ, "[...] then[177] comes the end, when He hands over the kingdom to the God and Father, when He has abolished all rule and all authority and power. For He must reign until He has put all His enemies under His feet" (1 Corinthians 15:24–25). It appears that the last trumpet at Christ's coming not only announces His coronation in heaven but also signals the beginning of His millennial kingdom on earth. He must reign until He has put all His enemies under His feet, after which He will hand over the kingdom to God the Father.

Ever since the fall of man, death has had the final word over every human being ever born. From the stillborn child to the aged centenarian, in the end, death has always won. But not anymore! Through His own death and resurrection, Jesus has won the victory over sin and death forever. And so Paul writes,

---

[177] The Greek word translated "then" (*eita*) means "then; next; after that" (*The Online Bible Thayer's Greek Lexicon and Brown, Driver & Briggs Hebrew Lexicon*) and indicates sequence of time. (Liddell and Scott Abridged Greek Lexicon. PC Study Bible formatted electronic database Copyright © 2014 by Biblesoft, Inc. All rights reserved.)

[...] the trumpet will sound, and the dead will be raised imperishable, and we will be changed. But when this perishable will have put on the imperishable, and this mortal will have put on immortality, then will come about the saying that is written, "DEATH IS SWALLOWED UP in victory. O DEATH, WHERE IS YOUR VICTORY? O DEATH, WHERE IS YOUR STING?" The sting of death is sin, and the power of sin is the law; but thanks be to God, who gives us the victory through our Lord Jesus Christ.

1 Corinthians 15:52b, 54–57

The resurrection at the coming of Christ will mark the final triumph over sin and death for the people of God, and death itself will ultimately be abolished from the earth forever (Revelation 21:1–7).

Paul's words of victory reach back into the Old Testament and echo the words of the ancient prophets who looked forward to this future day of resurrection for the people of God. Living in the eighth century BC, Isaiah said, "Your dead will live; their bodies will rise. You who dwell in the dust, wake up and shout for joy. Your dew is like the dew of the morning; the earth will give birth to her dead" (Isaiah 26:19, NIV). Using two complementary metaphors, Isaiah envisions the dead waking in the morning with a shout of joy and the ground giving birth and new life to those who were dead.

In a different passage, Isaiah adds to the hope of resurrection the promise that not only will the dead be raised to life but that God will abolish death itself when he says, "On this mountain he [God] will destroy the shroud that enfolds all peoples, the sheet that covers all nations; he will swallow up death forever. The Sovereign LORD will wipe away the tears from all faces; he will remove the disgrace of his people from all the earth. The LORD has spoken" (Isaiah 25:7–8, NIV). It is this prophetic word from Isaiah that

Paul references when he says, "But when this perishable will have put on the imperishable, and this mortal will have put on immortality, then will come about the saying that is written, 'DEATH IS SWALLOWED UP in victory'" (1 Corinthians 15:54).

Paul was well aware of the ancient prophecies of future resurrection before he ever took pen in hand to write these words to the Corinthian believers. In fact, he goes on to reference the prophet Hosea, a contemporary of Isaiah, using his own paraphrase when he says, "O DEATH, WHERE IS YOUR VICTORY? O DEATH, WHERE IS YOUR STING?" (1 Corinthians 15:55). Speaking through the prophet Hosea, the *Lord* says, "I will ransom them from the power of the grave; I will redeem them from death. Where, O death, are your plagues? Where, O grave, is your destruction?" (Hosea 13:14, NIV)[178] Paul is simply building his case for the victory of Christ over sin and death by drawing upon the testimony of the ancient prophets who, looking through their prophetic lens, saw this victory coming centuries before Paul ever penned these words.

Most people in our world today are terrified at the prospect of dying. I think it was the comedian Woody Allen who said, "I'm not afraid of dying—I just don't want to be there when it happens!" Most people would probably agree with that. This is because most people have no hope in the face of death. My father once told me about a couple he knew who bought a cemetery plot located on a hill overlooking a beautiful valley. They were so excited because they had a plot with a view. Seriously. I'm not kidding. I've always wondered how they expected to enjoy the view when they would be lying in their

---

[178] New Testament writers often reference passages from the Old Testament with their own paraphrase translation. Even modern translators differ in how they translate the original Hebrew text into English in the Hosea and Isaiah passages. For example, compare how Hosea 13:14 reads in the NASB, NIV, NLT, NKJV, and, if you read Greek, the Greek Septuagint translation.

caskets buried six feet under the ground. Sadly, these were people with no hope beyond the grave.

Those who belong to Christ have a hope that the world just doesn't understand. They know that at the coming of Christ, they will be resurrected from the dead. "In a moment, in the twinkling of an eye," Paul says, they will receive brand new spiritual bodies that are immortal, indestructible, powerful, and glorious beyond imagination. And those who belong to Christ and are still alive at His coming will find their bodies immediately transformed into the same immortal, indestructible and glorious spiritual bodies as those who are raised from the dead. At that very moment, as Paul says, Isaiah's prophecy will be fulfilled, saying that God will swallow up death in victory. (Isaiah 25:8).

In the meantime, how should this future hope of resurrection and glory make a difference in the way we live our lives right now? As Paul concludes his teaching on the resurrection in the book of 1 Corinthians, he ends with this final word—"Therefore, my beloved brethren, be steadfast, immovable, always abounding in the work of the Lord, knowing that your toil is not in vain in the Lord" (1 Corinthians 15:58). In light of our hope of future resurrection and the glory to follow, Paul says that we are to be steadfast and immovable. A steadfast and immoveable faith is rock-solid so that when it comes under pressure of any kind, it doesn't budge even an inch. If the reality of Christ's resurrection and the hope of our future resurrection isn't enough to make our faith steadfast and immovable, then I don't know what else is. When we face the pressures of life, we need to stand firm in our faith and not budge from our confidence in God and His Word.

But as we remain solid in our faith, we are also to be abounding in the work of the Lord. God has prepared beforehand the good works that He has for us to do. We don't have to figure out what God wants us to do. We just have to be on the lookout every day for the works that He's already prepared and placed in our path. A friend of mine once described these good works as "works of significance that will change the landscape of eternity."[179] That gives the whole idea of good works an entirely different twist, doesn't it? If my words and actions can impact other people's lives in ways that have the potential to change the landscape of eternity, it should motivate me to get busy doing these works of significance that God has prepared for me to do.

But this is only true if the resurrection of Christ and the future resurrection of believers and the glory to follow are true—not just some fairy tale or a figment of someone's overactive imagination. Again, Paul says,

> If there is no resurrection of the dead, not even Christ has been raised; and if Christ has not been raised, then our preaching is vain, your faith also is vain [....] and if Christ has not been raised, your faith is worthless; you are still in your sins. Then those also who have fallen asleep in Christ have perished. If we have hoped in Christ in this life only, we are of all men most to be pitied.
>
> 1 Corinthians 15:13–14, 17–19

We can thank God that Paul doesn't stop there. He says, "But now Christ has been raised from the dead, the first fruits of those who are asleep [and] after that those who are Christ's at His coming" (1 Corinthians 15:20, 23). This is why Paul can urge us on not just to do works of significance but to abound in those works of significance. Because of Christ's resurrection and our own future resurrection and glory, we can have confidence that our faith is not in vain. Neither is our toil in vain when it's in the Lord. As we'll see in chapter 17, nothing we ever do for the Lord will go unrewarded in the day

---

[179] Dax Romaine, Pastor of Live Oak Christian Fellowship, Ocala, FL.

when we stand before the judgment seat of Christ (2 Corinthians 5:9–10). Let this be our motivation in the present as we keep our eyes focused on what is yet to come.

Chapter 16

The Justice of God

Let the trees of the forest rustle with praise before the LORD, for
he is coming! He is coming to judge the earth. He will judge the
world with justice, and the nations with his truth.

Psalm 96:12–13 (NLT)

Try to imagine living in a world without justice. I'm talking about a world
where everyone is free to do whatever he wants with no regard for how it
might hurt other people. Imagine living in a world where there are no laws
and no way to enforce them if there were. Imagine living in a world in which
there is no reward for doing what is good, kind, and loving toward others and
no penalty or accountability for doing evil and hateful acts. Imagine living in
a world where right is never rewarded, and criminal acts are never punished.
You may be surprised to know that there are actually places in our world
today where you can get just a little taste of how terrible and dreadful such a
world would be.

> These are the world's most lawless countries, according to the
> World Justice Project's Rule of Law index. The index judges how
> the rule of law is experienced by members of the public in everyday
> situations in 113 countries and jurisdictions. It measures a number
> of indicators, including constraints on government power, levels
> of corruption, security, open government and criminal justice,
> to consider how laws are used and enforced. The WJP uses the
> testimonies of local residents and legal experts to compile their
> data—the aim being to accurately collate the experiences of the

general population, including marginalized groups. Denmark was found to be the most lawful country, demonstrating the strongest adherence to the rule of law, and the UK was tenth. In the most lawless countries, the report found that criminal activity goes unchecked, laws are not applied equally, corruption is apparent, and foreign investment does not reach the people who needed it. These are the ten countries where the rule of law was applied the least effectively.[180]

According to the WJP, the ten most lawless countries in the world are Venezuela, Cambodia, Afghanistan, Egypt, Cameroon, Zimbabwe, Ethiopia, Pakistan, Uganda, and Bolivia. Imagine spending your vacation in one of these exotic locations around the world. You literally might not come back alive.

In addressing the subject of justice, here's the reality: there could not possibly be a just God, nor could a morally just universe even exist, if God were tolerant of sin and lawlessness, allowing them to go unpunished or unchecked. God has given mankind His moral laws for our good (Deuteronomy 10:13) because He loves us. For our sake, He wants to prevent the utter chaos and devastation that unchecked sin would bring upon our world and the human race. There is no place in a moral universe governed by a morally just God for those who bring chaos and destructiveness upon the world because they stubbornly refuse to live according to His moral law. Because of God's love, He gives us His law. And because God is just, He must punish sin. It really is that simple! It's because of man's sin that the world is in such a mess. It's the reason why the news is filled with accounts

[180]"These Are the Most Lawless Countries in the World," Yahoo News, October 25, 2016, https://www.yahoo.com/gma/most-lawless-countries-world-110913024.html (accessed 27 April 2022)

of war, fraud, murder, robbery, assault, oppression, sexual abuse, human trafficking, and so much more.

It is never God's will for us to sin, but God has given the human race the freedom of choice, which includes the freedom to sin if we so choose. He allows this freedom of choice so that we might come to see the utter folly of sin with its wake of devastation and destruction. However, the Scriptures are clear that a day of reckoning will come. The apostle Paul says to a rebellious and unbelieving world—

> Do you show contempt for the riches of his kindness, tolerance and patience, not realizing that God's kindness leads you toward repentance? But because of your stubbornness and your unrepentant heart, you are storing up wrath against yourself for the day of God's wrath, when his righteous judgment will be revealed.
>
> Romans 2:4–5 (NIV)

This day of God's wrath is that future day when God will judge those who arrogantly despise God's kindness and tolerance and patience toward them, refusing to repent of their rebellion and unbelief.

But what exactly is this wrath of God that Paul is talking about? Is God a cranky, mean old man sitting up in heaven and having a temper tantrum every time someone on earth steps out of line? That's not the picture we find in the Bible. Nelson's Bible Dictionary accurately describes the true nature of God's wrath when it says,

> The personal manifestation of God's holy, moral character in judgment against sin. Wrath is neither an impersonal process nor is it irrational and fitful like anger. It is in no way vindictive or malicious. It is holy indignation—God's anger directed against sin.

235

God's wrath is an expression of His holy love. If God is not a God of wrath, His love is no more than frail, worthless sentimentality; the concept of mercy is meaningless; and the Cross was a cruel and unnecessary experience for His Son.[181]

The ironic part about God pouring out His wrath and judgment against sin is that this is not the way God ever intended it to be. The apostle Paul explains why this is true when he says,

This is good and acceptable in the sight of God our Savior, who desires all men to be saved and to come to the knowledge of the truth. For there is one God, and one mediator also between God and men, the man Christ Jesus, who gave Himself as a ransom for all, the testimony given at the proper time.

1 Timothy 2:3–6

At the cross, God has revealed His heart for man, even in our sinful and fallen state. When Jesus, the incarnate Son of God, gave His own life to pay the ransom for our sin, God provided a way for us to be forgiven and never have to face His wrath. As the apostle Paul describes it so clearly—"But God demonstrates His own love toward us, in that while we were yet sinners, Christ died for us. Much more then, having now been justified by His blood, we shall be saved from the wrath of God through Him" (Romans 5:8–9).

The reason God has delayed the coming wrath in the day of judgment for so long is explained by the apostle Peter when he says, "The Lord is not slow about His promise, as some count slowness, but is patient toward you, not wishing for any to perish but for all to come to repentance" (2 Peter 3:9). But Peter doesn't stop there! He continues, "But the day of the Lord will

---

[181] "Wrath," Nelson's Illustrated Bible Dictionary

come" (2 Peter 3:10). And in that day, God's wrath will be poured out in His righteous judgment upon those who have rejected His mercy and grace. The only reason that the day of judgment has been delayed is God's patience. God has been extending the day of salvation (2 Corinthians 6:2) now for a very long time because He wants all men to repent and be saved. But the day is coming when God's patience will run out, and in perfect justice, He will finally judge the world for their rebellion and unbelief.

However, the wrath of God is only one side of God's justice. God's justice is not just about punishing the wicked for their evil deeds but also about rewarding the righteous for their good deeds. In describing the day of judgment, the apostle Paul says,

> [God] WILL RENDER TO EACH PERSON ACCORDING TO HIS DEEDS: to those who by perseverance in doing good seek for glory and honor and immortality, eternal life; but to those who are selfishly ambitious and do not obey the truth, but obey unrighteousness, wrath and indignation. There will be tribulation and distress for every soul of man who does evil, of the Jew first and also of the Greek, but glory and honor and peace to everyone who does good, to the Jew first and also to the Greek. For there is no partiality with God.
>
> Romans 2:6–11

In His Olivet Discourse, Jesus helps us to understand how God's justice works, and particularly what criteria He will use when He comes to judge the world. Everyone loves a good story. And Jesus' disciples are no exception. He tells them a parable, which is simply a story with a purpose. As the Holman Bible Handbook explains,

A parable has been defined as a comparison from nature or daily
life designed to teach a spiritual truth...Jesus developed stories
from familiar images and ideas that reveal truth about the nature
of God, prayer, spiritual values, stewardship, judgment, and the
kingdom of God. He used parables as a teaching device with His
disciples, antagonistic religious leaders, and ordinary people.[182]

In this parable, Jesus puts Himself directly into the story, portraying
Himself as a shepherd who is separating the sheep from the goats in his flock
before they lie down to rest for the night.[183] He says,

> But when the Son of Man comes in His glory, and all the angels
> with Him, then He will sit on His glorious throne. All the nations
> will be gathered before Him; and He will separate them from one
> another, as the shepherd separates the sheep from the goats; and
> He will put the sheep on His right, and the goats on the left.
>
> Matthew 25:31–33

According to this parable, when He comes to judge the world, He will
be like a shepherd as He separates the entire human race into two groups,
designated in the parable as sheep and goats.[184] Those whom He describes

---

[182] "Parable," *Holman Bible Handbook*, David Dockery, editor, Holman Bible Publishers, 1992

[183] The idea of separating sheep and goats would have been a familiar one because it was a commonplace practice in the culture of that day. Even though sheep and goats would often graze together during the day, at night, a shepherd would normally separate the sheep from the goats because the goats needed warm shelter at night while sheep preferred sleeping outdoors in the open air (Bruce B. Barton, Mark F. Fackleer, et. al., "MATTHEW," *The Life Application Commentary*, Bruce Barton, general editor [Livingstone Corporation, 2000, produced with permission of Tyndale House Publishers, Inc.]).

[184] We find a similar scenario in another of Jesus' parables—the parable of the wheat and tares (Matthew 13:24–30; 36–43).

as sheep will be gathered on His right side, and those whom He describes as goats will be gathered on His left.

Why does Jesus use sheep and goats to make His point in this parable? I suspect that it has something to do with the differences in how sheep and goats generally behave. As Chris Palusky explains in his blog, "Goats are typically pushy, self-reliant animals. They are independent and think they know best. Goats do not respond well to shepherding...In contrast to goats, sheep are gentle, they stick together, and they rely on their shepherd."[185] To put it simply, sheep tend to be more submissive and willing to follow the shepherd, while goats are more independent and more likely to stray and go off on their own. It shouldn't surprise us, then, that Jesus describes those who have chosen to follow Him as "My sheep" when He says in the Gospel of John, "My sheep hear My voice and I know them, and they follow Me" (John 10:27). Jesus also describes the sheep in this parable as being the righteous (Matthew 25:37), meaning that they live right because, by faith, they have a right relationship with Him. Righteousness, simply defined, is "purity of heart and rectitude of life; being and doing right."[186]

Who are these sheep in the parable? They are true believers—those throughout the ages who have faithfully followed God and walked in His ways. The goats, on the other hand, represent a rebellious and unbelieving world made up of people throughout the ages who have rejected God and chosen to live their own way rather than God's way. Together, the sheep and the goats represent all of humanity throughout history up until that final day of judgment. To the sheep (the people of God), Jesus says, "Come, you who are blessed of My Father, inherit the kingdom prepared for you from the foundation of the world" (Matthew 25:34). But to the goats (the rest of

---

[185] Chris Palusky, president and CEO of Bethany Christian Services
[186] "Righteousness," *The New Unger's Bible Dictionary*

humanity who are rebellious and unbelieving), He says, "Depart from Me, accursed ones, into the eternal fire which has been prepared for the devil and his angels" (Matthew 25:41). Later in the parable, He summarizes, "These [the goats] will go away into eternal punishment, but the righteous [the sheep] into eternal life (Matthew 25:46).

So, why are the sheep privileged to enjoy the presence of the King in His kingdom forever, while the goats are banished from the presence of the King forever into the eternal fire prepared for the devil and his angels?[187] Jesus is very clear in His answer. He doesn't speak in abstract theological terms but lays it out very plainly. To the sheep, He says, "For I was hungry, and you gave Me something to eat; I was thirsty, and you gave Me something to drink; I was a stranger, and you invited Me in; naked, and you clothed Me; I was sick, and you visited Me; I was in prison, and you came to Me (Matthew 25:35–36).

But to the goats, He says, "For I was hungry, and you gave Me nothing to eat; I was thirsty, and you gave Me nothing to drink; I was a stranger, and you did not invitee in; naked, and you did not clothe Me; sick, and in prison, and you did not visit Me (Matthew 25:42–43). Both groups are clearly confused by what Jesus says, and both parties want to know when they did or failed to do these things for Him. Now is where it really gets interesting–and maybe just a little bit confusing. Jesus says to the sheep, "Truly I say to you, to the extent that you did it to one of these brothers of Mine, even the least of them, you did it to Me" (Matthew 25:40). Then He turns to the goats and says to them, "Truly I say to you, to the extent that you did not do it to one of the least of these, you did not do it to Me" (Matthew 24:45).

Jesus has been talking about two groups of people designated as sheep and goats. Now He introduces a third group of people into the parable whom he

---

[187] We will talk more about "eternal fire" in chapter 18.

describes as "these brothers of Mine." It was how they treated "these brothers of Mine" that would serve as the criteria for whether Jesus identified them as a sheep or a goat. So who are "these brothers of Mine"? Commentators don't seem to agree on the identity of who "these brothers of Mine" are. However, the explanation that I find most compelling is that Jesus is identifying with the poor and needy in our world, regardless of who they are, by simply referring to them as "these brothers of Mine." They could be anybody, though nobody in particular, who is hurting and in need. I'm inclined to agree with William Barclay when he says,

> This is one of the most vivid parables Jesus ever spoke, and the lesson is crystal clear—that God will judge us in accordance with our reaction to human need. His judgment does not depend on the knowledge we have amassed, or the fame that we have acquired, or the fortune that we have gained, but on the help that we have given.[188]

In other words, the criteria for judgment in this parable appear to be the way a person treats his neighbor. More specifically, it is how a person responds to the desperate needs of others around him. It's the way a person responds to human suffering when He is in a position to do something about it. How has that person treated those around him who are poor, needy, disenfranchised, helpless, or oppressed? Has that person responded with compassion or complacency? Has that person extended mercy or shown apathy—even disdain?

The book of Proverbs says, "The righteous is concerned for the rights of the poor; the wicked does not understand such concern" (Proverbs 29:7).

---

[188] William Barclay, *Daily Study Bible*

Again, the book of Proverbs says, "He who is kind to the poor lends to the LORD, and he will reward him for what he has done" (Proverbs 19:17, NIV). God so identifies with hurting people in our world, whether they live across the street or across the ocean, that whatever we do to help them or neglect to do to help them is the same as if we have done it or neglected to do it for God Himself.

What Jesus is saying, then, really echoes the words of the ancient Hebrew prophets, who speak often about how much God cares for the poor and oppressed in this world. In the Old Testament, the Jewish people were commanded to fast on the Day of Atonement. But for most of the people of Israel, this had become merely a religious ritual of going through the motions of religion. Their religious observances stood out in stark contrast to the way they were treating the poor and the needy in their midst. As He speaks through the prophet Isaiah, the *Lord* says to the people of Israel,

> This is the kind of fasting I want: Free those who are wrongly imprisoned; lighten the burden of those who work for you. Let the oppressed go free, and remove the chains that bind people. Share your food with the hungry, and give shelter to the homeless. Give clothes to those who need them, and do not hide from relatives who need your help.
>
> Isaiah 58:6-7 (NLT)

Isn't this exactly what the book of James is talking about? James says, "Pure and genuine religion in the sight of God the Father means caring for orphans and widows in their distress[189] and refusing to let the world corrupt you" (James 1:27, NLT). And isn't this exactly what Jesus is telling us in

---

[189] In that day, there was no safety net for orphans and widows, making them entirely dependent on the generosity of others.

the parable of the sheep and goats? Caring for those who are poor, needy, disenfranchised, helpless, or oppressed is simply the practical expression of what Jesus means when He says, "You shall love your neighbor as yourself" (Matthew 22:39). In case you're not sure exactly what it means to love your neighbor as yourself, Jesus defines it for us when He says, "So in everything, do to others what you would have them do to you, for this sums up the Law and the Prophets" (Matthew 7:12, NIV). If you were personally in the condition of being poor, needy, disenfranchised, helpless, or oppressed, how would you want people to treat you? There's what it means to "love your neighbor as yourself."

If you want to see all of this fleshed out in living color, read the parable of the Good Samaritan (Luke 10:30–37). Then imagine yourself being the poor man lying beside the road, and pay close attention to the way the good Samaritan treated him. Loving your neighbor doesn't mean just doing good for a specific group of people, but doing good to anyone and everyone as God gives you opportunity, regardless of who they are. In the case of the Good Samaritan, the man who needed help was from a different nationality, ethnicity, and religion than the man who helped him. This is why Paul says in the book of Galatians, "Let us not lose heart in doing good, for in due time we will reap if we do not grow weary. So then, while we have opportunity, let us do good to all people, and especially to those who are of the household of the faith" (Galatians 6:9–10). Notice that he says we are to do good to all people, regardless of who they are. That's what it means to love your neighbor as yourself, and that's exactly what Jesus is telling us in this parable of the sheep and the goats.

But wait a minute? Is Jesus saying then that the sheep enter the kingdom of God because of their good works, and the goats are consigned to eternal fire because they lack the necessary good works to make the cut? Certainly not! The apostle Paul makes this crystal clear when he says, "For by grace you have been saved through faith; and that not of yourselves, it is the gift of God; not as a result of works, so that no one may boast. For we are His workmanship, created in Christ Jesus for good works, which God prepared beforehand so that we would walk in them" (Ephesians 2:8–10). Let there be no mistake—our salvation is not based on our merit but on His mercy. Not on our goodness but on His grace. Our salvation is a gift to be received, not a work to be performed. Yet the concept of salvation by grace through faith does not negate the importance of good works, nor does it contradict or nullify the commandment to love your neighbor as yourself.

Good works are not the means to obtain salvation but the means to express the reality of salvation that is already ours because of our response in faith to the grace of God. Jesus says, "The good man brings out of his good treasure what is good; and the evil man brings out of his evil treasure what is evil" (Matthew 12:35). In other words, outward actions reflect and reveal the true condition of the heart in terms of our relationship with God. A truly regenerated heart is going to motivate us to treat people very differently than an unregenerate one. When we truly experience the love and grace of God, it will begin its transformative work in our hearts and lives. That transformative work will begin to show in our actions as we express God's love and grace toward the poor and needy around us. Remember that it was when we were poor and needy, helpless to help ourselves, that Christ extended His love and grace toward us (Romans 5:6–8; 1 Corinthians 8:8).

Loving our neighbor by extending God's love and grace to the poor and needy cannot and will not save us. But loving our neighbor by extending God's love and grace to those in need will demonstrate the reality of having a genuine life-transforming faith in Christ. Claiming to have faith in Christ without showing it by how we treat other people, especially those who desperately need the help we can give them, should raise some serious doubts about the legitimacy or genuineness of that faith. This is why James can say,

> What use is it, my brethren, if someone says he has faith but he has no works? Can that faith save him? If a brother or sister is without clothing and in need of daily food, and one of you says to them, "Go in peace, be warmed and be filled," and yet you do not give them what is necessary for their body, what use is that? Even so faith, if it has no works, is dead, being by itself.
>
> James 2:14–17

Again, the apostle John says, "But whoever has the world's goods, and sees his brother in need and closes his heart against him, how does the love of God abide in him?" (1 John 3:17)

We're not talking here about faith versus works, or faith plus works, but a faith that works. We're talking about the kind of faith that produces a changed heart and a transformed life, one that extends the love and grace of God that we've experienced in salvation to the needy people all around us. As Tim Keller puts it so eloquently,

> If a person has grasped the meaning of God's grace in his heart, he will do justice.[190] If he doesn't live justly, then he may say with his lips that he is grateful for God's grace, but in his heart he is far from Him. If he doesn't care about the poor, it reveals that at best

---

[190] Tim Keller is talking about social justice. According to an article published by the San Diego Foundation, "Social justice is the view that everyone deserves equal economic, political and social rights and opportunities." Or to put it another way, **"Social justice means equal rights and equitable opportunities for all." ("What Is Social Justice?", March 24, 2016, San Francisco Foundation** [https://www.sdfoundation.org/news-events/sdf-news/what-is-social-justice], **accessed 27 April 2022).**

he doesn't understand the grace he has experienced, and at worst he has not really encountered the saving mercy of God ...If you look down at the poor and stay aloof from their suffering, you have not really understood or experienced God's grace.[191]

That sounds like a pretty severe indictment of people who call themselves Christians but have no regard for the needs of the people around them. And that's something to stop and think about. I wonder how many people who would call themselves Christians and believe they truly are Christians have never really experienced the saving grace of God at all? Or, at the very least, they have never really understood what that saving grace of God is all about.

I wonder how many people who would call themselves Christians and believe they truly are Christians will, in the day of judgment, find themselves among the goats rather than among the sheep because they never truly experienced the life-transforming grace of God through genuine saving faith in Christ. As Mother Teresa once said,

At the end of our lives, we will not be judged by the diplomas we have received, how much money we have made or how many great things we have done. We will be judged by "I was angry and you gave to eat. I was naked and you clothed me. I was homeless and you took me in."[192]

Jesus says in the Sermon on the Mount,

A good tree cannot produce bad fruit, nor can a bad tree produce good fruit. Every tree that does not bear good fruit is cut down

---

[191] Timothy Keller, *Generous Justice*, Riverhead Books published by the Penguin Group, 2010
[192] Email from Mark Beto, mark.beto@cyberdefenses.com

and thrown into the fire. So then, you will know them by their fruits. Not everyone who says to Me, "Lord, Lord," will enter the kingdom of heaven, but he who does the will of My Father who is in heaven will enter. Many will say to Me on that day, "Lord, Lord, did we not prophesy in Your name, and in Your name cast out demons, and in Your name perform many miracles?" And then I will declare to them, "I never knew you; DEPART FROM ME, YOU WHO PRACTICE LAWLESSNESS."

Matthew 7:18–23

As you think about this parable of the sheep and the goats, I would encourage you to consider which group you would be in and where you would stand before Christ in that day. Speaking to a group of people who would have considered themselves Christians, the Apostle Paul says, "Test yourselves to see if you are in the faith; examine yourselves! Or do you not recognize this about yourselves, that Jesus Christ is in you—unless indeed you fail the test" (2 Corinthians 13:5). These words are not intended to give us reason for doubting our salvation but to encourage us to make sure that our faith is real. Just remember that we are saved by grace through faith. But the faith that saves is a faith that works. What kind of faith do you have? If your faith isn't really working, maybe you need to take a closer look to see if your faith is real. Where you stand in the day of judgment may depend on it.

Chapter 17

The Reward of the Righteous

Behold, I am coming quickly, and My reward is with Me, to render
to every man according to what he has done.

Revelation 22:12

One of the great rags to riches stories in the Bible is that of a man born
as a slave in Egypt during the second millennium BC. Through circumstances
that could only have been orchestrated by God Himself, as a child born into
a Hebrew slave family, Moses was adopted into the Egyptian royal family
as the son of Pharaoh's daughter. In that day, Egypt was the most powerful
kingdom on earth, and Pharaoh was the most powerful man in Egypt. The
princess took Moses to live with her in the palace where, as the book of Acts
explains, Moses was educated in all the learning of the Egyptians, and he was
a man of power in words and deeds (Acts 7:22). He experienced the best that
Egypt had to offer, including wealth, power, and prestige. Yet Moses turned
his back on it all to identify with the Hebrew slaves and become God's man
to lead them out of slavery.

Why would Moses deliberately, by his own choice, go from rags to riches
back to rags? Most people would look at the story of Moses' life and say that
he achieved everything that the world could possibly offer. Yet he gave it all
up. And for what? The writer to the Hebrews answers that question when he
says,

> By faith Moses, when he had grown up, refused to be called the
> son of Pharaoh's daughter, choosing rather to endure ill-treatment
> with the people of God than to enjoy the passing pleasures of sin,

considering the reproach of Christ greater riches than the treasures
of Egypt; for he was looking to the reward.

Hebrews 11:24–26

Moses willingly chose to turn his back on all that the world had to offer
because he was single-mindedly focused on the one thing that mattered
more to him than anything else—the eternal reward that he would receive
from God for his faithful obedience to God's calling on his life. Moses had
an eternal perspective that was focused on eternal values. His priorities and
corresponding behavior in the present were not determined by the temporary
rewards that Egypt could provide—rewards that would ultimately pass away.
That's because he was looking forward to the eternal reward that he would
receive from God at the end of his life journey here on earth—a reward that
would last forever.

Moses had the wisdom to understand just how temporary our life on this
earth really is and how quickly it passes. This is why Moses says in the book
of Psalms, "As for the days of our life, they contain seventy years, or if due to
strength, eighty years, yet their pride is *but* labor and sorrow; for soon it is
gone and we fly away. So teach us to number our days, that we may present
to You a heart of wisdom" (Psalm 90:10, 12). One day we will all step out of
this life into eternity and, if we are trusting in Christ as our Savior, we will
step into the presence of Christ Himself, where we will live with Him forever.

The apostle Paul also clearly understood the brief and temporary nature
of this present life on earth when he describes our present mortal body here
on earth as our earth-tent where we live briefly and temporarily until we
finally go home to be with Christ. It is this temporary nature of life on earth
that Paul is talking about when he says, "Therefore, being always of good
courage, and knowing that while we are at home in the body we are absent

from the Lord—for we walk by faith, not by sight—we are of good courage, I say, and prefer rather to be absent from the body and to be at home with the Lord (2 Corinthians 6:6–8). So, what are the practical implications of what Paul is saying here? Paul answers this question when he says, "Therefore we also have as our ambition, whether at home or absent, to be pleasing to Him" (2 Corinthians 5:9). According to the Collins English Dictionary, the word "ambition" means an earnest desire for some type of achievement or distinction, and the willingness to strive for its attainment."[193]

Isn't it true that we all have certain ambitions in life—things that we strive for because they're important to us and worth the effort? It may be to make a lot of money or to become a famous athlete or to have a wonderful family or even to pursue a fruitful ministry for Christ. There are all sorts of goals in life that we may be ambitious to attain. Certainly, there's nothing wrong in any of these goals in and of themselves. For Paul, however, there is only one ambition that surpasses all others because he knows that at the end of this brief and temporary life on earth, only one thing will really matter—knowing he has lived a life that is truly pleasing to Christ. Like Moses, he was looking to the reward.

We all need to understand that this promise of reward is not just for Moses or for Paul, but for everyone who is a follower of Christ through saving faith in Him. In the final chapter of the book of Revelation, the risen Christ, who is coming again to rule the earth, says, "Behold, I am coming quickly, and My reward *is* with Me, to render to every man according to what he has done" (Revelation 22:12). This is Paul's motivation in making it his ambition to live a life that is pleasing to Christ. He goes on to say, "For we must all appear before the judgment seat of Christ, so that each one may be recompensed for

[193] https://www.collinsdictionary.com/us/dictionary/english/ambition (accessed 27 April 2022)

his deeds in the body, according to what he has done, whether good or bad" (2 Corinthians 5:10).

The Scriptures do not clearly indicate when this judgment of believers will take place. However, it will probably occur immediately or soon after the resurrection of the righteous (Luke 14:14) at the beginning of Christ's millennial reign. John may be alluding to this when he says in the book of Revelation,

> Then I saw thrones, and they sat on them, and judgment was given to them. And I saw the souls of those who had been beheaded because of their testimony of Jesus and because of the word of God, and those who had not worshipped the beast or his image, and had not received the mark on their forehead and on their hand; and they came to life and reigned with Christ for a thousand years. [...] This is the first resurrection [i.e., the resurrection of the righteous]. Blessed and holy is the one who has a part in the first resurrection; over these the second death has no power, but they will be priests of God and of Christ and will reign with Him for a thousand years.
>
> Revelation 20:4–6

In the Roman world of Paul's day, the "judgment seat," sometimes referred to as the "bema seat,"[194] was simply "the official seat of a judge."[195] It's true that in the culture of that day, the term "judgment seat" often was used in a judicial sense of the place where an accused prisoner would be pronounced innocent

---

[194] In the original language of the Greek New Testament, the word translated "judgment seat" is simply the Greek word "bema" (*The Online Bible Thayer's Greek Lexicon and Brown, Driver & Briggs Hebrew Lexicon*).
[195] *The Online Bible Thayer's Greek Lexicon and Brown, Driver & Briggs Hebrew Lexicon*

or guilty. Such was the case of Pilate, who was "sitting on the judgment seat" ("bema seat") when He sentenced Jesus to death (Matthew 27:13). However, that is not the way Paul is using the term "judgment seat" in this passage.

> Paul was picturing the believer as a competitor in a spiritual contest. As the victorious Grecian athlete appeared before the *Bema* to receive his perishable award, so the Christian will appear before Christ's *Bema* to receive his imperishable award. The judge at the *Bema* bestowed rewards to the victors. *He did not whip the losers.* We might add, neither did he sentence them to hard labor.

> In other words, it is a reward seat and portrays a time of rewards or loss of rewards following examination, but it is not a time of punishment where believers are judged for their sins. Such would be inconsistent with the finished work of Christ on the Cross because He totally paid the penalty for our sins.[196]

We are already considered righteous before God because, as Paul makes so very clear when he says, "He [God] made Him [Christ] who knew no sin to be sin on our behalf, so that we might become the righteousness of God in Him" (2 Corinthians 5:21). We are considered righteous not because of anything we have done but because of what Christ has already done for us in His mercy and grace. Again, Paul makes this clear when he says,

> He saved us, not on the basis of deeds which we have done in righteousness, but according to His mercy, by the washing of regeneration and renewing by the Holy Spirit, whom He poured

---

[196] "The Doctrine of Rewards: The Judgment Seat (Bema) of Christ," https://bible.org/article/doctrine-rewards-judgment-seat-bema-christ (accessed 27 April 2022)

out upon us richly through Jesus Christ our Savior, so that being justified by His grace we would be made heirs according to the hope of eternal life.

Titus 3:5–7

For us, the judgment seat of Christ, we will be to determine our eternal reward based on the life that we've lived on earth as those who have already received by faith God's gracious gift of salvation in Christ.

Picture in your mind a group of highly-skilled and well-trained athletes in the ancient Isthmian games poised and ready to run the race that lies before them as hundreds of spectators cheer them on. They've all been in strict training for months just for this day. Then the signal is given, and with a burst of speed, the runners begin drawing upon every ounce of strength they have to come in first at the finish line. They are giving the race everything they have for one simple reason—they know there can only be one winner. And each one is determined to be that winner.

Why is this so important to them? Will they receive great wealth for being the winner? Will they get to marry the princess? No! What they will receive is the winner's crown. Does that mean a crown of gold studded with precious jewels? Again, *no*! Their reward was nothing more than a braid of oak leaves with no monetary value whatsoever. Eventually, the leaves would shrivel up and turn to dust. But wearing that braid of oak leaves meant the one wearing it was the champion who had won the race. This is the metaphor that Paul is using when he says, "Do you not know that in a race all the runners run, but only one gets the prize? Run in such a way as to get the prize. Everyone who competes in the games goes into strict training. They do it to get a crown that will not last; but we do it to get a crown that will last forever" (1 Corinthians 9:24–25, NIV).

Whether we like it or not, as believers, we are all in the race of life, and we will all be judged based on our performance to determine the prize that will be awarded to us. In the case of the judgment seat of Christ, however, we are not competing against other competitors based on how well we do compared to how well others have done. We are competing against ourselves in the sense that we will be judged for our faithfulness and devotion in obedience and service to the Lord. That judgment will be based on the resources, abilities, and opportunities that God has given us. Is it our ambition to please the Lord by making the most of these resources, abilities, and opportunities to serve and please Him? If an athlete in the ancient Greek games wanted to win the prize, then he would have to put in the effort to win. He would run his best with his eyes fixed on the prize, waiting for the person who crossed the finish line first. The same is true for us in living the Christian life: if we want to win the prize, then we have to put in the effort to be a winner with our eyes fixed on the prize. Our works do not determine our salvation, but they do determine our reward.

So, what exactly does Paul mean when he says that our works will be judged on the basis of whether they are good or bad? You might be inclined to think that he's talking about what is morally good versus what is morally evil. But that's not the case. He's using the word "good" in the sense of something being worthwhile—something that is found worthy of a reward because it has eternal value.[197] On the contrary, he's using the word "bad" in the sense of something being worthless with no eternal value and thus not worthy of any reward at all.[198] Our works will not be judged on the basis of whether they are morally

---

[197] The Greek word translated "good" (*agathos*) is being used to describe that which is "good in its character or constitution [and] is beneficial in its effect" (*Vine's Expository Dictionary of Biblical Words*), and something "of the highest quality and character" (*The Online Bible Thayer's Greek Lexicon and Brown, Driver & Briggs Hebrew Lexicon*).

[198] The Greek word translated "bad" (*phaulos*) "[...] primarily denotes 'slight, trivial, blown about by every wind'; then, 'mean, common, bad, in the sense of being worthless, paltry, or contemptible, belonging to a low order of things'" (*Vine's Expository Dictionary of Biblical Words*).

good or evil since that issue was settled at the cross. They will be judged on the basis of whether our works are worthwhile or worthless from the perspective of what has eternal value and is worthy of reward. Like Paul, our ambition ought to be that we will be able to present to the Lord works that are found worthy of reward in the day of judgment. Is that your true ambition in life? Or are you settling for some lesser ambition that has no real eternal value at all?

Here's another question to consider. What exactly are these good works that God is looking for in our lives—the kind that will be found worthy of reward at the judgment seat of Christ? Let's take a closer look! I can tell you, first of all, that it's not religiosity that will be found worthy of reward. It's not just about going to church on Sunday and reading your Bible and putting money in the offering plate when it's passed, or, as many people might say, just being a good Christian—whatever that means.

That's exactly what the people of Israel thought in the time of Isaiah the prophet. Speaking through Isaiah, the *Lord* says to them,

> "What makes you think I want all your sacrifices?" says the LORD. "I am sick of your burnt offerings of rams and the fat of fattened cattle. I get no pleasure from the blood of bulls and lambs and goats. When you come to worship me, who asked to parade through my courts with all your ceremony? Stop bringing me your meaningless gifts; the incense of your offerings disgusts me! As for your celebrations of the new moon and the Sabbath and your special days for fasting—they are all sinful and false. I want no more of your pious meetings. I hate your new moon celebrations and your annual festivals...They are a burden to me. I cannot stand them! When you lift up your hands in prayer, I will not look..."
>
> Isaiah 1:11–15a (NLT)

It's not that these things have no value, but when it's all empty religiosity, then it all becomes worthless.

Isaiah talks about this again when he says of the people of Israel in his day, "Then the Lord said, 'This people draw near with their words and honor Me with their lip service, but they remove their hearts far from Me, and their reverence for Me consists of tradition learned *by rote*'" (Isaiah 29:13). The same is true with all our religious church activities if they're not accompanied by the kind of "good works" that are truly pleasing to the *Lord*. It's significant that immediately on the heels of telling us that our salvation is by grace through faith and not on the basis of our good works; Paul goes on to say, "For we are His workmanship, created in Christ Jesus for good works, which God prepared beforehand so that we would walk in them" (Ephesians 2:10). As we saw in the last chapter, these good works that God has for us to do are "works of significance that will change the landscape of eternity."[199] God has not only prepared "works of significance" for us to do but He's also prepared us for doing these "works of significance." He's done that by giving us the abilities, resources, and opportunities we need to get the job done. All He asks is that we do the best we can with the abilities and resources we have to make the most of the opportunities He provides.

This is why Paul says, "So be careful how you live. Don't live like fools, but like those who are wise. Make the most of every opportunity in these evil days. Don't act thoughtlessly, but understand what the Lord wants you to do" (Ephesians 5:15–17, NLT). Jesus illustrates what this would look like in practical terms through a parable. As we saw in the previous chapter, a parable is a story with a purpose—an imaginary story that illustrates an important spiritual truth. This particular parable is commonly known as the parable of the talents (Matthew 25:14–30). In this parable, Jesus introduces

---

[199] Dax Romaine. See chapter 15, footnote 180

us to three servants whose master is about to go on a long journey to a distant land. Each of these servants is entrusted with a certain sum of money to invest for their master based on his ability to invest well. The servants have no idea how long their master will be gone or how soon he will return. All they know is that they have been entrusted with a sum of money to invest while he's gone. And when he returns, they can expect to give an accounting to their master of how well they have done with the money entrusted to them.

When the master returns, he discovers that with the first two servants, although each has received a different amount of money to invest based on his ability, both have doubled the money entrusted to them. And in each case, the master is pleased, as seen in his response to both servants—"Well done, good and faithful servant!" (Matthew 25:23, NIV) He praises them both, not just for what they have accomplished with the money entrusted to them, but for their faithful obedience that is evident in what they have done. Accordingly, both are richly rewarded. Not so with the third servant. The master is angry with him because he didn't invest his master's money at all—he simply buried it in the ground. The third servant makes all kinds of excuses, but there is no excuse for being unfaithful and disobedient. The master is no fool and gets right to the heart of the problem when he says to the third servant, "[...] You wicked and lazy servant!" (Matthew 25:26, NIV) The master is angry not because the servant failed to produce the return on his money that the other two servants had but because he had been unfaithful and disobedient to his master.

As much as the Lord may be pleased with the good works that we do, what pleases Him is not just the works we have done but the faithfulness that prompts our obedience in doing them. And that will be reflected in the reward that we receive or fail to receive at the judgment seat of Christ in the day of His coming. So what are these good works that God has prepared for us to do? They are acts of faithful obedience and loving service motivated by our own loving devotion to Him. To put it another way, the good works that God rewards are actions that express what it truly means to love God with all our heart, soul, mind, and strength (Matthew 22:37–38). That also includes loving our neighbor as ourselves, which is treating other people the way we, ourselves, would want to be treated (Matthew 22:39; 7:12).

So, what does this look like on a practical level? Again, speaking through the prophet Isaiah, the *Lord* gives us practical examples of what He's looking for when He says, "Wash yourselves and be clean! Get your sins out of my sight. Give up your evil ways. Learn to do good. Seek justice. Help the oppressed. Defend the cause of orphans. Fight for the rights of widows" (Isaiah 1:16–17, NLT). This is hardly an exhaustive list, but it provides some practical examples that reflect what He's looking for. Along the same lines, the apostle Paul says, "So let's not get tired of doing what is good. At just the right time we will reap a harvest of blessing if we don't give up. Therefore, whenever we have the opportunity, we should do good to everyone—especially to those in the family of faith" (Galatians 6:9–10, NLT).

Religious people are sometimes referred to as do-gooders, but truly godly people actively go about doing good, just as Jesus did (Acts 10:38). Just remember that why we do what we do is just as important—even more important—than what we do. Jesus warns about this when He says, "Beware of practicing your righteousness before men to be noticed by them; otherwise you have no reward with your Father who is in heaven" (Matthew 6:1). If your motive is wrong, even when you're doing what is right, you risk forfeiting the kind of reward that could have been yours at the judgment seat of Christ.

The apostle Paul expands our understanding of this theme of judgment and reward in another passage of the New Testament using a different metaphor—

not an athlete competing for the prize—but a builder constructing a house that is built to last. Of course, if you're building a house, it all has to begin with a firm foundation upon which to build. He says, "According to the grace of God which was given to me, like a wise master builder I laid a foundation, and another is building on it. But each man must be careful how he builds on it. For no man can lay a foundation other than the one which is laid, which is Jesus Christ" (1 Corinthians 3:10–11).

I have to wonder if Paul may have had in mind the parable that Jesus tells about two men, one who built his house upon the rock and the other who built his house upon the sand. When the rains fell, and the floods came, and the winds blew, the house built on the rock stood firm, while the house built on the sand was swept away. Jesus likens the man who built his house on the rock to someone who hears His words and, in faithful obedience, acts upon them. In stark contrast to the first man, He likens the man who built on the sand to someone who hears His words and then simply walks away (Matthew 7:24–27). There is only one solid foundation upon which to build our life, and that is the person and teaching of Jesus. Unless we build our life on Christ and His teaching, our so-called good works really won't do us any good at all.

Assuming, however, that we are building our life on that firm foundation of Jesus and His teaching, what comes next? Paul continues, "Now if any man builds on the foundation with gold, silver, precious stones, wood, hay, straw, each man's work will become evident; for the day will show it because it is to be revealed with fire, and the fire itself will test the quality of each man's work" (1 Corinthians 3:12–13). I remember a time when I was driving on a road near my home when up ahead, the road was blocked off as firefighters were trying to extinguish a roaring house fire. The house was built of wood and had quickly turned into a roaring inferno. The next day I was driving on that same road, and when I looked to see where that house had been, all that remained was a smoldering pile of ashes. Even when we build on the right foundation, the issue then becomes the quality of the building materials that we're using to build on that foundation.

The same thing is true when it comes to living the Christian life. The gold, silver, and precious stones represent those works of faithful obedience to God and loving service to others motivated by our own loving devotion to Him. They are practical expressions of our love for God, as seen in our love for our neighbor. The wood, hay, and straw represent anything else that doesn't fit that description—things that simply have no eternal value and do nothing to change the landscape of eternity. Paul continues, "If any man's work which he has built on it remains, he will receive a reward. If any man's work is burned up, he will suffer loss; but he himself will be saved, yet so as through fire" (1 Corinthians 3:14–15).

The irony is that we can live our whole life even with Christ as our foundation and doing works that we would consider good but still end up with nothing more than a smoldering pile of ashes in terms of the eternal reward that could have been ours. We'll end up just like the people whose house I saw burned to the ground. We cannot lose our salvation, but we may end up entering into eternity smelling like smoke. Good works don't save us, but that doesn't mean that good works don't matter. Every day we can expect God to provide opportunities for us to do the good works that He has already prepared for us and equipped us to do (Ephesians 2:10). Our job is to make the most of the opportunities as we make it our ambition to consistently please God by loving Him and loving people. If we do that, we'll end up receiving a reward, not being filled with remorse over what otherwise might have been.

So, what is this future reward to be received at the judgment seat of Christ? The Scriptures don't provide a clear answer to this question, although there has been much speculation among biblical scholars on the subject. I think that Scripture's lack of clarity on the subject of rewards is deliberate on God's part to increase our eager anticipation over the coming of that future day when we will find out. It would be similar to the eager anticipation and excitement of a child over the coming of Christmas as he thinks about the gifts that will be under the tree. Not knowing what's wrapped up in those boxes under the tree gives that child opportunity to think about and imagine what wonderful treasures might be there. Having said that, I think it's wonderful to be able to use our imagination and think about what this future reward to be ours at the judgment seat of Christ might be.

Could it be that our future reward is simply the capacity to glorify our God throughout all the ages of eternity? This would mean, then, the greater our reward, the greater would be our capacity to glorify God. This is certainly consistent with the words of the apostle Paul when he says twice in the book of Ephesians that God's ultimate purpose in redemption is that we should be "[...] to the praise of His glory" (Ephesians 1:12, 14). However, I think there's more to it than that. Coming back to the parable of the talents, I think it's very significant that the master expresses his praise to the first two servants in saying to each of them, "Well done, good and faithful servant." (Matthew 25:21). Why does he praise them? Because they have demonstrated faithfulness in their obedience by the way, they have invested the resources and opportunities entrusted to them. The same will be true for us as we stand before the judgment seat of Christ. How awesome a reward it will be to receive praise from the mouth of the Savior whom we praise for all He is and all He's done for us.

This is what Peter is talking about in speaking about the outcome of the trials that we endure as followers of Christ. He says,

In this [the promise of a future inheritance of glory] you greatly rejoice, even though now for a little while, if necessary, you have been distressed by various trials, so that the proof of your faith, being more precious than gold which is perishable, even though tested by fire, may be found to result in praise and glory and honor at the revelation of Jesus Christ.

1 Peter 1:6–7

We will receive praise and glory and honor from our Savior when we stand before Him because, by our good works, we have brought praise and glory and honor to God with our faithfulness and obedience in doing the good works that God has prepared for us to do. This is what Jesus means when He says, "Let your light shine before men in such a way that they may see your good works, and glorify your Father who is in heaven" (Matthew 5:16).

But that's not all! Praise is not the only thing that these servants receive for their faithfulness and obedience to their master. He also says to them, "[...] You have been faithful with a few things; I will put you in charge of many things" (Matthew 25:21b, NIV). Not only does the master praise these servants for their faithfulness in serving him, but he gives them greater responsibility and, with that responsibility, greater opportunity to serve him because of that faithfulness. In the same way, at the judgment seat of Christ, our reward will not only be the praise of our Master for our faithful works of service for Him but also increased responsibility and greater opportunity to serve Him through our acts of service in His eternal kingdom. And through these greater opportunities to serve Him, we will be able to glorify God all the more throughout all eternity. I have no idea what these future acts of service may look like, but I am confident that they will be more awesome than we could ever imagine.

Coming back to the parable of the talents, not only does the master praise his faithful servants and give them increased responsibility and opportunity to serve him, but he also says to them, "[...] enter into the joy of your master" (Matthew 25:21, 23). Apparently, the reward that we receive at the judgment seat of Christ for our faithful service to Him is not only greater capacity to glorify God through greater opportunity to serve Him in His eternal kingdom but also greater capacity to glorify God through greater capacity to experience the fullness of His joy forever.

Apparently, there is a close connection between our capacity to enjoy God and life in His kingdom and our capacity to glorify Him. The Westminster Assembly in England agreed with this when they wrote the Westminster Shorter Catechism back in the seventeenth century. The Shorter Catechism asks the question, "What is the chief end of man?" and then answers the question by saying, "Man's chief end is to glorify God, and to enjoy him forever."[200] God created us for a relationship with Himself in which we would not only glorify Him but enjoy Him both now and forever. The psalmist tells us that in God's presence is "fullness of joy" (Psalm 16:11). Furthermore, Jesus makes it clear that God wants us to share in this same fullness of joy that fills His presence when He says, "These things I have spoken to you so that My joy may be in you, and that your joy may be made full[201]" (John 15:11).

There is clearly a connection between the glory that God receives from us and the joy that we receive from Him. John Piper sums it up well when he says, "God is most glorified in us when we are most satisfied in Him."[202] In other

---

[200] "Westminster Shorter Catechism," https://en.wikipedia.org/wiki/Westminster_Shorter_Catechism (accessed 27 April 2022)

[201] The Greek word translated "made full" (*pleroo*) means "to make full, to fill, to fill up, to render full, ie., complete, properly to fill up to the top" (*The Online Bible Thayer's Greek Lexicon and Brown, Driver & Briggs Hebrew Lexicon*).

[202] John Piper, *Desiring God* (Sisters, OR: Multnomah Press, 1986, Copyright, John Piper, 1996)

words, we glorify God the most when we enjoy Him the most—when our greatest delight is in Him—when He, above all other things, is our greatest treasure. I believe that part of the eternal reward that God has in store for all faithful believers is simply the capacity to enjoy Him and to enjoy living with Him forever in His everlasting kingdom. It will be something far better and far beyond anything we could ever begin to imagine. And the greater our capacity to enjoy Him and life in His kingdom, the greater our capacity to glorify Him because the two go hand in hand. Our capacity for experiencing this kind of joy that glorifies God in eternity is determined by how we live our lives as believers right now. The more we seek God with our whole hearts in faithful and loving devotion reflected in our faithful obedience and service to Him, the greater our capacity will be to experience His joy and to magnify His glory forever.

You can fill both a bucket and a thimble with water right to the top. Both are full, but the bucket will clearly hold more water than the thimble. The one with the greater capacity will hold more water than the other, even though both are full. Even so, in eternity, we may all experience fullness of joy, but that fullness will only be to the degree that we have the capacity to receive it. So, in eternity how great do you want your capacity to glorify God and enjoy Him forever to be? That will be determined by the way you live your life right now.

Yes, we receive salvation by faith as a gift of God's grace, but our capacity to glorify God and enjoy Him forever will depend on our faithfulness in doing the good works that God has prepared for us to do as the outward expression of our faith and our faithfulness. So in this race of life, we need to keep our eye on the prize and run to win. The reward we receive will be worth the effort! What you and I need to remember, as Moses did and as Paul did, is that this present earthly life is not all there is. Beyond this life is eternity! And how we live now is going to determine what that eternity will look like.

Sadly, for unbelievers, their eternity is going to look pretty bleak. But what about those of us who are genuine followers of Christ. What does eternity hold for us? What will our eternity look like? That will depend on how we live our lives right now. The question of *where* we will live in eternity was settled for us at the cross. But the question of *how* we will live in eternity will be determined by how we live right now.

The reason this is true is that we, too, will be judged for our works, just as unbelievers will. The difference is that our judgment is not to determine punishment—that has already been settled at the cross. Our judgment is to determine the reward we will receive for a life well-lived. Moses understood this and lived the life that he did because he was "looking to the reward." Paul understood this and made it his highest ambition in life to live in a manner that was pleasing to the Lord. So what about you? What are you living for? Your answer will determine not where you will spend eternity as a follower of Christ but how you will spend eternity. So choose wisely!

Chapter 18

The Judgment of the Unrighteous

Rest in the LORD and wait patiently for Him; [...] For evildoers will
be cut off, but those who wait for the LORD will inherit the land.

Psalm 37:7a, 9

For those who are weary of living in a world where evil and violence so
often seem to run rampant and wrongdoers often seem to go unpunished,
waiting patiently for the coming of a new world that will be "filled with God's
righteousness" (2 Peter 3:13, NLT) can be a difficult challenge. And yet that's
exactly what God asks us to do. The psalmist says,

> Rest in the LORD and wait patiently for Him; [...] For evildoers
> will be cut off, but those who wait for the LORD, they will inherit
> the land. Yet a little while and the wicked man will be no more; [...]
> But the humble will inherit the land and will delight themselves in
> abundant prosperity.

Psalm 37:7a, 9–11

At Christ's coming, He will send His angels to gather together His saints
so that we may live and reign with Him forever. But in that day, the angels will
also be doing another kind of gathering—it's what Jesus talks about as He
tells the parable of the wheat and the tares. Remember, as we saw in chapter
sixteen, a parable has been defined as "a comparison from nature or daily life
designed to teach a spiritual truth.[203] Jesus says,

---

[203] "Parable," *Holman Bible Handbook*, David Dockery, editor, Holman Bible Publishers,
1992

"The kingdom of heaven may be compared to a man who sowed good seed in his field. But while his men were sleeping, his enemy came and sowed tares among the wheat, and went away. But when the wheat sprouted and bore grain, then the tares became evident also. The slaves of the landowner came and said to him, 'Sir, did you not sow good seed in your field? How then does it have tares?' And he said to them, 'An enemy has done this!' The slaves said to him, 'Do you want us, then, to go and gather them up?' But he said, 'No; for while you are gathering up the tares, you may uproot the wheat with them. Allow both to grow together until the harvest; and in the time of the harvest I will say to the reapers, 'First gather up the tares and bind them in bundles to burn them up; but gather the wheat into my barn.'"

Matthew 13:24–30

Certainly, this is a picture that would have been familiar to the people of that day living in a primarily agricultural economy. However, it's one thing to understand the story itself, but something altogether different to grasp its spiritual implications. Even the disciples didn't get it, and as soon as they were alone with Jesus, they asked Him to explain the meaning of this parable. In response to their request, Jesus explains,

The one who sows the good seed is the Son of Man, and the field is the world; and as for the good seed, these are the sons of the kingdom; and the tares are the sons of the evil one; and the enemy who sowed them is the devil, and the harvest is the end of the age; and the reapers are angels. So just as the tares are gathered up and burned with fire, so shall it be at the end of the age. The Son of Man will send forth His angels, and they will gather out of His kingdom all stumbling blocks, and those who commit lawlessness, and will throw them into the furnace of fire; in that place there will be weeping and gnashing of teeth. Then THE RIGHTEOUS WILL SHINE FORTH AS THE SUN in the kingdom of their Father.

Matthew 13:37–43

Jesus is using the metaphor of a farmer gathering the weeds out of his field and casting them into the fire as a vivid picture describing the judgment of the unrighteous in the day of His coming. Even as the righteous will be gathered together to meet Him as their Rescuer, so the unrighteous will also be gathered together to meet Him as their Judge.[204] The apostle Paul develops these same two themes of deliverance for the righteous and judgment for the unrighteous in his second letter to the Thessalonians. At the time this letter was written, the Thessalonian believers were suffocating at the hands of those who were mercilessly persecuting them because of their faith in Christ.

This intense suffering they were enduring should not come as a surprise to us in light of Jesus' own words to His disciples (and to us) in the Upper Room Discourse when He says,

"If the world hates you, you know that it has hated Me before it hated you. If you were of the world, the world would love its own; but because you are not of the world, but I chose you out of the world, because of this the world hates you. Remember the word

---

[204] If this parable has a familiar ring to it, it's probably because we find the same theme in the parable of the sheep and goats in chapter 16. In both parables, there is a separating of the righteous from the unrighteous in the day of judgment, with the righteous receiving their just reward and the unrighteous receiving their just punishment.

that I said to you, 'A slave is not greater than his master.' If they persecuted Me, they will also persecute you; if they kept My word, they will keep yours also. But all these things they will do to you for My name's sake, because they do not know the One who sent Me."

John 15:18–21

This will especially be true during the great tribulation that will precede Christ's coming when He says, "Then you will be handed over to be persecuted and put to death, and you will be hated by all nations because of me" (Matthew 24:9, NIV)

In an effort to encourage the Thessalonians in the midst of their suffering, Paul commends them for their perseverance and steadfast faith, even to the extent of telling them that he boasts about them to the other churches. Clearly, they are setting an example for other believers facing similar circumstances (and certainly for us today). Furthermore, he says, "All this is evidence that God's judgment is right, and as a result you will be counted worthy of the kingdom of God, for which you are suffering" (2 Thessalonians 1:5, NIV). Don't misunderstand what Paul is saying here. Our perseverance in suffering does not make us worthy of God's kingdom. On the contrary, we are made worthy of God's kingdom only because of God's grace put on display at the cross when we put our trust in Christ. We are not made worthy of God's kingdom by our perseverance but by a faith that perseveres. And such was the case with the Thessalonians in their time of suffering.

You might be wondering why God allows the wicked to do the things they do and seemingly get away it. Where is the God of justice? If God is truly just, then why doesn't He punish the wicked for their wicked deeds? I can only imagine how these very questions must have plagued the minds of the Thessalonian believers in the midst of their suffering. The simple fact is that judgment day hasn't come yet—but we can rest assured that it will. The apostle Paul makes this clear in his first letter to the Thessalonians when he reminds them of something they already know but need to be reminded of (as do we) about the coming of the Lord. He says,

> For you yourselves know full well that the day of the Lord will come just like a thief in the night. While they are saying, "Peace and safety!" then destruction will come upon them suddenly like labor pains upon a woman with child, and they will not escape. But you, brethren, are not in darkness, that the day would overtake you like a thief. For God has not destined us for wrath, but for obtaining salvation through our Lord Jesus Christ, who died for us, that whether we are awake or asleep, we will live together with Him.
>
> 1 Thessalonians 5:2–4, 9–10

For a rebellious and unbelieving world, the day of the Lord will be a day when they experience God's wrath in judgment. But for the people of God, it will be a day when they experience God's grace in deliverance, not only from persecution but from the wrath of God's judgment against sin. Now, in his second letter to the Thessalonians, Paul reminds the Thessalonians again about what will happen in the day of the Lord, pointing out that God's justice will prevail in that day. He says,

> God is just: He will pay back trouble to those who trouble you and give relief to you who are troubled, and to us as well. This will happen when the Lord Jesus is revealed from heaven in blazing fire

271

with his powerful angels. He will punish those who do not know
God and do not obey the gospel of our Lord Jesus.

2 Thessalonians 1:6–8 (NIV)

Apparently, this judgment that Paul is speaking about is not a judgment of all unbelievers living on the earth at the time of Christ's coming. Rather, it is a judgment that specifically targets those who have been responsible for the terrible persecution of the Jewish people and followers of Christ during the great tribulation. To be more specific, Paul says that God, in His justice, will "pay back trouble" to those who have troubled the people of God—that is, those who have persecuted the people of God. This is clear from the meaning of the word translated as "trouble" in the original Greek text.[205]

Furthermore, Scripture seems to indicate that there will be unbelieving Gentiles still living on the earth during the millennial reign of Christ. Though these unbelieving Gentiles will not be permitted to participate in Christ's kingdom, because of God's amazing grace, God will continue to extend to them the offer of salvation throughout the millennial period. During this time, many of these unbelieving Gentiles will actually come to faith in Christ and be saved. James speaks of this in the book of Acts as he quotes from a prophecy of Amos spoken hundreds of years before the birth of Christ. Apparently, early on in the Jerusalem church, there was a controversy over whether only Jews could be saved or whether salvation was also available to the Gentiles. As a result, a special council was called to address this controversial subject. In responding to this critical question, James is making reference to the prophecy of Amos, where the *Lord* says, "'After this I will return and rebuild David's fallen tent. Its ruins I will rebuild, and I will restore it, that the remnant of men may seek the Lord,

---

[205] See 1 Thessalonians 2:13–15

272

and all the Gentiles who bear my name,' says the Lord" (Acts 15:16–17, NIV).[206]

When David ruled as king over the nation of Israel in the tenth century BC, the *Lord* made a covenant promise to David in which He said, "Your house and your kingdom shall endure before Me forever; your throne shall be established forever" (2 Samuel 7:16). Yet, David's dynasty lasted only slightly more than four hundred years until the Babylonians captured the city of Jerusalem in 586 BC, removing the last of David's descendants from the throne and taking the Jewish people into exile in Babylon. Most people would probably think that this covenant promise that a descendant of David would rule forever over the nation of Israel simply will never happen. But it will happen at the coming of Christ when Jesus, a descendant of David (Matthew 1:1), will take His rightful place on David's throne to rule not only the nation of Israel but the entire world.

According to the prophecy of Amos, as related by James, many unbelieving Gentiles still living on the earth in that day when Christ comes to take His rightful place upon the throne of David will see this obvious miracle and seek the Lord. As amazing as it sounds, during the millennial reign of Christ, God will graciously offer His gift of salvation to all who will receive it. According to the prophet Isaiah, God will even send His own people as missionaries to the nations during the millennial period, giving everyone throughout the world opportunity to hear the message of the gospel and believe. The *Lord*,

---

[206] James is quoting the prophecy found in Amos 9:11–12 as it reads in the Greek Septuagint translation of the Old Testament, which was commonly used in the Church of that day. The Septuagint dates back to the mid-third century BC and is based upon manuscripts of the Hebrew Old Testament that are hundreds of years older than the Hebrew manuscripts of the Old Testament available today, which date back only to the AD twelfth century. For this reason, in some instances the Septuagint may represent a more accurate rendering of the Hebrew Old Testament. Clearly, James, speaking by the Spirit of God, had full confidence in the accuracy and trustworthiness of the Septuagint, or he would not have quoted from it.

speaking of this offer of grace to those who are still unbelieving, says, "I will set a sign among them and will send survivors from them to the nations [...] to the distant coastlands that have neither heard My fame nor seen My glory. And they will declare My glory among the nations" (Isaiah 66:19).

The prophet Zechariah tells us, "[In that day] the LORD will be king over all the earth; in that day the LORD will be the only one, and His name the only one" (Zechariah 14:9). The prophet Isaiah describes His kingdom as one characterized by everlasting peace, justice, and righteousness (Isaiah 9:6–7). During this time, Christ will rule the nations with a rod of iron (Psalm 2:27; Revelation 12:5; 19:15). In other words, Christ will be quick to judge sin and to put down any rebellion against His rule among the still unbelieving Gentiles. Under the rule of Christ, there will be zero tolerance for sin on the earth, without which a kingdom of righteousness, justice, and peace would not even be possible.

You might think that in such a perfect environment on earth, everyone would finally see the benefits of living under Christ's rule and welcome Him as their Savior and King. You might expect to see everyone turn from their unbelief and come to faith in Christ. Yet beneath the surface, a spirit of rebellion will be brewing in the hearts of those unbelieving Gentiles who give lip service to Christ as their King but who persist in their unbelief and in their hearts remains a spirit of rebellion toward the rule of Christ on earth.

As God pulls back the curtain and allows us to look into the spiritual realm, He reveals that after Christ has ruled on the earth for a thousand years, Satan will be released from his imprisonment in the abyss[207] (Revelation 20:7). The outcome should not be hard to predict. Satan will immediately do what he's done ever since the garden of Eden—something he is a master

---

[207] The "abyss" in the New Testament represents "the prison of disobedient spirits or the world of the dead" (Luke 8:31; Romans 10:7) ("Abyss," *Nelson's Illustrated Bible Dictionary*).

at doing. John writes, "When the thousand years are completed, Satan will be released from his prison, and will come out to deceive the nations which are in the four corners of the earth, Gog and Magog, to gather them together for the war; the number of them is like the sand of the seashore" (Revelation 20:7–8). Satan will deceive the nations once again by convincing them to attempt a coup against the rule of Christ (Revelation 20:8). Once again, the remaining Gentile unbelievers among the nations will gather their armies together in a coalition that has one common purpose—to overthrow God's anointed King so that they may no longer have to live under His rule. In their arrogant pride and unbelief, they will still refuse to see the utter folly and futility of attempting to overthrow the King.

This is exactly what the book of Psalms is talking about when it says,

> Why are the nations in an uproar and the peoples devising a vain thing? The kings of the earth take their stand and the rulers take counsel together against the Lord and against His Anointed, saying, "Let us tear their fetters apart and cast away their cords from us!" He who sits in the heavens laughs, the Lord scoffs at them. Then He will speak to them in His anger and terrify them in His fury, saying, "But as for Me, I have installed My King upon Zion, My holy mountain." "I will surely tell of the decree of the Lord: He said to Me, 'You are My Son, Today I have begotten You. Ask of Me, and I will surely give the nations as Your inheritance, and the very ends of the earth as Your possession. You shall break them with a rod of iron, You shall shatter them like earthenware.'"
>
> Psalm 2:1–9

The outcome of their attempted rebellion will be horrendous as fire falling from the sky consumes them all. One minute there will be a huge army preparing to launch an insurrection against the rule of Christ on earth. The next minute all that's left of this mighty army will be piles of ashes and acrid smoke ascending to the heavens (Revelation 20:9). And what of Satan? He will be cast into the lake of fire forever (Revelation 20:10). At this point, only those who are truly believers in Christ will remain on earth. All those who refused to put their trust in Christ and surrender their hearts to Him as their King will be gone. As the psalmist writes, "Yet a little while and the wicked man will be no more; and you will look carefully for his place and he will not be there. But the humble will inherit the land and will delight themselves in abundant prosperity" (Psalm 37:10–11).

Let's pause for a moment and ponder why God would even allow this rebellion against the rule of Christ to occur after He's ruled over the entire earth for an entire millennium? Scripture doesn't provide a clear answer to this question, but it's likely that God's purpose is to demonstrate to the angels of heaven and to His people on earth that a spirit of rebellion and lawlessness still lies deep in the heart of those who choose personal autonomy over loving, faithful obedience to God. This is in spite of living in a world under the benevolent reign of Christ where everyone in it has been flourishing as God intended from the beginning.

This brings us to the final judgment. Without a doubt, the book of Revelation is a pretty scary book of the Bible. Visions of hideous creatures that look like locusts but sting like scorpions. Visions of a mountain burning like a torch falling from the sky and setting the world on fire. Visions of two hundred million soldiers engaged in a war that kills a third of the human race. Visions of famines and pandemics and earthquakes that topple mountains and bring great cities crashing to the ground. These are the kinds of things that haunt us in our worst nightmares. These are the kinds of things that can make a grown man blubber like a baby in abject terror. And yet none of these scenes can produce the kind of debilitating terror that John's vision of dead men walking can conjure up as the dead are awakened out of the sleep of death to face the fury of a holy God at the final judgment.

As we've already seen in chapter seventeen, the resurrection of the righteous occurs at the beginning of the millennial reign of Christ when He sends forth His angels to gather His elect. Jesus refers to this resurrection as a "resurrection of life" (John 5:29). Likewise, Daniel, speaking five hundred years earlier, says that those who participate in this resurrection will be raised to "everlasting life" (Daniel 12:2). This is the same resurrection that Paul is talking about when he says,

> For the Lord Himself will descend from heaven with a shout, with the voice of the archangel and with the trumpet of God, and the dead in Christ will rise first. Then we who are alive and remain will be caught up together with them in the clouds to meet the Lord in the air, and so we shall always be with the Lord.
>
> 1 Thessalonians 4:16–17

Again, as we've already seen in chapter 17, this is likely the time when the righteous will stand before the judgment seat of Christ to be rewarded for their good deeds (Luke 14:14). John talks about this same resurrection "to everlasting life" in the book of Revelation when he says,

> Then I saw thrones, and they sat on them, and judgment was given to them. And I saw the souls of those who had been beheaded because of their testimony of Jesus and because of the word of God, and those who had not worshipped the beast or his image, and had not received the mark on their forehead and on their hand; and

they came to life and reigned with Christ for a thousand years. [...] This is the first resurrection. Blessed and holy is the one who has a part in the first resurrection; over these the second death has no power, but they will be priests of God and of Christ and will reign with Him for a thousand years.

Revelation 20:4–6

But what about those who do not participate in this first resurrection? John answers this question when he says, "The rest of the dead did not come to life until the thousand years were completed" (Revelation 20:5a). These are the people who, Daniel says, will be raised "to disgrace and everlasting contempt" (Daniel 12:2) and whom Jesus says will participate in the "resurrection of judgment" (John 5:29). John tells us the fate of those who miss on the first resurrection when he says,

Then I saw a great white throne and Him who sat upon it, from whose presence earth and heaven fled away, and no place was found for them. And I saw the dead, the great and the small, standing before the throne, and books were opened; and another book was opened, which is the book of life; and the dead were judged from the things which were written in the books, according to their deeds. And the sea gave up the dead which were in it, and death and Hades gave up the dead which were in them; and they were judged, every one of them according to their deeds.

Revelation 20:11–13

In describing this judgment, John says that books will be opened, and then another book—a different book—will be opened as well, which is the book of life. Apparently, the books that are opened contain the names of all

278

the unrighteous who have lived throughout the ages from the very beginning of time, as well as a record of all their works during their life on earth. The other book, the book of life, apparently contains the names of all the righteous (God's true saints) who have lived throughout the ages from the very beginning of time.[208] Those whose names are found in the book of life will be exempt from judgment. For them, the penalty for sin has been dealt with at the cross. The only reason they escape the judgment of God is that they have relied in humble faith upon God's mercy and grace as revealed at the cross, not upon their own works. Because of the work of Christ, all their sins have been blotted out forever.

As David expresses it so well, speaking of the righteous, he says, "He [God] does not treat us as our sins deserve or repay us according to our iniquities. For as high as the heavens are above the earth, so great is his love for those who fear him; as far as the east is from the west, so far has he removed our transgressions from us" (Psalm 103:10–12, NIV). And as Paul says in the book of Titus,

> He [God] saved us, not on the basis of deeds which we have done
> in righteousness, but according to His mercy, by the washing of
> regeneration and renewing by the Holy Spirit, whom He poured
> out upon us richly through Jesus Christ our Savior, so that being
> justified by His grace we would be made heirs according to the
> hope of eternal life.
>
> Titus 3:5–7

When the wicked stand before a holy God in judgment, they will see with total clarity the reason that they stand condemned before Him. They

---

[208] See chapter 11 for more information about the book of life

will know that they have been judged fairly and justly deserve the judgment they receive because of their sinful thoughts, words, and deeds recorded in the books. The penalty for all will be the same because God doesn't grade on a curve. According to the book of James, "The person who keeps all of the laws except one is as guilty as a person who has broken all of God's laws" (James 2:10, NLT). It only takes one sin—one evil thought, word, or deed—to render a person guilty before God. And, as Paul makes clear in the book of Romans, "the wages of sin is death" (Romans 6:23). John calls it here "the second death" (Revelation 20:14).

John is using powerful language to describe the eternal destiny of the wicked that he saw in his vision, just as does Jesus in His parable of the sheep and goats. He says, "Then death and Hades were thrown into the lake of fire. This is the second death, the lake of fire. And if anyone's name was not found written in the book of life, he was thrown into the lake of fire" (Revelation 20:14–15). Using similar language in His parable of the sheep and goats, Jesus says to the goats, "Depart from Me, accursed ones, into the eternal fire which has been prepared for the devil and his angels" (Matthew 25:41).

Certainly, one cannot deny that both Jesus and John explicitly describe the punishment of the wicked in terms of burning fire. Yet, this raises a significant issue that cries out to be addressed. Are these references to the wicked burning in a lake of fire meant to be understood literally? Or are they intended to serve as a poignant metaphor to describe the horrible consequences of sin? There is certainly a danger when we interpret as a metaphor what is intended to be understood literally. We don't want to make that mistake. But there's also real danger when we interpret literally what is intended to be understood as a metaphor.

As those who are committed to the truth, it's essential that we make every effort to get it right. We need to be extremely careful in the way we interpret

Scripture as we seek to remain true to the text and, at the same time, discern the intent of the original writer when he wrote it. Did the original writer intend for it to be understood in a literal sense or as a metaphor? This is something we need to think about as we seek to understand what these passages about eternal judgment truly mean. And if it isn't meant to be understood literally, then what does the metaphor represent? If we take it literally, then the meaning is clear, whether we like it or not. But if we understand the idea of "eternal fire" or a "lake of fire" as a metaphor—powerful imagery but not to be taken literally—then what does this imagery mean?

In the Gospels, Jesus makes reference to hell ten times, describing it as "the fiery hell" (Matthew 5:22; Mark 18:9) and a place of "unquenchable fire" (Mark 9:43). It's likely that this is what Jesus is referring to in the parable of the sheep and goats when he says to the goats (the unrighteous), "Depart from Me, accursed ones, into the eternal fire which has been prepared for the devil and his angels" (Matthew 25:41). The Greek word translated as "hell" (Gehenna) refers to an actual place that existed in Jesus' day. It was a ravine just south of the city of Jerusalem, originally known as the Valley of Hinnom.

According to Nelson's Illustrated Bible Dictionary,

> In the time of Jesus the Valley of Hinnom was used as the garbage dump of Jerusalem. Into it were thrown all the filth and garbage of the city, including the dead bodies of animals and executed criminals. To consume all this, fires burned constantly. Maggots worked in the filth. When the wind blew from that direction over the city, its awfulness was quite evident. At night wild dogs howled and gnashed their teeth as they fought over the garbage. Jesus used this awful scene as a symbol of hell. In effect he said, "Do you want to know what hell is like? Look at the valley of Gehenna." So hell

may be described as God's "cosmic garbage dump." All that is unfit for heaven will be thrown into hell.[209]

This certainly gives some credence to the possibility that the "eternal fire" that Jesus is speaking about is metaphorical rather than literal. Gehenna, with its burning trash heaps, represented a dreadful place where no one would ever want to go to spend eternity.

Furthermore, we dare not overlook the significance of the fact that Paul never uses the imagery of fire in describing the destiny of the wicked. Writing to the Thessalonians, the apostle Paul describes the eternal punishment of the unrighteous a little differently when he says, "They [the unrighteous] will be punished with everlasting destruction and shut out from the presence of the Lord and from the majesty of his power" (2 Thessalonians 1:9, NIV). We might be inclined to think that when Paul talks about "eternal destruction," he's referring to annihilation—where the unrighteous would simply cease to exist. But such is not the case. When an insurance adjuster says that an automobile that has just been in a serious accident has been "totaled," he means that it has been totally destroyed to the point that it cannot be repaired and restored to usefulness again. He doesn't mean that the car doesn't exist anymore, but that it's been reduced to a pile of twisted metal that is totally ruined. As such, it will never again serve any useful purpose nor be anything more than scrap metal on a junk pile.

In the same way, when Paul talks about "everlasting destruction[210]," he's talking about something that will continue to exist in a state of ruin

---

[209] "Valley of Hinnom," *Nelson's Illustrated Bible Dictionary*

[210] The Greek word translated "destruction" (*olethros*) means "ruin, destruction" (*Vine's Expository Dictionary of Biblical Words*). This word is translated "ruin" in 1 Timothy 6:9 and refers to the love of money "ruining" a person's life (*The Online Bible Thayer's Greek Lexicon and Brown, Driver & Briggs Hebrew Lexicon*).

or destruction, totally useless or worthless for anything other than being thrown on the scrap pile of eternity. The penalty of persistent, unrepentant sin is a ruined life forever. So what does everlasting destruction actually mean if not annihilation? Paul provides the answer when he says that they will be "[...] shut out from the presence of the Lord and from the majesty of his power."

According to the Westminster Shorter Catechism, "the chief end of man is to glorify God and to enjoy Him forever."[211] This means that the primary purpose for which man exists, for which he has been designed, and which alone can satisfy the deepest longings of his heart is to know God (John 17:3), to enjoy God (Psalm 37:4), and live for the glory of God (1 Corinthians 10:31). The very essence of what it means to experience eternal death is being forever banished from God's presence and the glory of His power. Those separated eternally from God will experience unimaginable ruin and loss because they will never experience the relationship with God for which they were created to experience with Him forever. Instead of experiencing the life they were created to live, they will experience the emptiness and destructiveness of a ruined life, wholly self-centered and given over to satisfying the desires of the self. They will experience forever the self-inflicted torment of a life wholly given over to the self, meaningless and empty, without purpose or hope. What a horrible way to live for all eternity.

If indeed references to "eternal fire" and to "the lake of fire" as God's punishment for sin are meant to be understood as a metaphor rather than taken literally, then they present a vivid and terrifying picture of just how awful a ruined life lived forever "shut out from the presence of the Lord and from the majesty of his power" will be. In reality, the penalty of sin that God

---

[211] "Westminster Shorter Catechism," https://en.wikipedia.org/wiki/Westminster_Shorter_Catechism (accessed 27 April 202 2022)

will impose on a rebellious and unbelieving world is giving them over to the very thing they want—or think they want—an existence where God is totally absent from their life, allowing them to live totally for themselves with no interference from Him. In thinking this is what they really want, they will be in for a very unpleasant surprise. You've probably heard people say that they would rather go to hell than to heaven because then they can spend eternity partying with their friends. By saying such a thing, they demonstrate the depth of their own ignorance. They have no idea what it will mean to be eternally separated from God—banished from His presence forever.

This is not the first time in Scripture that we read about God punishing people for their sin and rebellion by simply giving them what they want. In the Old Testament, we see God doing this with the people of Israel when He says,

> My people did not listen to My voice, and Israel did not obey Me.
> So I gave them over to the stubbornness of their heart, to walk
> in their own devices. Oh that My people would listen to Me,
> that Israel would walk in My ways! I would quickly subdue their
> enemies and turn My hand against their adversaries. [...] I would
> feed you with the finest of the wheat, and with honey from the
> rock I would satisfy you.
>
> Psalm 81:11–14, 16

We see this again in the New Testament when Paul says,

> For the wrath of God is revealed from heaven against all
> ungodliness and unrighteousness of men who suppress the truth
> in unrighteousness. For even though they knew God, they did not
> honor Him as God or give thanks, but they became futile in their

speculations, and their foolish heart was darkened. Therefore God gave them over in the lusts of their hearts...

Romans 1:18, 21, 24a

Those who foolishly think that they are better off without God in their lives will discover that life without God is utter ruin and destruction. Their life will end up as worthless as a pile of smoldering ashes even as "the smoke of their torment rises forever and ever" (Revelation 14:11, NIV). Those who have been banished from the presence of God and His majestic glory will discover that their eternal existence will be totally devoid of all that makes life worth living.

Facing the wrath of God in the final judgment will be a terrifying experience for those who have flaunted God's moral laws and thought that they would never be held accountable for their actions. This will be equally true for those who, in their ignorance of God and His ways, thought that He would be grading on a curve that would allow them to escape His wrath. They will all discover the reality of what the prophet Nahum is talking about when he says, "The LORD is slow to anger and great in power, and the LORD will by no means leave the guilty unpunished. [...] Who can stand before His indignation? Who can endure the burning of His anger? His wrath is poured out like fire..." (Nahum 1:3a, 6)

The only ones who will have no reason to fear God's wrath in the day of judgment are the people of God who trust in Him, and in Him alone, to save them from the punishment that they deserve. As the apostle Paul makes perfectly clear—"God has not destined us for wrath, but for obtaining salvation through our Lord Jesus Christ, who died for us, so that whether we are awake or asleep, we will live together with Him. Therefore encourage one another and build up one another, just as you also are doing" (1 Thessalonians

5:9–11). There will be no wrath for us because we have God's promise that the Savior whose coming we are eagerly waiting for "rescues us from the wrath to come" (1 Thessalonians 1:10). Yes, the prophet Nahum says that the *Lord* will not leave the guilty unpunished, but he continues, "The LORD is good, a stronghold in the day of trouble, and He knows those who take refuge[212] in Him" (Nahum 1:7).

If you have put your trust in Christ to save you from God's wrath, then you will have no reason to worry and every reason to rejoice in that day. But if you have not yet put your trust in Christ to save you from God's wrath, then you have every reason not to delay any longer in making that decision. Remember Jesus says, "Whoever believes in the Son has eternal life, but whoever rejects the Son will not see life, for God's wrath remains on him" (John 3:36, NIV).

---

[212] The Hebrew word translated "take refuge" (*hasah*) means "to seek refuge, flee for protection and thus figuratively put trust in [God]." Harris, Archer, & Waltke (Eds.), *Theological Wordbook of the Old Testament*.

Chapter 19

The Grand Finale

And He who sits on the throne said, "Behold, I am making all things new."

Revelation 21:5

If you've ever witnessed a fireworks display, you know how awesome it can be to see exploding rockets filling the night sky with a kaleidoscope of color cascading out of the heavens. You also know that nothing could compare with the grand finale at the end when the entire night sky lights up like daylight as hundreds of rockets explode, one right after the other only seconds apart. Like the encore at the end of a concert, so with the grand finale of a fireworks display, the best is always saved for last. The same principle holds true as we come to the grand finale of God's redemptive story for planet earth. It will include the most extravagant fireworks display the world has ever seen, with a solar eclipse, a blood moon, and stars falling from the sky. And that spectacular light display in the heavens will be followed by something far more spectacular than anything that we could ever picture in our wildest imagination.

Looking back over God's redemptive story as it has been unfolding through the centuries, we've seen how the climax of the story begins to reach a grand crescendo with the unfolding of what the ancient Hebrew prophets described as the "day of the Lord." They foretold how one day, God, Himself, would once and for all intervene in human history to establish His kingdom rule on the earth forever in justice, righteousness, and peace. As that day begins to unfold, the inhabitants of earth will look up to the sky and witness the coming of Jesus Christ, God's anointed King, in all the fullness of His glory. When He comes, Christ will send His angels throughout the earth to search out, find, and gather all of His elect, those who have been His faithful people down through the ages from the time of Adam to the time of His coming. Those who have died will be raised from the dead and, together with those still living, will rise to meet Christ in the air.

When Christ comes, we will all share His glory as He triumphantly enters into our world as King of kings and Lord of Lords. We will all receive new immortal bodies so that we might live forever in His kingdom. At last, after years of wars, famines, pandemics, and earthquakes have brought unprecedented death and destruction to the planet, the whole world will thrive and flourish under Christ's benevolent rule. Yet, as glorious as all this may sound, this is still not the end of God's redemptive story for our planet. As the story continues to unfold, we come at last to the final chapter, God's grand finale, starting with the most incredible fireworks display the world has ever seen.

The apostle Peter speaks of this as he warns the church of his day about false prophets and teachers, scornfully challenging the very idea that this same Jesus who died and rose from the dead would be coming again to establish His kingdom on the earth. These false prophets and teachers were putting doubts in the minds of believers and even leading some of them astray. They asked in a mocking tone dripping with sarcasm, "Where is the promise of His coming? For ever since the fathers fell asleep, all continues just as it was from the beginning of creation" (2 Peter 3:4). Remember, in writing to the Thessalonians, Paul warned them about a deceptive lie that the day of the Lord had already come, implying that they had missed it. Paul's response to the Thessalonians was, "Don't you believe it!" Now the lie being circulated was not that Jesus had already come but rather that He wasn't coming at all. And because Jesus wasn't coming, by implication, it didn't matter how a person lived because there wouldn't be any day of judgment either. And like Paul, Peter's response is, "Don't you believe it!"

Peter challenges these mockers in a way that demonstrates their ignorance of the truth. He points out something obvious that was clearly revealed in the Old Testament Scriptures. He says, "For when they maintain this, it escapes their notice that by the word of God the heavens existed long ago and the earth was formed out of water and by water, through which the world at that time was destroyed, being flooded with water" (2 Peter 3:5–6). I suspect that Peter may be doing a little mocking of his own in pointing out how ignorant they are concerning the Old Testament Scriptures. So he gives them a little history lesson to remind them of something they should already know, if they're as intelligent and informed as they make themselves out to be. He reminds them that not long after creating our planet, God turned around and brought destruction upon the very planet He had created. It was an expression of His righteous judgment because mankind's unbelief and rebellion against Him had gone just too far.

In the days of Noah, God destroyed the world with a global flood reaching beyond the tops of the highest mountains. Only Noah and his family were spared because they trusted God and were obedient to Him. No, all has not continued just as it was from the beginning of creation (Genesis 6–8; Matthew 24:37–39). Furthermore, He adds that, just as there was judgment for an unbelieving and rebellious world in Noah's day, so "[...] the present heavens and earth are being reserved for fire, kept for the day of judgment and destruction[213] of ungodly men" (2 Peter 3:7). When Peter talks about the

---

[213] The Greek word translated destruction (*apoleia*) here is not the same Greek word (*olethros*) that Paul uses in 2 Thessalonians 1:9, but both words have essentially the same meaning. In commenting on the meaning of *appollumi*, from which the word *apoleia* is derived, Vine states, "The idea is not of extinction, but of ruin, loss, not of being, but of wellbeing" (*Vine's Expository Dictionary of Biblical Words*).

"destruction of ungodly men," he's talking about the same thing as Paul when he says of the ungodly on the day of judgment, "These will pay the penalty of eternal destruction, away from the presence of the Lord and from the glory of His power" (2 Thessalonians 1:9). For those who will stand before him in judgment in the future day of wrath, it will definitely not end well.

Peter explains the reason for the apparent delay in Christ's coming. The Church of that day expected the coming of Christ to be soon, and they looked expectantly for that day. Yet here we are nearly two thousand years later, and still, Christ has not come. Could some of us who are followers of Christ even today entertain the same questioning doubts about why so much time has passed since the promise was given?

Peter points out two reasons for this apparent delay. First, an eternal God who dwells outside of time looks at time differently than we do. Peter says, "But do not let this one fact escape your notice, beloved, that with the Lord one day is like a thousand years, and a thousand years like one day" (2 Peter 3:8). Think about it from God's perspective, and it hasn't been all that long, has it? The second reason for this apparent delay is God's patience. Peter says, "The Lord is not slow about His promise, as some count slowness, but is patient toward you, not wishing for any to perish but for all to come to repentance" (2 Peter 3:9). Every day that Jesus delays His coming is another day of opportunity for individuals to repent of their unbelief and rebellion so that they will not have to face the coming judgment. This is not about God being slow to act upon His promise but about God being gracious in extending the opportunity for sinful and rebellious people to experience His mercy instead of His wrath.

We dare not make the mistake, as those in Peter's day did, thinking that because of the apparent delay in Christ's coming that He's not coming at all or that there will be no final judgment of mankind. Peter continues, "But the day of the Lord will come like a thief" (2 Peter 3:10a). Make no mistake! Jesus is coming. And when He does, He will be right on time according to God's timetable, not yours or mine.

The day of the Lord will take a rebellious and unbelieving world completely by surprise, just like a thief breaking into someone's home. As Paul says in writing to the Thessalonians, "For you yourselves know full well that the day of the Lord will come just like a thief in the night. While they are saying, 'Peace and safety!' then destruction will come upon them suddenly like labor pains upon a woman with child, and they will not escape (1 Thessalonians 5:2–3).

Yet, we who are Christ's followers need not be taken by surprise when He comes because we have been forewarned of His coming (1 Thessalonians 5:3–4). Furthermore, Jesus has told us what to be looking for as an indication that His coming is near (Matthew 24:32–35, 42–43). But even as followers of Christ, if we allow ourselves to become so caught up in the things of this world that we have no interest in His coming and are not looking for His coming, we may easily be taken completely by surprise by His coming just like the rest of the world. Don't let that happen to you!

Not only will God judge the world in the day of the Lord, but Peter goes on to say that in the day of the Lord, "[...] the heavens will pass away with a roar and the elements will be destroyed with intense heat, and the earth and its works will be burned up" (2 Peter 3:10b). This might be a reason for alarm to think that the present heavens and earth would be destroyed if it were not for God's promise that He will create new heavens and a new earth in their place. We find this promise in the ancient prophecy of Isaiah dating back nearly eight hundred years before the birth of Christ. In this prophecy, God declares, "For behold, I create new heavens and a new earth; and the former things will not be remembered or come to mind" (Isaiah 65:17).

Peter is referring to this very promise in Isaiah's prophecy when he says, "But according to His promise we are looking for new heavens and a new earth, in which righteousness dwells" (2 Peter 3:13).

Our present world is a mess, just as it was in Isaiah's day and just as it has been since the time of the Fall in the garden of Eden. The apostle Paul describes the condition of our present world as it has been since the time of the Fall when he says,

> The creation was subjected to frustration, not by its own choice, but by the will of the one who subjected it, in hope that the creation itself will be liberated from its bondage to decay [...] We know that the whole creation has been groaning as in the pains of childbirth right up to the present time.
>
> Romans 8:20–22 (NIV)

The whole creation is still groaning today as it continues to yearn for liberation from corruption and decay. It's no different from the yearning of people in Europe during World War II for that future day when the Allied forces would liberate them from the horrors of Nazi occupation. But just as that day of liberation finally came to the people of Europe, so the day of liberation will finally come to the people of God to deliver us from the mess that we've made of our world. It will come when God creates new heavens and a new earth that will replace the present heavens and earth that are so messed up because of sin. He will create new heavens and a new earth so grand and glorious that we will have no reason to remember or even think about the way things used to be in our present world. This, in a nutshell, is the grand finale of God's redemptive story!

In creating new heavens and a new earth, God will do a complete renovation[214] to restore our entire world to the same pristine perfection and beauty as it was in the beginning when God looked upon all that He had made and pronounced it very good (Genesis 1:31). This is exactly what the apostle Peter is talking about in speaking to the Jewish people, probably only days after the ascension of Christ into heaven. He said, "He [Christ] must remain in heaven until the time comes for God to restore everything, as he promised long ago through his holy prophets" (Acts 3:21, NIV). When Peter says that Christ will "restore" everything at the time of His coming, he's talking about the same thing that Jeremiah has in mind in describing the work of a potter when he says, "Then I went down to the potter's house, and there he was, making something on the wheel. But the vessel that he was making of clay was spoiled in the hand of the potter; so he remade it into another vessel, as it pleased the potter to make" (Jeremiah 18:3–4). Another translation says, "But the pot he was shaping from the clay was marred in his hands; so the potter formed it into another pot, shaping it as seemed best to him" (Jeremiah 18:4, NIV).

The point is that when the potter sees that his vessel has an imperfection, he doesn't trash the old piece of clay but transforms it into a brand new vessel. In the same way, God will take the present heavens and earth that have become encrusted with corruption and devoured by decay, and, using

---

[214] The Hebrew word in Isaiah 65:17 translated "new" (*hadash*) does not have the idea of removing something and replacing it with something else but rather repairing something and restoring it to its previous and preferable condition. This Hebrew word hadash "[...] is used in the sense of 'repair' or 'rebuild' referring to cities (Isaiah 61:4), the temple (2 Chronicles 24:4, 12), and the altar (2 Chronicles 15:8)." It is also used figuratively. Under Samuel, the kingdom was renewed at Gilgal (1 Samuel 11:1). David wanted a right spirit, equivalent to a clean heart, renewed within him (Psalm 51:10). The prophet asked for renewal as of old (Lamentations 5:21). God renews the face of the ground, that is, gives it new life (Psalm 104:30), and he renews one's youth (Psalm 103:5). Harris, Archer, & Waltke (Eds.), *Theological Wordbook of the Old Testament*.

the same "lump of clay," He will make them into something brand new. God won't trash the present heavens and earth but will transform them into new heavens and a new earth that will be the same and yet different. That's because God will repair the damage caused by sin and restore them to what they were originally intended to be before sin entered God's story.

When the *Lord* says, "The former things will not be remembered, nor will they come to mind" (Isaiah 65:17), I don't think this means that God will erase all memory of this present earth from our minds. That would mean erasing from our memory the entirety of God's redemptive story up until that point. How could we possibly appreciate or even understand the totality of God's redemptive story if all but the last chapter of the story were missing? How could we possibly appreciate or even understand the magnitude of God's love, mercy, and grace in redemption, if we had no recollection of how bad it was and what God had to do to accomplish our redemption? It's not that we won't be able to remember the present heavens and earth but that we will be so caught up in the grandeur and glory of the new heavens and earth that we will have no longing or desire to think about or remember the way it used to be. Our recollection of how the world used to be will only make our appreciation and gratitude for how much greater and grander our new world has become by comparison. We won't look back longingly and with regret, but with a sigh of relief that those previous days are gone forever. And our hearts will be filled with joy that God has restored our world to the way it was always meant to be and that it will remain this way forever.

In trying to imagine what this marvelous transformation of earth will look like, listen to what N'dea Yancey-Bragg describes in *USA Today* as "one of the most destructive volcanic eruptions in U.S. history." She writes,

At 8:32 a.m. on May 18, 1980, a 5.1 magnitude earthquake hit and within minutes the volcano's north flank collapsed, creating the largest landslide in recorded history, according to the U.S. Geological Survey. That landslide triggered powerful explosions that sent ash, steam, rocks and volcanic gas upward and outward. The lateral blast scorched and flattened about 230 square miles of dense forest, blanketing the area in hot debris. Within 15 minutes, a plume of volcanic ash rose over 80,000 feet. Over the next few days, winds blew the 520 million tons of ash east across the U.S. causing complete darkness 250 miles away in Spokane. The ash circled the globe in 15 days."[215]

Seeing what happened when Mount St. Helens erupted back in 1980 provides us with just a hint of the total devastation that Peter says will engulf our entire planet in the day of the Lord. Yet within just a few years, the healing properties that God has built into His creation began to reverse the damage resulting from the eruption of Mount St. Helens, revitalizing and restoring the land to its previous pristine beauty. In the same way, in the future day of the Lord, our world will be completely revitalized and restored. This will occur even after it is destroyed by a fire burning with such intensity that it will literally melt the elements that are the building blocks of our planet. Yet, like the potter taking a marred vessel and remaking it into something new and so much better than the original, so God will take the marred vessel called earth and remake it into something new and so much better than the original because God will

---

[215] N'dea Yancey-Bragg, "Photos show Mount St. Helens historic eruption: Cars sunk in volcanic ash, people wearing masks," *USA Today*, May 18, 2020, https://www.usatoday.com/story/news/nation/2020/05/18/mount-st-helens-photos-deadly-eruption-40-years-ago/5211478002/

create "new[216] heavens and a new earth in which righteousness dwells[217]" (2 Peter 3:13).

The complete destruction of the earth in a fiery conflagration so intense that it will literally melt the elements may sound like the end of the world, but it's really only preparation for a brand new beginning. It will be the day when the creation itself will be liberated from its bondage to decay and brought into the freedom of the children of God (Romans 8:21). Out of the destruction of an earth that is currently in bondage to decay—out of the rubble and ashes of the old earth—God will reconstruct a brand new earth just as perfect as it was before the entrance of sin into the world. This new earth is something that we should be anxiously looking forward to. Unlike our present earth, which has been corrupted by sin, this new earth will be a place where righteousness dwells. As the NIV puts it, the new earth will be "the home of righteousness" (2 Peter 3:13).

What does it mean that the new earth will be "the home of righteousness"? To answer this question, we must first understand what the Bible means by righteousness. First of all, righteousness does not mean being a religious do-gooder. It has nothing to do with faithfully following a set of rules or doing our church thing flawlessly. It is not something we achieve by trying as hard as we can in our own strength and ability to make it happen. All this is a misconception of what righteousness looks like to many people who call themselves Christians. Righteousness is "purity of heart and rectitude

---

[216] In the New Testament, there are two different Greek words translated "new"—neos and kainos. "The difference in meaning between kainos and neos is, in the main, that kainos denotes new in respect to quality, the new as set over against that which has seen service, the outworn, the effete, or marred through the ages; neos, new (in respect of time), that which has recently come into existence" ("New, Newness," *International Standard Bible Encyclopedia*).

[217] The Greek word translated "dwell" (*katoikeo*) means "to dwell; to live in; to inhabit; to be more and more at home. It means permanent residence; to live in a home; to enter, settle down, and be at home" (*Practical Word Studies in the New Testament*).

of life."[218] It is being right and doing right, with God defining what is right because we have been made right with God. It is being and doing right in our thoughts, words, or deeds. It is being right and doing right in our relationship with God and in our relationships with people. It is being right and doing right in how we respond to every circumstance of life. Living in a sinful body in this present world corrupted by sin where Satan is actively seeking to destroy us may make being perfectly righteous seem an impossibility. But on the new earth where we will live forever in glorified, sinless bodies in a perfect and sinless environment from which Satan and his minions have been banished forever, this will be the new normal.

This is why Peter can say that the new earth will be "the home of righteousness." On the new earth, being and doing what is right will be as natural as breathing—so much so that we won't even have to think about it. Every day we all will naturally live out the perfect character of a holy God and treat one another just as God treats us. We will all naturally love God with all our hearts and love our neighbor as we love ourselves. On the new earth, we will all live in perfect freedom the way God has always intended for us to live from the very beginning according to His design and for His glory in conformity with His perfect character. In that day, we will experience incredible joy in our relationship with God and with each other as we serve one another in love. And that will be true for everyone who will spend eternity in God's new world on God's new earth. Now that's something we can really look forward to! And that's just the beginning because God's new world will be a place that will be incredible in every way beyond imagination.

If you were asked to name the most beautiful city in the world, which would you choose? According to Tom Marchant, contributing travel editor for *Harpers Bazaar* magazine,

---

[218] "Righteousness," *The New Unger's Bible Dictionary*

The world is home to some 4,416 cities—from the crumbling grandeur of Rome to the bristling, ultra-modern towers of Shanghai. It includes tiny Adamstown, a microscopic settlement in the Pitcairn Islands with a population of only 48; it includes Venice, a floating city laced by idyllic canals and breathtaking palazzos. And like the people who inhabit them, each has its own distinctive personality [and] allure..."[219]

Yet among all the cities in the world, Tom Marchant lists Florence, Italy, as the most beautiful of all.

As beautiful as these cities may be, none, not even Florence, Italy, can compare to a city on the new earth that will far outshine them all. The name of that city is the New Jerusalem. John describes this glorious city that will serve as the capital city of the new earth and from which Christ will rule the universe. He says in the book of Revelation, "Then I saw a new heaven and a new earth; for the first heaven and the first earth passed away, and there is no longer any sea. And I saw the holy city, new Jerusalem, coming down out of heaven from God, made ready as a bride for her husband" (Revelation 21:1–2). If you've ever attended a wedding, you know that there is nothing more beautiful than a bride as she walks down the aisle wearing her wedding dress in full view of the man with whom she will soon hear the words, "I now pronounce you husband and wife." What an appropriate metaphor to describe what it will be like when we are privileged to gaze upon the city that God has prepared for His people, where we will live forever with Him forever.

The beauty of the New Jerusalem will be so incredible that it will

[219] Tom Marchant, "These Are the Most Beautiful Cities in the World," *Harper's Bazaar*, December 10, 2019, https://www.harpersbazaar.com/culture/travel-dining/g12244524/most-beautiful-city-in-world/ (accessed 28 April 2022)

immeasurably surpass the beauty of even the most beautiful city in our present world. John describes it as "having the glory of God" and says that in his vision, "her brilliance was like a very costly stone, as a stone of crystal-clear jasper" (Revelation 21:11). He continues,

> The material of the wall was jasper; and the city was pure gold, like clear glass. The foundation stones of the city wall were adorned with every kind of precious stone. And the twelve gates were twelve pearls; each one of the gates was a single pearl. And the street of the city was pure gold, like transparent glass.
>
> Revelation 21:18–19a, 21

The New Jerusalem will surpass all the cities of today's world not only in beauty but in size as well. John writes, "The city is laid out as a square, and its length is as great as the width; and he measured the city with the rod, fifteen hundred miles; its length and width and height are equal" (Revelation 21:16). Apparently, the city of New Jerusalem will be a cube, measuring 1500 miles wide, 1500 miles long, and 1500 miles high. Just to put this in perspective, if you were to drive from Pittsburgh to Denver, the distance would only be about 1450 miles and would take nearly twenty-four hours driving nonstop.

In terms of area, the largest city in the world today is Beijing, China, measuring 6,400 square miles in area. Yet, comparing the size of Beijing, China, with the size of the New Jerusalem would be like comparing a tiny pebble with a huge mountain. I say this because the New Jerusalem will measure 2,250,000 square miles. In other words, the New Jerusalem will be more than 351 times larger than the largest city in the world today.

The New Jerusalem is not only immensely larger in area than the largest city in our present world, but it's also immensely taller than the tallest building ever built. Currently, the tallest building in the world is the Burj Khalifa in

Dubai, which soars a grand 2,717 feet. But the New Jerusalem, at 15,000 miles high, will be so tall that it would be the equivalent of 2,915 buildings as tall as the Burj Khalifa stacked one upon another ascending into the sky. Skeptics may say that designing and constructing such a city on the earth would be technologically and architecturally impossible. But just remember that this is a city "[...] whose architect and builder is God" (Hebrews 11:10). The prophet Jeremiah says, "Ah Lord God! Behold, You have made the heavens and the earth by Your great power and by Your outstretched arm! Nothing is too difficult for You" (Jeremiah 32:17). If that's true—and it certainly is—then God constructing the New Jerusalem on the new earth would be child's play, like a toddler playing with his LEGO. Such a great and mighty God is He. And what a marvelous city He will build for His people to enjoy on the new earth forever.

How wonderful it will be to live in a world that is the home of righteousness. How magnificent it will be to live in a city as awesome as the New Jerusalem. Yet these are not the best part of living on the new earth. The best part will be that God Himself will live with us there, and we will enjoy perfect fellowship with Him forever. According to the Genesis account of the fall of man, after Adam and Eve had deliberately disobeyed God by eating the forbidden fruit, Adam heard the voice of the *Lord* as He was walking in the garden calling to Him, "Adam, where are You?" (Genesis 3:8–9). This reveals the relationship that God and mankind had with each other in the beginning—one of intimate fellowship in which God appeared visibly to Adam and Eve, walked with them in the garden, and spoke audibly with them. After the fall of man, such an interaction as this between God and men became extremely rare and eventually ceased altogether. Yet this is the very kind of relationship that God intended from the beginning for all of us to experience with Him.

A. W. Tozer provides an insightful observation on this when he says,

> God formed us for His pleasure, and so formed us that we, as well as He, can in divine communion enjoy the sweet and mysterious mingling of kindred personalities. He meant for us to see Him and live with Him and draw our life from His smile. But we have been guilty of that "foul revolt" of which Milton speaks when describing the rebellion of Satan and his hosts. We have broken with God. We have ceased to obey Him or love Him, and in guilt and fear have fled as far away as possible from His presence...So the life of man upon the earth is a life away from His presence, wrenched loose from that 'blissful center' which is our right and proper dwelling place, our first estate, which we kept not, the loss of which is the cause of our unceasing restlessness. The whole work of God in redemption is to undo the tragic effects of that foul revolt, and to bring us back into right and eternal relationship with Himself.[220]

The apostle John talks about this restored relationship with God and man in the book of Revelation as he describes how we as the people of God will live forever on the new earth. He says, "And I heard a loud voice from the throne, saying, 'Behold, the tabernacle of God is among men, and He will dwell among them, and they shall be His people, and God Himself will be among them'" (Revelation 21:3). This fulfills the prophecy of Ezekiel dating back to the sixth century BC regarding the new covenant that God will one day make with His people. Here the *Lord* says to them,

---

[220] A. W. Tozer, *The Pursuit of God* (Abbottsford, Wisconsin: Aneko Press, Life Sentence Publishing, 2015), 22–23

> I will make a covenant of peace with them; it will be an everlasting covenant with them. And I will place them and multiply them, and will set My sanctuary in their midst forever. My dwelling place also will be with them; and I will be their God, and they will be My people. And the nations will know that I am the LORD who sanctifies Israel, when My sanctuary is in their midst forever.
>
> Ezekiel 37:26–28

What does John mean when he says that God will dwell among His people on the new earth forever? I believe that He will live in the midst of His people in the person of Jesus Christ. He is the One who Himself is God incarnate, King of kings and Lord of lords. Jesus will sit upon His throne in the New Jerusalem, and from there, He will rule over the kingdom of this world forever. In that day, we will actually see the face of God (Revelation 21:4) in the face of Jesus Christ. On the new earth, not only will our world be restored as in the beginning, but our face-to-face relationship with God will be restored as well.

Finally, on the new earth, the curse caused by sin will be gone forever. In the beginning, immediately after the Fall of man, God said from that point on, the earth would be under the curse of sin—in bondage to corruption, decay, and death. From then until now, the entire creation has been groaning as it longs for the day when God will set it free from its bondage to the curse. In that day, we will step into the perfect freedom of being all that God originally created us to be. God has given us a promise of redemption and restoration, not only for mankind but for our entire world. While Satan's grand design and work all along has been to bring destruction and death to God's creation, John tells us, "The Son of God appeared for this purpose, to destroy the works of the devil" (1 John 3:8b).

This promise will be fulfilled on the new earth when, as the book of Revelation tells us, "He [God] will wipe every tear from their eyes. There will be no more death or mourning or crying or pain, for the old order of things has passed away" (Revelation 21:4, NIV). At last, the curse of sin with its bondage to corruption, decay, and death will be gone—and that forever. In that day, the prophecy of Isaiah will be fulfilled when he says,

> He will swallow up death for all time, and the Lord GOD will wipe tears away from all faces, and He will remove the reproach of His people from all the earth; for the LORD has spoken. And it will be said in that day, "Behold, this is our God for whom we have waited that He might save us. This is the LORD for whom we have waited; let us rejoice and be glad in His salvation."
>
> Isaiah 25:8–9

This is our glorious hope for the future! But should this hope for the future make a difference in how we think and act right now in the present as followers of Christ? And if so, what would this difference look like? Peter doesn't leave us to our own speculation but rather states with great clarity when he says,

> Since all these things are to be destroyed in this way, what sort of people ought you to be in holy conduct and godliness, looking for and hastening the coming of the day of God, because of which the heavens will be destroyed by burning, and the elements will melt with intense heat! [...]. Therefore, beloved, since you look for these things, be diligent to be found by Him in peace, spotless and blameless, and regard the patience of our Lord *as* salvation...
>
> 2 Peter 3:11–15a

When I was a teenager, there was a popular saying that made a significant impression on my life, even as a young follower of Christ. It simply said, "Only one life, 'twill soon be past; only what's done for Christ will last." Think about these words in relation to what Peter has just said regarding the total destruction of this present earth. Think about these words in relation to how you might prepare to live on a new earth where the people of God will live with Christ forever. Would it make sense to spend our lives pursuing the things of this world, knowing that it's scheduled for demolition, when we can pursue the things of Christ, knowing that such things will count for eternity?

Remember that in writing these words, Peter was countering a false teaching infiltrating many of the churches of that day. False teachers were scoffing at the idea of Christ coming again to reward the righteous and to judge the unrighteous. For this reason, they were downplaying the importance of holy and godly living and encouraging believers to pursue the things of this world because, to them, that's all that mattered. Peter is saying just the opposite. In that day, everything that we may think matters in this world will disappear in a firestorm that will destroy the earth. This is why Peter encourages believers to live their lives pursuing the things of Christ. Indeed, only what's done for Christ will last beyond this dying world into eternity on the new earth.

What would living for Christ in this present world actually look like? Of course, it would have to begin with a personal relationship with God through saving faith in Jesus Christ, His Son, and His atoning work on the cross. But beyond that, it would involve cultivating and pursuing a holy life. Peter's not talking here about a superficial spirituality that involves keeping rules and observing religious rituals. Harmon sums it up well when he says, "Our lives should demonstrate that we are set apart for God's purposes in this world, not our own selfish agendas."[221] In addition to holiness, our lives are also to reflect godliness. Again, I like the way Matthew Harmon explains the meaning of godliness when he says, "'Godliness' is a Godward orientation of life expressed in thoughts, feelings, attitudes, speech, and action...Godliness captures the first and greatest commandment to 'love the Lord your God with all your heart and with all your soul and with all your mind'" (Matthew 22:37).[222]

If we truly believe that this present world will eventually disappear in a puff of smoke to be replaced by a new earth that will be the home of righteousness, then such a belief should motivate us to pursue this kind of holy and godly living as we look forward to the coming of that great day. The question is—do we really believe it? Or are we so entangled in the things of this world that we aren't even looking forward to that future day? These are questions that we seriously need to think about.

When I was a young child, I didn't have a deeply theological understanding of Christmas. All I knew was that on Christmas morning, I would get to open presents under the Christmas tree. And I waited with eager anticipation for that day to arrive. Do we look forward to the coming of a new earth that is the home of righteousness with the same eager anticipation of a child looking forward to Christmas? It's one thing to believe that this will happen, but it's something else altogether to be looking forward to it with enough eager anticipation that we would do anything to make that day come sooner if we could.

Where does that leave you, my friend? Even in our present day, there are still mockers who say, or at least are thinking, "Where is the promise of His coming?" Such people may profess to have faith in Christ, but they don't really believe that Christ is coming to reward the righteous and judge

---

[221] Matthew S. Harmon, "2 Peter," *ESV Expository Commentary*, Volume 12 (Wheaton, IL: Crossway, 2018*)*, 405
[222] Matthew S. Harmon, "2 Peter," *ESV Expository Commentary*, Volume 12, 371

the unrighteous. They don't really believe that He will establish His eternal kingdom on a new earth that will be the home of righteousness. And even if they did, they certainly wouldn't be looking forward to the coming of that day because of their entanglement in the things of this present world.

Would you be found among that crowd? Or do you believe that Christ will indeed come as He said He would to do what He said He would do? Are you eagerly looking forward to that day? I encourage you to be found among those who delight in holy and godly living, who are looking forward to the day of Christ's coming with the same eagerness as a young child who can't wait for Christmas. Think about what it will mean to live in a perfect world that will be the home of righteousness forever in the everlasting kingdom of Christ Jesus the Lord. Don't cling to the things of this present world that will one day disappear in a puff of smoke. Be looking forward to the inheritance of glory that will be yours forever with Christ.

Epilogue

Seeing the Big Picture

If there's one overriding theme that flows through this book from the first chapter to the last, it's that the coming of Christ is not incidental to the plan of God, but it's the very centerpiece of God's redemptive story for planet earth. And it's important for you, the reader, to understand that, like a single thread in a beautiful tapestry, your story is interwoven into God's story. That story can be summed up in five keywords—relationship, rebellion, rescue, restoration, and response. Unless you personally see yourself as part of God's redemptive story, you'll miss the incredible significance of what that story is all about. Let's go back in review and look together at the big picture of God's story as it relates to you and your role in His story.

Relationship

> This is eternal life, that they may know You, the only true God, and Jesus Christ whom You have sent.
>
> John 17:3

In the beginning, God created the first man (Adam) and the first woman (Eve) as personal beings made in His own image and likeness (Genesis 1:26–27). He did so that they might know Him in a personal relationship that would allow them to be fully satisfied in Him, to reflect His glory,[223] and to experience the joy of His presence forever. This included giving them a mind to know Him intimately, a heart to love Him passionately, and freedom of choice to trust Him implicitly, obey Him willingly, and serve Him faithfully.

---

[223] God's glory is the radiant beauty of His infinite perfection (definition my own).

307

Such was true for man then, and it is still true for man today. Such a relationship with man has always been, and still is, and always will be the desire of God's heart. We can try to find true joy and happiness in other things, but there is only one thing that can truly satisfy the deepest longings of our hearts. I'm talking about longings so deep we may not even recognize them for what they are. That one thing is having this kind of relationship with the God who designed us for this very purpose. Anything else will fall far short. As Saint Augustine, one of the early church fathers (AD 354–430), once said, "You have made us for yourself, and our hearts are restless, until they can find rest in you."[224]

Rebellion

> All of us, like sheep, have strayed away. We have left God's paths to follow our own.
>
> Isaiah 53:6a (NLT)

At first, Adam and Eve enjoyed this beautiful relationship with God, fully satisfied with Him and in Him. But everything changed when they began to entertain the idea that there might be something more in life that they were missing. Something that might enhance or enrich their lives even more than what they already had in their relationship with God. In their innocence and ignorance, they believed a lie that they could become equal to God Himself, living to satisfy their own selfish desires rather than living obediently according to God's design. They thought they could make their life better on their own apart from God. But they quickly discovered that they had believed a lie—something that would have tragic consequences not

---

[224] Dan Graves, "Article #15," Christian History Institute, https://christianhistoryinstitute.org/incontext/article/augustine (accessed 28 April 2022)

just for them but for all of their descendants yet to be born (which includes us today).[225]

As we saw in the previous chapter, A. W. Tozer, in describing what happened to us as the human race, says,

> God formed us for His pleasure, and so formed us that we, as well as He, can in divine communion enjoy the sweet and mysterious mingling of kindred personalities. He meant us to see Him and live with Him and draw our life from His smile. But...we have broken with God. We have ceased to obey Him or love Him, and in guilt and fear have fled as far as possible from His presence... So the life of man upon the earth is a life away from His presence, wrenched loose from that "blissful center" which is our right and proper dwelling place, our first estate, which we kept not, the loss of which is the cause of our unceasing restlessness.[226]

His words pretty much sum up the problem. We all, like Adam and Eve, have misused our freedom to go our own way rather than God's way, living as though we are equal with God and free to do whatever we want to do that will satisfy our own selfish desires. Our rebellion against God has erected an invisible wall that separates us from God, making it impossible for us to enjoy the relationship that we were meant to have with Him. Because of sin, we all have become alienated from the God who created us to know Him, to enjoy Him, and to live in relationship with Him forever.

Furthermore, one day we will all stand before God in judgment (Romans 14:12). The prophet Nahum makes this very clear when he says, "The LORD is slow to anger and great in power, and the LORD will by no means leave

---

[225] You can read the full account in Genesis 3:1–24.
[226] A. W. Tozer, *The Pursuit of God*, 22–23

the guilty unpunished" (Nahum 1:3a). The penalty for our sin is eternal banishment from the presence of God (2 Thessalonians 1:9) in a place totally of every good thing that makes life worth living. To be banished from the presence of God is to be banished from the true source of all that is good in this world and the next (James 1:17). Our only hope is that someone will rescue us from the crushing burden of sin and its guilt because there is absolutely no way that we can rescue ourselves.

Rescue

> For God so loved the world that He gave His only begotten Son,
> that whoever believes in Him shall not perish, but have eternal life.
>
> John 3:16

Imagine yourself walking through the woods in the dark along a path that you've never traveled before. You're tired and hungry and anxious to get home where you can sink into your favorite easy chair with a cool glass of iced tea in your hand. Suddenly, without warning, you find yourself falling down—down—down into a deep pit. The landing is a hard one, cushioned only by the soft, oozy mud at the bottom. The darkness is thick, the air is stale, the walls are high, and your clothes are covered with that oozy mud.

As your mind begins to clear, you come to realize that you are trapped at the bottom of that pit. But not to worry. You're sure you're smart enough that when morning dispels the darkness, you'll easily figure out a way to get out and get home. You try to sleep, but sleep escapes your grasp. Then, as the light of dawn begins to make its way slowly downward to the bottom of the pit, you begin to look around, only to discover that there is no hope of climbing up the slick, smooth walls of the pit. There really is no way out of that pit without help from above. "Surely someone will come along the path and hear my cries," you think to yourself.

Finally, when all hope is nearly lost, you hear a voice from above, "Hey, anybody down there?" Immediately you cry out for help. Thank God your rescuer has finally shown up. He throws down a rope and says, "Grab on to the rope, and I'll pull you out of the pit!" But then you begin to have second thoughts. "What if the rope isn't strong enough?" "What if the rope breaks and I fall back into the pit?" Can I really trust the rope?" "And what about the man?" "He's a complete stranger. What if he wants to rob me and then throw me back into the pit? Can I really trust the man?"

You decide that trusting the rope and the man is better than staying at the bottom of the pit. So you grab the rope and hold on tight as he pulls you out of the pit. As you climb out of the pit, you look into the face of your rescuer, and what you see are gentleness, kindness, and love. And you think to yourself, "Thank God my rescuer finally came."

You might think that because we have turned our backs on God by living to pursue our own selfish desires, God has turned His back on us. But that's not the case at all! In spite of our rebellion against Him, God wants to restore the relationship with Him that we have severed by our rebellion against Him. The apostle Paul makes this very explicit when he says,

> [God]...wants everyone to be saved and to understand the truth. For there is only one God and one Mediator who can reconcile God and humanity—the man Christ Jesus. Jesus gave his life to purchase freedom for everyone. This is the message God gave to the world at just the right time.
>
> 1 Timothy 2:4–6 (NLT)

Because of His love for us, in spite of our sin, God, Himself, in the person of Jesus Christ, came to rescue us from our alienation and our bondage to the corruption and death that are the consequences of sin. As the apostle Peter explains, "Christ suffered for our sins once for all time. He never sinned, but he died for sinners to bring you safely home to God" (1 Peter 3:18a, NLT). Mission accomplished!

Through His death, Jesus rescued us from the bondage of our sin and guilt, and through His resurrection, He rescued us from the ultimate consequence of sin, which is death. As a result, Jesus has made it possible for every human being to be restored to the relationship with God that we were created for. As the apostle Paul writes,

> When we were utterly helpless, Christ came at just the right time and died for us sinners. And since we have been made right in God's sight by the blood of Christ, he will certainly save us from God's condemnation. For since our friendship with God was restored by the death of his Son while we were still his enemies, we will certainly be saved through the life of his Son. So now we can rejoice in our wonderful new relationship with God because our Lord Jesus Christ has made us friends of God.
>
> Romans 5:6, 9–11 (NLT)

Now, because of what Jesus has done, we have the opportunity to experience a new life in Christ that not only abundantly satisfies the deepest longings of our hearts, but that lasts forever (John 10:10, 28–29). Jesus wants to give us a life that overflows with peace and joy more satisfying than we could possibly imagine. Jesus says, "Peace I leave with you; My peace I give to you; not as the world gives do I give to you. Do not let your heart be troubled, nor let it be fearful" (John 14:27). And again, He says, "These things I have spoken to you so that My joy may be in you, and that your joy may be made full" (John 15:11).

Debra Rienstra sums it up so beautifully when she says,

> You are loved enough [by God] that God will see you exactly as you are; and if you are willing, God will take it from there. God will begin to remove the burdens and distortions of sin, rescue you from the powerful downward forces of sin, recreate you into the person you were designed to be, and draw you into the kind of communion with himself that is our true life, our highest purpose.[227]

This is only the beginning of what God has in store for those who put their trust in Him. There's still more! Much more!

Restoration

> And He who sits on the throne said, "Behold, I am making all things new."
>
> Revelation 21:5a

To use the language of English poet John Milton (1608–74), the story of God's redemptive love begins in Genesis, the first book of the Bible, as "paradise lost," and ends in Revelation, the last book of the Bible, as "paradise regained." God's story begins on a note of tragedy with man's rebellion against God and its tragic consequences for the human race and the entire world. But it ends on a note of triumph with God's restoration of the human race and our entire world to all that it was originally intended to be—and more! Again, as Dina Rienstra puts it so well,

---

[227] Debra Rienstra, *SO MUCH MORE: An Invitation to Christian Spirituality* (San Francisco, CA, Josey-Bass, 2005), 60

When Christians use the word *salvation*, they are referring to a rich, multi-dimensional experience and a promise of that experience's fulfillment. For Christians salvation means both *rescue* from sin, death, and hell in their many manifestations and *restoration* to perfect relationship with God, each other, and creation. We feel this rescue and restoration happening here and now, and we are promised that it will be completed in the future.[228]

As the book of Revelation draws to a close, its author, the Apostle John, writes, "And He who sits on the throne said, 'Behold, I am making all things new'" (Revelation 21:5). This work of making all things new has already begun in the lives of those who have begun to experience God's grace in being rescued from sin's grip and its devastating consequences. The apostle Paul puts this in simple terms when he says, "[...] Though outwardly we are wasting away, yet inwardly we are being renewed day by day" (2 Corinthians 4:16b, NIV), and again, "[...] if anyone is in Christ, he is a new creation; the old has gone, the new has come" (2 Corinthians 5:17, NIV).

When we are rescued from sin and death, we are restored to the relationship with God that He intended for us to have with Him all along. But that's not all! He also begins a work of renewal right now within us so that we are no longer the same person we used to be and are becoming progressively more and more the person that God designed us to be. That work of renewal and transformation will continue throughout the course of our life until it is brought to completion in the day of Christ's coming. As Paul writes, "I am certain that God, who began the good work within you, will continue his work until it is finally finished on the day when Christ Jesus returns" (Philippians 1:6, NLT).

As I've already said, this is just the beginning of God making all things

---

[228] Debra Rienstra, *SO MUCH MORE: An Invitation to Christian Spirituality*, 62

new. Those who have experienced God's grace in being rescued from sin's grip and its devastating consequences in their lives still live in mortal bodies subject to disease, sickness, corruption, pain, and death. That, too, will change in the day of Christ's coming as Paul says,

> Behold, I tell you a mystery; we will not all sleep, but we will all be changed, in a moment, in the twinkling of an eye, at the last trumpet; for the trumpet will sound, and the dead will be raised imperishable, and we will be changed. For this perishable must put on the imperishable, and this mortal must put on immortality. But when this perishable will have put on the imperishable, and this mortal will have put on immortality, then will come about the saying that is written, "DEATH IS SWALLOWED UP in victory."
>
> 1 Corinthians 15:51–54

Yes, in the present, God brings restoration to our inner being by giving us a new heart. But in the future, at Christ's coming, He will bring restoration to our outer being by giving us a new body. It will be a brand-new body that is immortal, no longer subject to disease, sickness, pain, sorrow, corruption, or death. It will be a body that is indestructible and that reflects the magnificent glory of God. Those who have died will receive this new body through resurrection, and the bodies of those who are still alive at His coming will simply be transformed into brand new bodies. All this will happen "[...] in a moment, in the twinkling of an eye, at the last trumpet" (1 Corinthians 15:52). How awesome to think that each of us can experience the reality of becoming a brand new person with the promise of a brand new body that will live forever, no longer subject to disease, sickness, pain, sorrow, corruption, or death.

This, however, raises a significant question? How can this be true since clearly, we live on a planet that is subject to decay and death, not only among humans but in the animal and plant kingdoms as well? How can this be since we live in a world where, because of sin, everyone and everything eventually dies? The apostle Paul answers this question when he says, "Against its will, all creation was subjected to God's curse. But with eager hope, the creation looks forward to the day when it will join God's children in glorious freedom from death and decay" (Romans 8:20–21, NLT).

God's rescue and restoration plan is not just for the human race but for the entire planet on which we live. As we've already seen in the previous chapter, the apostle John describes what will happen in the day of Christ's coming when he says,

> Then I saw a new heaven and a new earth, for the first heaven and the first earth had passed away, and there was no longer any sea. I saw the Holy City, the new Jerusalem, coming down out of heaven from God, prepared as a bride beautifully dressed for her husband. And I heard a loud voice from the throne saying, "Now the dwelling of God is with men, and he will live with them. They will be his people, and God himself will be with them and be their God. He will wipe every tear from their eyes. There will be no more death or mourning or crying or pain, for the old order of things has passed away."
>
> Revelation 21:1–4

Such will be the new world that God has in store for those whom He will rescue from their bondage to corruption, sin, and death. We will live on a brand new earth where there is no more curse and everything is perfect in every way, just as it was in the beginning. We will dwell in a city that is bigger, better, and more beautiful than any city we've ever known. God, whose throne is now in heaven, will come to live on the new earth forever among His people in the person of His Son, Jesus Christ. No more sadness. No more pain. No more death. All the old stuff marred by sin will be gone, and everything will be new and better—far better—than ever before. Indeed, the old order of things will entirely be ancient history, as all things will have been made new. And this is the way it will be forever throughout the endless ages of eternity. Hallelujah!

Response

> "The time has come," he said, "The kingdom is near. Repent and believe the good news!"
>
> Mark 1:15 (NIV)

So how do we come to experience this new life in Christ and this new hope of a glorious future forever? Jesus tells us in His own words when He says, "Repent and believe the good news!" (Mark 1:15, NIV) Repentance is "[...] a fundamental paradigm shift: an inward change of mind...that results in a change in the way we live."[229] In this case, repentance is a reversal of what happened in the garden of Eden. It is choosing to trust God to enable us to turn away from living life our own way according to our own design in order to embrace living life God's way according to His design. Believing the good news involves taking God at His word and trusting Him to do what He's promised to do. In this case, it's trusting God to restore us to a brand new relationship with Him and to give us a brand new life in Christ that is both abundant and eternal. This is the life that we were created to have from the beginning. It's the life that our hearts have longed for all along, but we just didn't know it.

Are you willing to take this step of repentance and faith to receive new

---

[229] Mary Jo Leddy, *Radical Gratitude* (ORBIS, 2014)

life in Christ? If you've never done so, there's no better time than right now. What the apostle Paul wrote to the Corinthians nearly two thousand years ago is still true today when he says, "Indeed, the right time is right now. Today is the day of salvation" (2 Corinthians 6:2b, NLT). When you make this decision, it will change your life. To put off this decision is to do so at your own peril. Do it today!

Appendix 1

Some might wonder how any of the Jews could have been expecting the Messiah to come in AD 33. There are several reasons to think that this expectation is possible, even probable:

1. The Jews—at least many, if not most, of the godly ones—would have known their ancient Scriptures well, which would have included the prophecies of the Messiah's coming. How else could Matthew, Peter, James, and John quote so profusely from the Old Testament in the Gospels of Matthew and John or the letters of Peter, James, and John or the book of Revelation? These men were not formally educated, but they weren't ignorant either. They clearly were well acquainted with the ancient prophecies. Consider how often in the Gospels messianic prophecies besides Daniel's are quoted, such as Isaiah's prophecy of the virgin birth (Isaiah 7:14; compare Matthew 1:18–25; Luke 1:26–38) or Micah's prophecy of His birth in Bethlehem (Micah 5:2–3; compare Luke 2:1–20).

2. The Jews of that day had their own calendar and could easily have kept track of the number of years from the issuing of the decree in 444 BC—a year they would never forget—to the current year of AD 33. Consider also the examples of a man named Simeon and a prophetess named Anna, who were eagerly awaiting the coming of the Messiah at the time of Jesus' birth. When Jesus' parents brought Him to the temple to be presented to the Lord for circumcision, according to Jewish custom (Luke 2:25–38), somehow God, through the Holy Spirit, revealed to both Anna and Simeon that the true Messiah of Israel was the child Jesus. They would have been representative of many, if not most, of the godly Jews living at that time.

3. The Jewish religious leaders were certainly well aware of the ancient messianic prophecies. They immediately knew the answer when King Herod

asked them where the ancient prophecies said that the Messiah would be born, and they replied that it was to be in Bethlehem of Judea (Micah 5:2). Surely, they would have known the other messianic prophecies as well, including Daniel's prophecy of the precise year when the Messiah would appear. Although we may not be able to prove conclusively that the Jewish people, or even the majority of the godly Jews, knew that AD 33 was the year foretold for the coming of the Messiah, the evidence suggests a strong possibility of this expectation.

About the Author

Allan Stewart Maitha is a retired pastor who served churches over a period of forty years in Pennsylvania, New Jersey, New York, and Texas. He has also served as president of two Christian corporations, Servants of the Word, Inc. and White Fields, Inc., focusing on Christian education, poverty relief, and Christian counseling, as well as being founder and director of the Adirondack Christian Counseling Service.

He is a graduate of Cairn University (formerly Philadelphia Biblical University) with a bachelor's degree in Bible, a graduate of Dallas Theological Seminary with a master's degree in theology, and a graduate of Liberty University with a master's degree in biblical counseling.

He is currently living in north-central Florida with his wife, Joyce. They have three adult children and nine grandchildren.

And he is looking for "the blessed hope—the glorious appearing of our great God and Savior, Jesus Christ" (Titus 2:13, NIV).

To ask questions or make comments about the content of this book, go to the author's website at https://amaitha-author.com.

To contact the author, send email to allanmaitha9@gmail.com.